Zombie History

Fake history is not a harmless mistake of fact or interpretation. It is a mistake that conceals prejudice; a mistake that discriminates against certain kinds of people; a mistake held despite a preponderance of evidence; a mistake that harms us. In the following pages, I liken fake history to the Zombies in the mass media, for the fake fact, like the fictional Zombie, lives by turning real events and people into monstrous perversions of fact and interpretation. Its pervasiveness reveals that prejudice remains its chief appeal to those who believe it. Its effect is insidious, because we cannot or will not destroy these mischievous lies. Zombie history is almost impossible to kill. Some Zombie history was and is political. It's a genre of what Hannah Arendt called "organized lying" about the past. Its makers designed the Zombie to create a basis in the false past for particular discriminatory policies. Other history Zombies are cultural. They encapsulate and empower prejudice and stereotyping. Still other popular history Zombies do not look disfigured, but like Zombies walk among us without our realizing how devastating their impact can be. Whatever their purpose, whatever the venue in which they appear, history Zombies undermine the very foundations of the disinterested study of the past.

Peter Charles Hoffer is Distinguished Research Professor of History at the University of Georgia.

Zombie History

Lies About Our Past that Refuse to Die

PETER CHARLES HOFFER

UNIVERSITY OF MICHIGAN PRESS • ANN ARBOR

Published in the United States of America by
the University of Michigan Press
Manufactured in the United States of America
Printed on acid-free paper

First published January 2020

A CIP catalog record for this book is available from the British Library.

ISBN 978-0-472-07452-5 (hardcover : alk. paper)
ISBN 978-0-472-05452-7 (paper : alk. paper)
ISBN 978-0-472-12682-8 (ebook)

Contents

Note to the reader: Beware! Zombies often roam in packs. They find strength in numbers. To better identify the bonds that bind those evil bands, I have arranged the following chapters to identify groups of Zombies that travel together.

Digital materials related to this title can be found on the Fulcrum platform via the following citable URL https://doi.org/10.3998/mpub.11328466

Preface

At the close of the 1990s, when the fate of American history in the schools seemed up for grabs among liberal and conservative intellectuals, respected historian Eric Foner published a collection of his prior essays on the subjects of teaching and doing history. His title was perfectly suited to the tumult over the content of history in the classroom and the textbooks. "Who Owns History?" he asked. Foner recalled that his father and uncle, both historians, were victims of the post–World War II Red Scare "blacklist"—a far less colorful time than the words might conjure. They could not teach history in college because their views, to the left of center, were called subversive. They did not even own their own history, because they were not allowed to explain themselves. Foner learned then that history was a potent weapon to liberate minds, or to close them.

We live in similarly fraught times for ourselves and our idea of our history. Rival politicians disparage one another's "fake history." Media pundits and opinion leaders offer us history sound bites and blog posts so uninformed that knowledgeable students of the past can only groan and shake their heads. Amateur historians like Naomi Wolf and Cokie Roberts get key terms in past records so wrong in the media that they embarrass themselves. Flocks of bloggers descend on unwary contributors to history in newspapers and magazines, mobbing authors with "Twitter rage" and undermining the very idea of fact. Academic historians have joined the combat, jousting among themselves about the meaning and uses of our history. Should the classroom historians offer value-oriented lessons, and if so, which values should they advocate? Who among the profession is qualified by their ethnic identity or ancestry to teach a particular subject?

In the meantime, the number of history majors in our colleges plummets so steadily that we who teach history worry that no one will want to take our courses, or pay to train and find jobs for a new generation of history teachers.

Ironically, at the same time, popular history books continue to appear and sell at all-time highs, and history in public parks, museums, and battle-field sites attracts millions of visitors every year. Americans report that they love reading history. As Tyrion Lannister told the council at the end of the last episode of *Game of Thrones*—"What unites people? . . . Stories. There's nothing in the world more powerful than a good story." We want good stories—trustworthy and informative—to help us choose our leaders, to define us as a people, and to reveal our values. How can we be sure we are getting them, and not fake history?

If this is so, then are we, academic historians, the guarantors of sound history? Who appointed us? There are more episodes of misfeasance, mal-feasance, and downright fraud in our corner of academe than we want to admit. There were historians who pushed their theses far beyond their evidence or simply invented evidence to support their theses; journal editors and book publishers who should have been far more careful with what they accepted and what they turned away; and professors who did not bother to uncover plagiarism in their own students. Why then not welcome crowd-sourced history; is that not the truly populist way? Why should expertise—advanced degrees, archival research, years in the classroom or the institute—privilege scholars over commoners? Think about this when you, dear reader, are choosing a cardiothoracic surgeon to do your bypass. Would you go to a neighborhood meat butcher or an experienced, board-certified surgeon?

Fake history is not a harmless mistake of fact or interpretation. It is a mistake that conceals prejudice; a mistake that discriminates against certain kinds of people; a mistake held despite a preponderance of evidence; a mistake that harms us. In the following pages, I liken fake history to the Zombies we see in mass media, for the fake fact, like the fictional Zombie, lives by turning real events and people into monstrous perversions of fact and interpretation. Its pervasiveness reveals that prejudice remains its chief appeal to those who believe it. Its effect is insidious, because we cannot or will not destroy these mischievous lies. Zombie history is almost impossible to kill.

Some Zombie history was and is political, a genre of what Hannah Arendt called "organized lying" about the past. Its makers designed the Zombie to create a basis in the false past for particular discriminatory policies. Other history Zombies are cultural. They encapsulate and empower prejudice and stereotyping. Still other popular history Zombies do not look disfigured, but like Zombies walk among us without our realizing how devastating their impact can be. Whatever their purpose, whatever the venue in which they appear, history Zombies undermine the very foundations of the disinterested study of the past.

This book is an exploration of the history Zombies in the public mind and in academic writing. As Zombies go back and forth between the two, so shall we. In the latter, my examples are almost always drawn from historical sources. That I suppose is inevitable, because I have been teaching the history of historical writing for nearly fifty years.

I am grateful to Williamjames Hull Hoffer, who nearly a decade ago suggested the idea of fake history as a Zombie and has discussed it with me many times since then. He urged me to defend all of my opinions with copious notes. It is sound and caring advice, which I tried to take to heart, but something of the author's contrarian (old and grouchy but hopefully not churlish) nature has crept into the text, especially its latter stages. To my colleagues Steve Berry, Brian Drake, Claudio Saunt, and Michael Winship for reading chapters, and to the readers for the press, Vernon Burton and an anonymous reader, for their comments, I express gratitude. That they were not able to save me from any excess is no fault of their own. My editor, Elizabeth Demers, is a fellow historian and, fortunately for me, also a reader of great discernment. She saw merit in the manuscript and encouraged me to submit it to the University of Michigan Press. John Raymond did a wonderful job of copyediting, and Marcia LaBrenz, production editor for the press, was simply a wonder. Finally, I hope that those historians whose work I have faulted will take my criticisms kindly. That is how I intend them. Finally, I did not identify every Zombie—not even close. Keep a sharp eye for those I missed.

Introduction

How to Recognize a History Zombie

Is there anyone who watches horror movies or apocalyptic television series who does not know what a Zombie looks like? Unlike the erotic Dracula and the majestic Godzilla, the Zombie is an ugly caricature of humanity. He or she shuffles onto our screens mangled, bloody, and undead. Not content with their own miserable existence, Zombies threaten the living with unimaginable horror. In order to survive, the Zombie must consume living people's brains.

The fictitious Zombie has a history of its own. The word's origin is African, and it came to the New World in Afro-Haitian dialect. It meant someone raised from the dead. Although associated with Voodoo, the Zombie has nothing to do with any Afro-Christian religious rite, or indeed with Haitian history. No serious historian believes that Haitians made a pact with the Devil to aid in the uprising against the French, or that the result has been a curse on the Haitian people.

English-speaking students of the occult rediscovered the Zombie. The title character of Mary Shelley's *Frankenstein* was a Zombie. Zombies reappeared in science fiction and horror stories in the twentieth century, in movies following director George Romero's *Night of the Living Dead* (1968), in comics written by Robert Kirkman and illustrated by Tony Moore, and on television in *The Walking Dead*. The Zombie in popular fiction is a cousin of the Mummy, the Vampire, the Ghoul, and other creatures, but none of these so resemble the living as does the Zombie.

We know that Zombies do not exist. The dead stay dead. Except when they do not—in history books and articles. In works of historical scholarship, authors try to bring the dead back to life. Historians do not rely on occult ritual, but instead plumb historical records, weigh different accounts against one another, and deploy practiced skills to sift truth from fiction. Historians cannot avoid bias in the sources and their own biases, but, aware of bias, they can work hard to counter it. In short, historians avoid confusing the dead with the undead. Or should. For not every Zombie is old. Some are new, created today by journalists, politicians, bloggers, historians, teachers of history, guest lecturers in our history programs, and public intellectuals.

However created, history Zombies are palpably fake stories that refuse to die; theses that cannot be proved; or disfigured versions of past events. They wander through the halls of Congress and the White House, visit high school classes, infiltrate the pages of approved textbooks, and generally wreak havoc with Americans' understanding of their past. To save living history, one must cut off the heads and burn the bodies of the Zombies. That turns out to be difficult for reasons that are important for us to understand.

To prevent history Zombies from reproducing themselves, much less taking over our history, one must understand why history Zombies' existence means so much to so many, and why, despite evidence to the contrary, some people prefer the Zombie to the nuanced, complex explanations that mark model histories of past time.

To complicate matters, the reason why these untruths persist is not a Zombie itself, but a genuinely important part of our history. People clung to the old Zombies because they preserved or confirmed old prejudices. These falsities reassured us in times of trouble and uncertainty more than did hard, unpleasant facts and carefully documented interpretations. The old history Zombies are all the more dangerous for that reason. Disfigured versions of reality cater to prejudice and ignorance. Such wrongheaded history may lead to very real disasters. Younger history Zombies may not seem as dangerous. They may pass unnoticed, or even gain praise, for their bold reinterpretations or morally committed stances. When they rest upon unsubstantiated and unprovable assumptions about the inherent evil of American history, and the lasting onus that those evils place on future generations, they are Zombies.

A short survey of what post–Civil War leaders wrote about American history will help to explain how and why history Zombies came to occupy a vacuum in American cultural and psychological life. It begins with a time of trauma for Americans. In 1865, Americans had just concluded a horrific civil war, with over a million casualties. All of the time-honored stories about a shared national history seemed to have been deceptions. Worse, the incongruities of these stories seemed to have led to the nightmare of rebellion. A people dividing against itself, to borrow Abraham Lincoln's words, had produced two incompatible histories. In an 1858 campaign speech in Rochester, New York, Senator William Henry Seward warned, "Our country is a theatre, which exhibits, in full operation, two radically different political systems; the one resting on the basis of servile or slave labor, the other on voluntary labor of freemen." The result was an "irrepressible conflict." Democratic newspapers condemned the speech as fake history. At the Milledgeville, Georgia, secession convention, on November 12, 1860, delegate T. R. R. Cobb offered his own version of the preceding period of American history: "Can it be supposed that our fathers intended to allow our national elections to be controlled by men who were not citizens under the National Constitution? Never, never! Yet to elect Abraham Lincoln, the right of suffrage was extended to free negroes in Vermont, Massachusetts, Ohio, New York and other Northern States, although the Supreme Court has declared them not to be citizens of this nation. Yes! Our slaves are first stolen from our midst on underground Railroads, and then vote at Northern ballot-boxes to select rulers for you and me. The memory of our fathers is slandered when this is declared to be according to the Constitution." Cobb was referring to Supreme Court Justice Roger Taney's obiter dictum in *Dred Scott v. Sandford* (1857) that people of African ancestry could never be citizens because the framers of the Constitution did not think so—a view that abolitionists condemned as historically false and perniciously biased.

The problem with American history, it seemed to contemporaries after the carnage had ended, was that the two versions of our past competed for the allegiance of Americans. Both of these narratives not only proposed different accounts of secession and the Civil War, they derived opposite lessons from them. After the war was over, a Unionist version spoke in the solemn tones of the glories of the Union. As Andrew Dixon White, a New Yorker, first president of Cornell University and of the American Historical Association, created by Congress in 1884 to preserve and explain our history, told a meeting of the AHA in Saratoga Springs, New York, Americans should "recall another historical fact . . . to keep up the courage of our people." That fact was that "men of sterner purpose" must be put in charge of the nation for it to survive disunion. The second historical account found voice in the apologia of former Confederate president Jefferson Davis of Mississippi for his brief career as president of the Confederacy. His *Short History of the Confederate States of America* (1890) opened: "Believing the case to be one which must be adjusted finally by historical facts, the candid reader is asked, without favor or prejudice, to make a decision on the unquestionable record." That record, Davis continued, demonstrated the legitimacy of secession and the continuing sanctity of the Lost Cause of the Confederacy. For the experiment in Southern self-government based on racial purity and states' rights was not a failure, but a blueprint for a better America. Defenders of the both of these historical views cited the same founding fathers, the same founding ideology, and the same documentary evidence for the rightness of their cause.

What was to be done to save American history from endless rounds of fruitless recrimination over the causes of the war and the moral fiber of the two sections' people? In the 1880s, a new generation of teachers and scholars proposed that the end of sectional bitterness and a return to national harmony lay in a new kind of history. First, they would listen as a cadre of professionally trained historians got the story right and, second, they would require every pupil to study the new American history. The new kind of historian was a professor with a PhD from a university. Such men (few women were allowed to enter graduate study) would replace the passionate subjectivity of the amateur defenders of North and South and find the unquestionable facts that both sides could accept. The new, required course in American history would rest on history textbooks vetted by local and state school boards. The new history would elevate and inspire its students. As AHA president John Jay told the association's annual meeting in 1890, "It would seem clear from such testimony that there is no reason why the elementary principles of the improved methods of teaching history may not be wisely introduced into the education of our common schools; that there, as well as in our colleges and universities, history may become . . . an active instead of a passive process—an increasing joy instead of a depressing burden."

What were to be the themes of that newly refashioned history? Bear in mind that in this project both the popular view of American history and the writing of American history by experts came together. The foremost among the new themes was national unity. In fact, America in the 1880s and 1890s was increasingly becoming a nation of many nations, and not all of them got along with one another or even within their own membership. But the goal of national harmony required a rethinking of the actual diversity of peoples in America. For unity to work, the people must be uniform, melted down from their various origins in the national "melting pot." The term was already in use when David Zangwill, a British Jewish immigrant, made it the title of his play. The chief character explained: "There she lies, the great Melting Pot . . . the harbour where a thousand mammoth feeders come from the ends of the world to pour in their human freight . . . Celt and Latin, Slav and Teuton, Greek and Syrian, black and yellow. . . . Yes, East and West, and North and South, the palm and the pine, the pole and the equator, the crescent and the cross. . . . Here shall they all unite to build the Republic of Man and the Kingdom of God . . . where all nations and races come to worship and look back, compared with the glory of America, where all races and nations come to labour and look forward." This new man, the American, with all evidence of diversity melted away, was actually a Zombie, a deliberate caricature of the actual physical, cultural, and behavioral qualities of Americans.

The history Zombie had a face—he (women were not featured in this history) was English. As Frances Fitzgerald revealed in her study of the first textbooks, their focus was the English origins of American history. The continuity of English ideas was a little hard to promote, given the Revolution and the War of 1812, but the textbook authors were not deterred. David Saville Muzzey's *An American History* in 1911 was typical: "England's dauntless seamen, Hawkins, Davis, Cavendish, and above all Sir Francis Drake, performed marvels of daring against the Spanish." In fact, these "Sea Dogs" were little more than pirates, but according to the historians, and popular publications, their virtue exceeded the "moral degradation" of the Indians and the "despotic" covetousness of the Spanish.

World War I spurred history textbook authors' efforts to unite in the past what the wartime of 1917 had brought together—the United States and Great Britain. Historians like Woodrow Wilson, whose ten-volume *A Documentary History of the American People* (1918) was widely praised (the editor, Ripley Hitchock, called it "the most brilliant general version of the history of our country"), and whose author was one of the first presidents of the American Historical Association as well as president of Princeton University and later of the United States, went further. He wrote that, poised for its colonial adventure, "England had thrown off all slavish political connection with Rome" and "this self-helping race of Englishmen" showed the stuff of which they were made: "Bred to adventure . . . venturesome and hardy" they overmatched all who dared rival England.

Through the first half of the twentieth century, the textbooks revealed a uniformity of tone and content: brave and intrepid explorers came to a "vast and lonely land." With ax, Christian faith, and democratic institutions these men (again, women were rarely mentioned) built a great nation. In it, the values of individual entrepreneurs, far-seeing politicians, and an energetic, homogenous people prevailed over internal and external enemies. The Zombie walked straight into the US Naval Academy in 2018. As President Donald Trump put it to an audience of Naval midshipmen on Memorial Day weekend, "our ancestors trounced an empire, and tamed a continent." So the message of the textbooks, like nationalism itself, called forth Zombies, what historian James Axtell has called "half truths perhaps worse than falsehoods."

A historiography of the newest history Zombies is more problematic. I have attempted it in chapter 8 below. It will ruffle some feathers. I believe that the new history Zombies have the same birth story as their ancestors. In a time of crisis for our understanding of our history, some of our finest scholars have grasped at remedies to a national malady that are the very opposite of helpful. Young students, themselves beset with doubts about their own future and the future of the nation, have taken these Zombies to dinner, always a bad idea. But let the reader decide—after all, the reader is always the final judge.

The history Zombie purports to be real, a genuine fact or a legitimate interpretation of facts in the popular imagination and in the pages of history. (My subject in this book is Zombies in both settings.) What then distinguishes the Zombie from the mere error of fact or interpretation? Admittedly, errors of fact can creep into reputable historical accounts. Such errors include incorrect names, dates, places, and other historical data. These are of two sorts. The false fact is easy to spot and not dangerous. It is not a Zombie. The fake fact is a Zombie, an assertion of fact made for a purpose whose author knows or should know it to be fake. It often takes pains not to be recognized for what it is.

False facts are mistakes that purport to be facts. For example, "Paul Revere warned the Minutemen at Concord that 'the redcoats are coming.'" This is false for two reasons. Though Revere set out to warn them, he never got there. It was his fellow rider, Samuel Prescott, who reached the green at Concord. Second, Revere did not warn of redcoats, but "regulars," the British troops quartered in Boston.

The source of this commonly repeated error may be Henry Wadsworth Longfellow's 1860 poem "Paul Revere's Ride." Longfellow was an abolitionist and a Republican and wrote his poem in the tumultuous election year of 1860. He meant to wake up the free states of the North to the peril that slavery posed to the nation. He was right about the danger. Shortly before the poem was published in the *Atlantic Monthly*'s January 1861 issue, South Carolina seceded from the Union.

The poem exhibited the second kind of error, fake facts. A fake fact is not just a mistaken belief. It is a lie. Longfellow knew that Revere did not ride through the countryside rousing patriots of 1775 to the British raid. The poet wanted to stir patriots of 1860 to defend freedom against the "peculiar institution" of the slave states. Longfellow's details were lies, fraudulent statements, meant to serve a purpose. In his mind, his purpose was the higher good of abolitionism. Hence the lines, "And yet, through the gloom and the light, / The fate of a nation was riding that night; / And the spark struck out by that steed, in his flight, /Kindled the land into flame with its heat." There was no nation in 1775 and the British raid on Concord to seek a hidden cache of weapons and ammunition did not kindle the land into flame—unlike secession.

Whether false facts are or are not held strongly, they easily can be corrected. Fake facts are harder to undo, because they are deeply rooted in the mind of the author and strike a chord in the ear of the audience. They reinforce a strongly held prejudice or interest.

An elderly gentleman here in Athens, Georgia, not so long ago, insisted to me that the Army of Northern Virginia had occupied Baltimore. My offer to supply the evidence of Lee's defeat at Sharpsburg, Maryland, was not sufficient to convince him. "But, I read it in a book," he insisted, apparently mistaking Newt Gingrich's Civil War trilogy, works of fiction, for historical fact. (Gingrich had Robert E. Lee winning the battle of Gettysburg, marching on to Baltimore, and being converted to antislavery by a rabbi there.)

The case of Holocaust deniers is less quirky and far more ominous. The effort, expense, and time it took Emory University historian Deborah Lipstadt to prove that Holocaust denier David Irving was deliberately lying when he wrote that "Jews are not victims but victimizers" showed that history Zombies are very real indeed. She, and the truth, prevailed, but there are some, including American politicians like Arthur Jones of Illinois and John Fitzgerald of California, still find this Zombie worth reviving. Fake facts are Zombies.

A mistaken interpretation may result from false facts or fake facts. The former is not a Zombie. The latter is. "Well, that's your opinion, and I have mine" is the conventional defense of this Zombie. But all opinions are not equal. The expert opinion based on familiarity with subject and primary research should outweigh any other, but again, "I don't trust experts" is the response. "I trust my gut" more than "anyone else's brain" was another version, this from the lips of President Donald Trump to a *Washington Post* reporter.

Some interpretations of historical events are inherently contentious, but contestable. Was the sectional contest a struggle between an industrializing North and an agricultural South? Was states' rights a legitimate constitutional jurisprudence? Was secession illegal? Was the Union perpetual? These are tough to resolve because contemporaries in 1860 and 1861 did not agree on them. An interpretation of questionable facts asserted by contemporaries becomes, over the course of time, part of history. The fact that some political leaders in 1860 thought that secession was constitutionally permissible and other political leaders thought that the Union was indissoluble is neither false nor fake.

Of course, one must separate the assertions of past actors from the assertions of historians. Historians' interpretations of past events and ideas may be questionable. Historians engage in interpretation all the time. Interpretation, or analysis, tries to answer the why questions in history. Disagreement over interpretation happens all the time, and does not mean that there are Zombies present, although one may see them approaching in an interpretation that rests on fake facts. So, the assertion that the Confederacy lost the war because it could not compete with Union manufacturing is questionable. Confederate armies never ran out of ammunition or replacements for their lost muskets. The Union armies had the potential for technological superiority, for example in the introduction of repeating Henry or Spencer rifles, but did not take full advantage, because the bullets cost too much to manufacture and soldiers tended to use them up too quickly in battle. Succeeding generations of historians often revise the interpretations of their predecessors. While revisiting and rethinking older arguments may be condemned as revisionism, revision keeps historical scholarship fresh (and gives younger scholars something to publish on their way to tenure).

An aside: some interpretative errors may grow from logical mistakes. David Hackett Fischer's *Historians' Fallacies* (1970) catalogued these, including overgeneralization, tunnel vision, confusing cause and effect, and fallacious comparisons. To these one might add the error of overdetermination, when all things are explained by a single theory. These are errors that later historians will correct, though some are persistent. Errors of this kind include racial theories (for example explanations of imperialism based on racial superiority and inferiority) and class theories (based on some form of Marxism, about which more shortly). An increasingly common, and to me alarming, variant of these is the argument that only women can write women's history, only blacks can write black history, only the French can write French history, and so on. The problem with these is that, followed to their logical conclusion, no one can write history at all because no one alive can understand what it was like to be alive in previous times. Still, these are not Zombies.

Let us pause for a moment to think about what Zombies are not. They are not the bodily manifestations of mythical figures. Myths are a part of the cultural heritage of a people. People invented them, passed them down to younger generations orally and then in writing. The myth is not history proper because there is no evidence for the existence of the mythological figure, save in the imagination of the believer. Myth is thus a kind of sacred history, loved and prized, but not taken as literally true. Myths take place in a time before the day to day of human time. Thus myths are often part of the origin stories of a people. Myths can also involve animals and inanimate objects, giving to both human-like characteristics.

Zombies are not legendary figures. A legend is a story about real people who lived, and whose deeds have passed down through tales, a John Henry "the steel driving man" and Johnny Appleseed for example. Joseph Campbell's theory of the hero with a thousand faces is a bridge between myth and legend. Campbell surveyed a wide variety of myths and concluded that they all included a human being who bravely entered the supernatural world and there learned mysteries and gained prowess that he brought back to the people. His gift, sometimes his sacrifice, enabled the people to survive. Campbell was a mystic, and sometimes it is difficult to follow his point, but the motif seems to fit the real figures who were larger than life like Moses, Jesus, Mohammed, and Buddha. Legends may not have clearly documented biographies, but some factual evidence can be found if we look for it. For example, historian Scott Nelson has found a real John Henry, a tunnel worker leased by the C & O Railroad from a Richmond, Virginia, prison. The legend of John Henry then grew, along with his size, strength, and significance. The real Johnny Appleseed was John Chapman, one of the nation's first nurserymen and conservationists.

The most familiar class of legends are folktales, but Zombies are not folktale figures. In folklore, legends and myths overlap. Folktales can be told and retold for edification and amusement. Some of the characters are unsavory. For example, one figure in folklore who seems to appear regularly is the trickster. In oral cultures, he may be a spider, a coyote, or a rabbit. In *Uncle Remus: His Songs and His Sayings, The Folklore of the Old Plantation*, a collection of folktales the Georgia journalist Joel Chandler Harris published in 1881, the trickster is brer (brother) rabbit. Faced with danger from much more powerful animals like brer fox, brer wolf, and brer bear, brer rabbit uses cunning to evade their superior strength. For the Navaho, coyote was a much more dangerous trickster, waiting for men to fall into his clutches. Such tricksters became far more likeable in animated movie shorts—Bugs Bunny and the Road Runner, for example. Bugs and the Road Runner have magical powers that defy Elmer Fudd and Wile E. Coyote, powers that the viewer enjoys watching.

Magic is a common component of the folktale, but Zombies are not magic. The best example of the role of magic in folktales is Merlin, a magician whose aid to King Arthur enables the would-be king to obtain the magical sword Excalibur. The legends surrounding the sword, a symbol of rightful kingship, actually predated the legends of Arthur, an example of two legends combined in one story. The two are probably Welsh in origin, and crisscrossed one another as variants were fashioned over time. The sword is used to blind Arthur's enemies and knight his followers. When he returned the sword to its makers, the end of his realm followed. But he and the sword continue to represent what is best in the ideal of knighthood and the unification of a just and prosperous kingdom. Sometimes magical objects, like Aladdin's lamp and Jack's beans, have a dark side—for using magic without understanding it is dangerous.

So what is a history Zombie? Well, it comes in many shapes and sizes. The old Zombies, the subjects of the first seven chapters of this book, are a statement that is not only provably wrong, but a defacement of truth. They are not just honest mistakes, they are assertive errors, part of larger mischievous arguments. They propel a prejudice that refuses to countenance contradiction, perhaps because the correction is unpalatable, perhaps because the Zombie clings to an invalid bias. These old history Zombies are the manifestations of fake history. They can be an image, like the savage Indian or Jim Crow. They can be an argument, like "the war between the states." They can be a fake fact, like Thomas Jefferson never slept with Sally Hemings. They can be a fake interpretation, like white supremacy or the inferiority of nonwhite races. They can be streams of propaganda produced by a nation's intelligence services or individual efforts retweeted by social media indifferent to evidence. Inconvenient truths and unpopular views can be silenced by social media "callouts, draggings, and pile-ons," mobbing that may be planned or simply a result of mindless repetition of prejudices. Perhaps we can never know what is true about the past with the exactness of science, but we can know what is false. If we assume that we can arrive at reasonable readings of fact and falsity—a goal in today's climate of partisanship under attack from the left and right of the political spectrum—we can defeat the Zombies and save historical scholarship for the next generation. That is a worthwhile task, I think.

The final chapter of the book confronts what is for me an even more troubling aspect of Zombie history. It is the creation of new or young Zombies. It is easy enough for the modern historian to condemn the racial and misogynistic animus of past generations. It is not so easy for us to confront our own Zombies. For we, too, are Zombie makers. By setting aside our professional duty to listen to the many voices of the past, and instead mining sources or privileging arguments because they fit our political or social agenda, we make new Zombies.

I do not know if history teaches lessons that everyone must know, or if we are fated to repeat history if we do not master those lessons. I think we should concede that history is about the present as well as the past, for we live in the present. The future is in our own hands, not those of past generations of workers, framers, founders, heroes, villains, and whoever else we choose to teach and write about. In a country of so many people with so many different and sometimes conflict-filled histories, there is space (and yearning) for many different versions of the past. It is the value of history to each and all of us that makes capturing it such a prize, and all the more important to seek out and destroy Zombie history.

CHAPTER ONE

First Zombies

The first history Zombie shambles out of the mist of the distant past into the popular mind, the textbook, digital media, and the classroom. His or her shape is indistinct, because the farther back in history one goes, the fewer written sources there are, and the less we can be sure about. This makes it hard to know what shape the Zombie takes. Nevertheless, we can know that Zombies wander through the images and narratives of the peopling of North America, including the savage Indian, the haggard, sour-faced witch, and her persecutor, the mean-spirited Puritan.

Who were the first Americans? Calvin (of *Calvin and Hobbes*) was confident that "I always catch these trick questions," but even Calvin's self-assurance would have been tested by this question. In his introduction to the British Museum's display of North American Indian artifacts, Jonathan C. H. King admitted that "no other aspect of contemporary native North America is so contentious as, and in its own way, so interesting, as the naming of peoples." America (hence Americans) is the place name assigned to lands that European explorers found on the other side of the Atlantic. Italian voyager Amerigo Vespucci won pride of place, literally, by writing about his travels, and, even though some of these accounts were clearly fabricated, they convinced a German mapmaker, Martin Waldseemüller, to use the Latin version of Vespucci's first name for the new lands. Then were the first Americans the Europeans? Hardly. For thousands of years different peoples lived on the Western continents. When he first set foot in the Bahamas, Christopher Columbus named its inhabitants "Indios," because he wrongly thought he had reached the far eastern end of the Indies. Indians is the common term for the native peoples, a proof of how European newcomers have displaced native tongues. Other European colonizers in other continents called the natives aborigines, a term that soon came to mean primitives.

Today, advocates of native peoples' rights call original inhabitants of the islands and the continents "First Peoples," but this, like America and Indian, is actually an argument hidden in a name. It is a claim of priority and privilege over the land that its first explorers and settlers made, nearly two thousand years ago. "Only the Indian people really knew what was going on," writes Colin Calloway in his *First Peoples: A Documentary Survey of American Indian History* (2008), and today neither native people nor newcomer really can be sure what the first people called themselves. Such ignorance is an invitation to Zombie history.

To repeat, Native Americans, First Peoples, and Indians were not the names that the peoples who first came to the Western Hemisphere brought with them. Those names are lost. We can "upstream" to guess at them, however. Upstreaming is a technique that anthropologists use to reach back in time. The researcher takes existing customs, words, and objects and tries to follow them back to their origins. Thus the aboriginal peoples of the Far North, the most recent arrivals in the Western Hemisphere, call themselves Inuit, which is the plural of Inuk, meaning "person." Almost invariably the newcomers' words for themselves would have translated to "the people" or "us."

Instead of trying to find out what the first comers called themselves, European settlers gave them names. Naming is a kind of magic. By naming we try to control nature, turning novelty into familiarity. That is how a conquering people ensures their conquest—they replace the names of native peoples and places. The French called the Inuit peoples of the Far North "Eskimo" from the French *esquimaux*, meaning people who wear snowshoes. The first step that Columbus took to ensure the Spanish possession of the Bahamas was to ignore the native Lucani names and call the first place on which he set foot "San Salvador." He also read in Latin a document prepared by lawyers in Spain to make the conquest legal. The Indians, because of their custom of listening politely to oratory, did not interrupt even though they could not understand a word. When the English settlers of New York had to deal with the native peoples of the Finger Lakes region, they called them the "Five Nations." In fact, they were a confederation of villages, not nations at all. The French, who arrived before the English, called these people the Iroquois, a loose rendering (variant) of the Basque explorers of Canada's word for killers. Would a people call itself killers? Hardly. Instead, the French explorers allied themselves with the native Algonquin peoples of the St. Lawrence River area. Those people regularly warred with the Iroquois peoples. Hence the name the French gave to their allies' enemy. These names are the first Zombies.

Those we injure by theft we also insult. The Iroquois people who lived closest to the French Canadian Indians the French called "Mohawks." In the Algonquian language Mohawk meant eater of the dead or man-eater. The name implied that the Mohawks practiced cannibalism. The Mohawk called themselves the people of the eastern door, Kanienkahaka, and the confederacy of Iroquois who lived around the Finger Lakes to which the Mohawk belonged called themselves the Haudenausawnee, or people of the longhouse. The evil connotations of the terms "Iroquois" and "Mohawk" have disappeared with time, but so has much of the Iroquois language. It is spoken by a very few native people and survives largely in college anthropology courses.

Later accounts, justifying Indian removal, had a tragic but cynical cast. The model was Francis Parkman, a fine writer and thorough scholar whose view of the Indians was condescending at best, and at worst—well, consider his dismissal of Indian worship: "a chaos of degrading, ridiculous, and incoherent superstitions." Theodore Roosevelt's *Winning of the West* (1881) documented the spread of the English-speaking peoples "over the waste spaces" of the West. Characterized as "tireless, and careless of all hardship, they came silently out of unknown forests, robbed and murdered, and then disappeared again into the fathomless depths of the woods. . . . Without warning, and unseen until the moment they dealt the death stroke," Indians had to be conquered by the "bold and hardy" English newcomers. Zombies all; ironically portrayed as Zombies!

A People without a History?

Neolithic (new stone age) peoples did not leave written histories of themselves. It is thus ironic that the first of our history Zombies is a people without a history. For until the first ethnographers—students of Native American life—came along in the middle of the nineteenth century, it was assumed that little had changed in Native American ways. Nothing could be further from the truth.

The absence of a documentary record does not mean the absence of historical change. The First Peoples were not always here. They were not homogeneous. They did not all live in teepees, wear eagle feathers in their headbands, and use bows and arrows. In fact, over the long course of their fifteen thousand years in what we call America they had gone from small bands of hunter-gathers to villagers. Though they never gave up hunting and gathering, some among them discovered and cultivated maize and potatoes, invented pottery, and built mound cities of thousands of men and women. They had a history, their lives changed over time, their numbers grew, and some among them built cities, irrigation systems, and invented pictographic writing.

Peoples of the eastern woodlands thrived in an environment entirely different from peoples of the northern boreal forests and peoples of the semiarid southwestern mesas. Mound cities of the Mississippi, Ohio, and other river valleys did not resemble the pueblos (again a Spanish term for the many different names Hopi and other southwestern peoples gave their villages) of the peoples along the Rio Grande and the Colorado Rivers and their tributaries. The peoples of these regions spoke mutually unintelligible languages, though they traded turquoise and copper, animal skins and pots across thousands of miles.

The history Zombie is the savage Indian, always at heart a savage, primitive in speech and demeanor, who never adapts, never assimilates, and can never be trusted. He or she has no name and no history. Zombies do not have names. If you take away a people's name for themselves, or individuals' own names, or you call them by something other than their names for themselves, you begin to turn those people into Zombies. The wonderful actor Wes Studi, a Cherokee by birth, can be cast in movies as Geronimo, an Apache; Magua, a Huron; and a Pawnee warrior, even though the Apache were an Athabascan people of the Southwest, the Huron were an Iroquoian people of the Northeast, and the Pawnee were a plains people whose native tongue was Caddoan. (For his roles, he spoke the appropriate language.) Members of those peoples today do not particularly resemble one another. But then, the Indian with no name is a Zombie whose description easily shifts.

One study of western US history in secondary schools found textbooks with pictures of John Wesley Powell, sent west by the federal government, standing next to the Grand Canyon. It described him as the first American to visit the site on August 13, 1869. Next to him in the photograph is an unidentified individual, though by dress obviously a Native American. Native Americans visited the Canyon thousands of years before Powell. History educators later identified the individual as Tau Pu, a Paiute Indian chief whose people lived in the area. He was Powell's guide. How could history have erased him? Without a name, he ceased to have an identity and became a Zombie.

Every one of the Indians who charged the cavalry in John Ford movies, every one of the Indians who pursued the *Revenant*, all of the Indians who adopted Lieutenant Dunbar in *Dances with Wolves* had names. The Navajo men who stood in for Northern Cheyenne in *Cheyenne Autumn* had names, and to make a mockery of the substitution, spoke *diné bazaad*, their own Athabaskan dialect, rather than learn the Algonquian language of the characters they played. Early twentieth-century photographic portraiture of Navajo and Cheyenne demonstrates that the two peoples did not look like one another at all. The Navajo actors knew they were Zombies, and some of their offhand speech, captured by the cameras, does not bear repeating. In a finishing touch, John Ford cast the roles of the Cheyenne chiefs with Ricardo Montalbán and Gilbert Roland, both Mexicans of Spanish extraction—as if more Zombies were needed.

Of course, one way to avoid all of this mincing of words is to leave the Indians out of the account of the westward march of civilization, or at least make them cameo players on their own land. Their "menace" and their "atrocities" to one side (ignoring the notion that the resettlement of the Ohio Country was trespass with arms and home invasion on a massive scale), David McCullough's acclaimed best seller, *The Pioneers: The Heroic Story of the Settlers Who Brought the American Ideal West* (2019) returns us to a time when the settlers of the Old Northwest, "as would be observed by historians long afterward, the Northwest Ordinance was designed to guarantee what would one day be known as the American way of life." He could not quite do what the settlers had done—remove the Indians—but he could quote Charles Dickens on tour in Cincinnati, "'We met some of these poor Indians [displaced by the Removal Act of 1830] afterwards, riding on shaggy ponies,' Dickens continued. They looked to him like gypsies . . . Only the Indian names were to remain." Sad, even tragic, but then back to the really important story.

Red Men

The "Red Indian" or the "redskin" is a Zombie. In fact, no Native American is red, unless red ocher has been used as decorative paint. The first accounts of meeting with North American natives in European writings described them as "of a colour brown" or some variant of tanned, tawny, and similar terms. Firsthand observers like the English writers Thomas

Harriot and John Smith assumed that the Indian's skin darkened because of exposure to the sun. Others noted the "persistent application . . . of natural dyes mixed with walnut oil and bear's grease." Sometimes, the first English arrivals in America reported, Indians decorated themselves in red and black paint, but no one thought that the red was anything more than a dye.

Over time, however, the English began to assign malign meanings to colors like red. For color was already a potent signifier in English culture. The color black had already taken on a malign connotation when the English first met Africans. The terms blackguard, blackmail, blackhearted, black magic, and black sheep were in common usage, and disposed the English to see Africans as inherently evil. The color red was associated with the Irish, and was a commonly used insult during the Anglo-Irish civil wars of the 1550s and 1560s. The red color implied that the Irish were choleric and wild. As war with various groups of Indians became a fixture of colonial borderlands life, the "Red Indian" became a menace rather than a curiosity. Indians, it argued, were a different race from the Europeans; red instead of white, the Indian was inherently a savage, therefore inferior. The same logic was in the process of development to explain why dark-skinned Africans were intended by nature to serve Europeans as slaves.

Ironically, the colonists were not the only ones who were discovering that the Indian was red. Historian Nancy Shoemaker has found that Indians of the Southeast in the early eighteenth century began to call themselves red, to distinguish themselves from whites (Europeans) and blacks (Africans) penetrating Indian homelands. Daniel Richter's *Facing East from Indian Country* recounts how Indian spiritual leaders in the last decades of the eighteenth century tried to unite various native groups by preaching that all Indians were red. They adopted the colonists' racism to their own use. It was a difference in skin color that surmounted or should surmount older inter-Indian rivalries. According to this story, the red people were the first to leave the ground and walk as men. The white people were the junior brother, and should show deference to their elders. The message got about during the French and Indian Wars, and seemed to work for a time. Indian peoples who had raided one another's villages for a time joined in a common effort to drive the English and colonists from the Ohio Valley and the Upper Great Lakes. But the effort foundered after a few years.

The image of the Indian as the "Redman" or the "Redskin" persisted, however, and it gained a pejorative or evil connotation as the nineteenth century wore on. When novelist James Fenimore Cooper first referred to Native Americans as "Redskins" in the 1820s, he was using the term without malice, probably because the Indians of the Otsego Valley in New York where he was reared used the term to refer to themselves. But like usages of the n-word, when a term that people use to describe themselves is used by others, it becomes an insult. Redskin and redskins is today a racial epithet that refuses to die, although lawsuits like *Blackhorse et al. v. Pro Football* (2014) denied to the Washington Redskins football team trademark status for its offensive images of a Native American and the term "redskins": the trademark administrative court found that "by a preponderance of the evidence, the petitioners established that the term 'Redskins' was disparaging of Native Americans, when used in relation to professional football services, at the times the various registrations involved in the cancellation proceeding were issued. Thus, in accordance with applicable law, the federal registrations for the 'Redskins' trademarks involved in this proceeding must be cancelled."

Just when one had good reason to hope that the story of First Peoples was in trustworthy hands, a new form of prejudice has taken hold of the historical profession. In 2018, presidential candidate Elizabeth Warren was challenged to prove that she did, indeed, have indigenous ancestry. Her family had told her it was so, and a DNA test proved a distant connection. At a 2019 American Historical Association session, a group of historians identifying themselves by their tribal registrations, as well as their academic positions, questioned whether Warren's claims were sufficient to show what Warren wanted to show. One of the panel stressed that membership in an Indian nation (a categorization that many Indians did not accept until Congress attached various benefits to it) was politically superior to mere ancestry—one had to belong, not just identify. Nationality mattered, a claim that eerily echoed nineteenth-century European nationalist movements. It's not about what identity you claim, it's about who claims you, the panelists agreed. One should use Indian methods of identification (i.e., tribal), which, ironically, were imposed on native peoples by European colonizers. Elsewhere, Native American museum curators told their audiences that their aim was to "decolonialize" the exhibits: "Decolonizing practices . . . are collaborative with tribal communities, privilege Native perspective and voice, and include the full measure of history, ensuring truth-telling." "Truth-telling" is now synonymous in the new orthodoxy with privileging one perspective over another. The irony is almost overwhelming, although members of the panel and the museum curators did not see it. Worse still is the implication that scholars like my colleague Claudio Saunt should not be allowed to write Native American history unless he can show that he is a member of a federally recognized tribe.

Then it gets even more complicated—and problematic. Can a member of an eastern woodlands tribe, for example a member of the Oneida Nation, write with true understanding of the Northern Cheyenne? Identity politics does not map easily over professional credentials. If you claim a special privilege to write about your people, does it disqualify you from writing about others?

Columbus

Historians and geographers actually know quite a bit about the real Cristoforo Columbus. We know he was born and reared in Genoa when it had been transformed by the Mediterranean trade from a medieval Italian town into a thriving commercial center. He went to sea as a young man, during the wars between Christians and Turks. He married well, and later took his oldest son with him on the first voyage to America. He and his brothers were for a time imprisoned by authorities in Spain for misgovernment of the Spanish New World possessions, for jealousies at the Court of Ferdinand and Isabela made a foreigner like Columbus easily suspect.

Columbus was a man who greatly enjoyed the adventures that seagoing and exploration offered. He was a deeply pious Catholic, and a man on the make, looking for the wealth and fame that new discoveries could bring. In these ways he was a man with one foot in the past and one in the future. In hindsight, his ignorance was palpable and his view of the world gullible. At the time, the reportage of his voyages, what he brought back from them, and what he, and Spain, planned of them transformed the European world. A Europe long besieged by its Islamic enemies now sensed a turning point, a vast New World of riches that could be deployed against the old antagonist. Surely it is possible to admire such a man as a navigator and ship captain, judging him not by our own standards, but by those of his contemporaries.

Columbus's knowledge of navigation, marine engineering, and everything else was the product of his time and place. That time and place was the Renaissance in Europe, including the rebirth of higher learning, the introduction of printed books, the rediscovery of old maps, Europe's sharing of the treasures of Arab shipbuilding, the compass, the astrolabe, and the demand for spices and sugar that the Crusades had brought to Europe. Without these, there would have been no Columbus in our history books.

Columbus's personal journey from Genoa to the pilot school in Lisbon, to the Court of Isabel and Ferdinand in Spain, would not have happened without the rise of European trade with Asia and Africa. Portuguese explorers had already laid the way for Columbus. They had adapted technologies like the compass (for direction), the astrolabe (for latitude), and the lateen sail (to allow caravels to tack across the wind), all from Arab sources, to sail out from the Mediterranean into the Atlantic. Columbus had all of these courtesy of his Portuguese mentors, and three ships and crews, courtesy of Isabel, along with the knowledge that he would not fall off the edge of the Earth, courtesy of every mariner of the age. In short, he was a man of his times, and his actions and beliefs cannot be understood, whether they are celebrated or condemned, without understanding those times.

Columbus's first voyage took him from the Spanish port of Palos to the Bahamas, which he incorrectly thought were the eastern edge of the Spice Islands (the East Indies). In this and three subsequent voyages, he charted the Caribbean Sea and a bit of the coast of South America. He brought back to Spain captives and the flora and fauna of the New World, though he never understood that he had found new continents, or that an ocean, the Pacific, lay between those continents and Asia. He reported, based on his own observations, that the Lucayan people of what he named San Salvador would in time become good Christians and loyal subjects of the Spanish crown.

Can a real person become a Zombie? Columbus the real person now has two Zombie impersonators. The old claim that Columbus discovered America turns a genuine seafarer, pilot, mapmaker, and explorer into a Zombie, the avatar of Western civilization coming to a howling wilderness and transforming it. Columbus did not discover America. He was not even the first European to sail across the Atlantic. Vikings from Iceland did that (or, to believe another source, Neolithic peoples from the European continent arrived even earlier). He was not the first person to visit North America. Those were the First People from Asia. He was not the person who named the new continent (that was another Italian, Amerigo Vespucci). What did Columbus discover? He discovered the vastness of the New World, and his four voyages to what he called the Indies galvanized European interest in the new worlds. Nothing was the same after his return to Spain—the real Columbus, that is, not the Zombie. But as the late philosopher of history Hayden White wrote in his 1966 essay, "The Burden of History," quoting a critic of history, "history will justify anything." Historically, that is a sad truth. The first Columbus Zombie became the avatar of early modern European moral, religious, and technological superiority over all the other peoples of the earth. For this, and for the pride of Italian Americans, October 12 was made Columbus Day in 1934.

(Congress three years later assigned it the second Monday of October.) It helped that Italian Americans voted Democratic.

In 1992, the five-hundredth anniversary of his first voyage, the unintended consequences of Columbus's arrival turned him into a second history Zombie. He was saddled with everything that the newcomers did intentionally, or not. He brought with him the diseases, the rats, fleas, cockroaches, pigs, and other pests that decimated native populations. He stole men, becoming the model for mansteeling for the next three hundred years. On Hispaniola, his men treated the natives with disrespect, attempting to enslave them, something he did not want, but by then it was too late. His legend became part of the dark side of the conquest of the Indies. Enter the second Zombie Columbus, a demon to be cast into that darkness.

That is hardly fair, but history is a powerful weapon in the hands of those who feel aggrieved, this time the ancestors of some of the Indians, along with their allies in the academy. They had decided that all of the explorers, conquistadores, traders, and just about everyone else who came in the waves of immigration from Europe in the early modern era to the Western Hemisphere were evil. They had all been turned into Zombies. English Zombies like John Smith and Walter Raleigh, Spanish Zombies like Hernán Cortés and Francisco Pizarro; French Zombies, Dutch Zombies, Portuguese Zombies, a horde of disfigured Zombies descending on the land and ravishing it. All motivated by greed, false religion, and the desire to outdo one another in conquest.

Why get Columbus so wrong—either by pillory or by celebration? On the one hand, he is a convenient symbol for the victimization of the native peoples. In our charged partisan times, however, when historical scholarship seems on the verge of becoming a field within the general rubric of grievance studies, nuance falls to harsh generalization. The admiral of the ocean sea becomes the very Satan that he thought he was combating. The urge to celebrate him comes, ironically, from the same source as the urge to criticize him. For the Knights of Columbus he remains a man of deep religious conviction who loved and respected the Indians and told his men to treat them with kindness. It is almost too much for a real person to bear, these contrary images, and the result is Zombie history.

European Technology and Native People

Before native peoples took the measure of Columbus, they saw his ships. Peoples of the Bahamas were accustomed to canoes, some of which were the size of Viking longboats. But Columbus's ships must have impressed the natives. And when push came to shove, surely Western technology made defeat of the Indians inevitable? What chance could they have against the newcomers' metallurgy, writing, and gunpowder? True, North American native peoples did not have the wheel, books or writing tools, or steel armor. When the Europeans arrived, they brought tools and weapons unlike any the natives possessed. Indian wood and stone weapons could not pierce European armor and European steel swords and steel-tipped spears could cut through Indian wooden armor. European guns and cannons reduced Indian fortifications to rubble. Europeans had the alphabet, books, and writing. Indians were awed by the way that European letters could convey information precisely over long distances. In the eyes of the first Europeans to encounter the native peoples, and in the eyes of many generations of historians, the absence of these technologies made the Indians primitive and ripe for conquest by more technologically sophisticated Europeans. All of this seems to make intuitive sense. When you look closer, however, you find a Zombie in a steel helmet and breastplate.

The Zombie is not technology itself, nor is it the difference between the conquistadors' gear and the Indians' technology. The Zombie is the idea that technological advances (and the Western civilization that they came to represent in the history of contact) made conquest of North America inevitable. And what is inevitable is not subject to moral criticism. The inevitability, in turn, allegedly rested on the superiority of European technology. Again, superiority is a code word for preeminence and authority. The implication is that Western civilization was better than native customs. The savage or innocent native peoples (depending on whose contemporary account one reads) simply had to bow to the dominance of Western ways.

It is true, if one believes the missionaries' accounts, that native peoples were amazed that Europeans could communicate information over great distances by writing on pieces of paper. North American Indians did not have the alphabet, but as early as AD 800 Indians of the Mexican plateau had a writing system. Indians used all manner of local materials like deerskins to fashion maps and pictorial histories like Egyptian hieroglyphics. Europeans brought metallurgy and chemistry to the Americas, on which were based plate armor and firearms. But the Mexica deployed weapons whose obsidian tips could piece European plate armor. Europe in 1492 could boast cities of some size, like Paris, Naples, and Venice, none of which were any larger than Cahokia in the Mississippi Valley or Tenochtitlan on the Mexican Plateau.

European trade depended on roads, the wheel, and sailing ships. Indians built roads and large canoes, but did not invent the wheel. The reason is simple. Wheels are valuable when one has oxen, horses, or other large animals to pull wagons, chariots, and other wheeled vehicles. Indians did not domesticate dray animals. But the absence of wheels did not deter Indians from trading over long distances or exchanging pottery, hides, food, and valuable ornaments in turquoise and copper. Had the Europeans not arrived, Indian civilizations might have progressed to rival those of Africa, but who can know what did not happen.

When the Europeans arrived on the eastern coasts of North America, Indians very soon began adapting and transforming trade goods and firearms to fit Indian ways. In the course of the encounter, Indians adapted European trade goods to Indian uses. For example, cheap Italian colored beads, a favored trade item, were cherished by Indians because they showed the status of the natives who could trade for them. Europeans adopted wampum, strings of quahog and whelk shells, already valued by Indians, as a medium of trade. Indians became better hunters with European firearms than the Europeans. In return, Indians' local knowledge, for example of hunting and local plant culture, far exceeded that of the Europeans. The result at first was mutual borrowing and sometimes mutual respect. Europeans learned about the new land and its flora and fauna from the Indians, even adopting Indian place names. The states of Massachusetts, Connecticut, Alabama, Mississippi, Missouri, Ohio, and Illinois, for example, all come from Indian dialects. So too did staples of the modern American diet like corn, potatoes, tomatoes, and chocolate, which are all of Indian origin and transformed European tastes, population growth, and commerce.

At the same time, what historians have called the "Columbian Exchange" had a terrible side. To the New World the Europeans brought the rat, the cockroach, and a veritable chest of drawers of diseases like measles, chicken pox, smallpox, and malaria that raced through Indian populations, in some places killing off more than 90 percent of the native inhabitants. They had no immunities to these diseases. Europeans also brought pigs that ate their way through Indian gardens, cattle that grazed on the grasses that fed the deer, and a demand for beaver skins (beaver hats were all the rage in European fashion) that induced Indians to trap and kill many of the woodlands' beaver. The result was that beaver dams fell into disrepair and the waters contained behind them rushed over the land, carrying its nutrients away. Contact with the Europeans was an ecological holocaust in America.

On top of which, Europeans became experts at playing on existing Indian rivalries. There was nothing new in that. Julius Caesar's account of the Roman conquest of Gaul explained how he pitted one tribe against another. The English and the French along the St. Lawrence River pitted Canadian Huron and Ottawa against New York Iroquois peoples. The Virginia government used the Susquehannock against the Iroquois, and the Pennsylvania government, despite its promises of fair treatment of the indigenous Delaware, used complex diplomatic maneuvers to drive the Delaware from their ancestral lands. Indians tried their best to reverse these polarities, pitting the French against the English, and, in the Mississippi Valley, the French and Spanish against the English. But long-standing animosity between powerful Indian alliances like the Creek and the Cherokee in the Southeast and the Iroquois and the Algonquian in the Northeast gave the Europeans the upper hand in the game of divide and conquer.

Why is the conquest by technology story so compelling, then, so common a Zombie, pushing the ecological and diplomatic stories to the edges of the page, if it simply was not true? The answer lies first in our own commitment to technological improvement. We believe in technology and embrace it almost unhesitatingly. "Progress Is Our Most Important Product" was the slogan of one of the great American manufacturing companies, General Electric, and both concepts seemed to go hand in hand. Progress was what made the conditions of life more bearable to each generation, as the standard of living for most Americans rose. The production of goods, particularly consumer durables like home appliances, automobiles, and more recently electronics, drove the economy. Today, go to any college campus when classes are changing and watch the students as they leave the classrooms. They are all on their smartphones. In the classroom the instructor is turning off the electronic devices she has used to present the online and other instructional materials. Twenty years ago one would not have seen any of this. Colleges routinely advertise their computer-friendly campuses, and provide free laptops and tablets to incoming students. Webinars and other online educational programs keep faculty up to date. Textbooks arrive as web-based content, and e-books on tablets are the rage for educational and recreational diversion.

Like the Indians' abandonment of older collective customs of the hunt, of sharing food, and giving gifts in favor of individualistic customs of trade, the losses technology imposes on time-tested pedagogies are obvious. Reading a book is not the same as viewing content on a screen. Face glued to a smartphone or following a MOOC (massive open online course) is not a conversation with a fellow student or a face to face chat with an instructor. Replacement of the face to face with the online may represent economic gains, but that is not the reason they have swept across the campuses. (In fact, studies have shown that face to face instruction and taking notes with a pen and a pad is a more effective pedagogy than viewing and typing.) But the infatuation with more and more sophisticated technologies seems unstoppable.

Which brings us to the second reason why we embrace the technology made conquest inevitable and right Zombie. The United States was late into the business of conquest of foreign nations, but once engaged in it, joined with fervor. A federation of republican states abandoned its aversion to imperialism, and gobbled up pieces of the Mexican Republic and the Spanish Empire. Where corporate interests found natural resources, arable land, or customers, the flag followed. Some Americans were repulsed by this avarice, but presidents and politicians defended these exercises of economic and military power in terms very similar to those that early modern European colonizers used. Technological superiority not only guaranteed supremacy, it made conquest a moral duty. And a Zombie.

Pilgrims, Puritans, and Religious Freedom

Many of the first English visitors to the New World were only nominally religious. By contrast, the Pilgrims and the Puritans of New England were passionate Protestant believers and brought that passion to their settlements. As a result, there are two Zombies fighting for control of the religious history of early New England. The first is that the Pilgrims and the Puritans came to America for religious freedom. The Mayflower Compact of 1620 and Roger Williams's later sermons are the touchstones of this claim. A monument to the first Pilgrim settlers, at what was their burying ground, proclaims, "history records no nobler venture for faith and liberty than that of the Pilgrim band. . . . they laid the foundations of a state, wherein every man, through countless ages, should have liberty to worship God in his own way." Williams, who after much travail, largely at the hands of his Puritan brethren, came to believe that civil authority should have no power to cabin the religious beliefs of the people, has been elevated by historians to a station far above what he held in his lifetime. Literary historian Vernon Parrington proclaimed that Williams's view of the separation of church and state "must be reckoned the richest contribution of Puritainism to American political thought." Colonial historian Edmund S. Morgan not only extolled Williams's "original mind," the historian credited the preacher with "demolishing" the very idea of an established church. In fact, Williams was an important thinker, one of the founders of Rhode Island, whose laws (which he largely wrote) would in time welcome a mixed multitude of worshipers. But he was an outsider, and the Rhode Island experiment remained an exception to the laws of church and state in the rest of New England.

The second Zombie is that the Pilgrims and the Puritans came to set up a state ruled by the church. In fact, they fled from a state church that they found tainted at best and illegitimate at worst. One should not conflate all their leaders' opinions on these questions into a single generalization, a caution that historian Michael Winship ably offers. On the other hand, Thomas Jefferson Wertenbaker's *The First Americans* (1927), a well-regarded survey by one of the most prolific colonial historians of his day, was certain that the Massachusetts Bay Colony was a "theocracy." Sidney Mead's *The Lively Experiment: The Shaping of Christianity in America* (1963) had little good to say about the "Puritan theocrats on the Charles [River]," and seventy years after Wertenbaker's essay, Darren Staloff found the notion of theocracy still floating around. Both ideas of liberty and theocracy are wrong, though they persist. Insofar as this does violence to a more sensible account of the settlement of New England, they are Zombies.

Caught in the heat of the Protestant Reformation and the religious wars between Protestants and Roman Catholics at the end of the sixteenth century, the Pilgrims were a group of religious separatists from farms in the northeast of England who traveled illegally to Leyden in the Netherlands. They wanted no part of a state religion, and rejected the Church of England. The idea that they wanted a theocracy is nonsense, and they did not allow churchmen to rule when they did travel to the part of the Massachusetts Indian lands they called Plimouth Plantation. In fact, for much of their first years they did not have the services of an ordained minister. The compact they drafted and signed on the *Mayflower* did not mention a state church.

Did they then come for religious liberty? That concept was foreign to them. Indeed, it was foreign to the ideas of all the radical reform Protestants of England. They came to worship God in a single congregation, but did not throw open the colony to anyone who differed from their ideas of sanctity and conformity. Although the Netherlands from which they had come did allow Protestants of various sects to worship relatively freely, and even welcomed Jews if they behaved themselves, Dutch toleration was not based on the ideal of religious liberty. The Dutch needed all the help they could get in their ongoing war for independence from Catholic Spain, and that included practical toleration of Protestants of various sects and Jews.

Now we come to the Puritans, often confused (on history exams at least) with the Pilgrims. The Puritans were not primarily farm folk. They were a mixed multitude of substantial families from London and the surrounding countryside. They did not reject the English monarchy. When one of them, Roger Williams, tried to do that in 1635, he was chased out of the Massachusetts Bay colony. They did not separate from the English state church. Instead, they wanted to be a distant (hence safe) model for the reform of the church and state—"a city on a hill," according to Jonathan Winthrop, the first governor of the colony, for all to see and emulate. Winthrop and his fellow voyagers, according to the leading modern student of early Puritanism, Michael Winship, "in their own minds . . . were always on stage, before their jealous deity and before an earthly audience of whom the greatest, wicked, part . . . was hoping for them to fail." So Winthrop's speech was as much warning as it was celebration.

Winthrop's leadership was important, but the stars of the Puritan experiment in self-government were ministers like John Cotton of Boston, Thomas Shepard of Newtowne (later Cambridge), and Thomas Hooker, who would leave Massachusetts to found the new Connecticut colony. Their preaching was widely reported and greatly admired and "magistrates worked hand in hand with learned minister to enforce, protect, and direct [religious] reformation," but the Puritans did not believe in theocracy. Busybodies in black gowns like Shepard and later John Norton could poke their noses into civil matters, but the final decisions were not theirs. No minister in Massachusetts held political office. No minister sat on juries or laid down laws. The magistrates, including the governor, might and did consult the ministers on matters of church governance, but the ministers' advice was no more than that.

But the colony was not a hive of religious diversity. Even more than the Pilgrims, the Puritans hated heresy. They would not allow religious dissidence to flourish. They would not allow settlers to practice anything other than the official version of radical reform Protestantism. Controversies over what that version was did disturb the harmony of the colony. Who could expect anything else where so many fervent believers were gathered together. But if harmony was not appreciated, open defiance was never permitted. It was not until 1689 that the Puritans had to swallow hard and allow ministers of the Church of England to preach and build churches and members of the Society of Friends (Quakers), Baptists, and other Protestant sects to worship in their midst. The exception was Roger Williams's colony of Rhode Island, a collection of four towns of religious sectaries around Narragansett Bay. Williams thought that magistrates should not be allowed to tell believers what to believe or how to worship. But even his tolerance had limits: no Catholics need apply.

Historians have long understood that the pious men and women who came to New England were zealots, but not avatars of religious freedom and not believers in theocracy. Why then do popular sources cleave to one of the other of the incorrect interpretations? The answer lies in our civic and religious values rather than our respect for historical truth. One of those values is the First Amendment protection of religious liberty. It has two prongs. The first is a guarantee of freedom of worship. The second is a bar to the establishment of a state religion. In historical fact, they do not have a pedigree that goes back to the first settlements. The very opposite is true. The First Amendment was pressed on James Madison and others in Congress by dissenting sects like the Baptists and the Quakers, long the victims of religious persecution by established churches in the colonies. The First Amendment was a reaction against zealotry and bigotry. Today, we face the return of these very old and divisive religious tendencies, and advocates of establishing a state religion once again look to the Puritans and Pilgrims for legitimacy. They abet the Zombies.

The Witches of Salem

Who could better resemble a Zombie than a witch? Were not witches supposed to be ugly hags, with goober eyes and mottled skin? Today, public figures are prey to the witchfinders. The witchhunt victim is remade in the media to look a lot like the old image of the witch. Sometimes the investigation itself is a kind of Zombie fashioned to hound an innocent person. Mobbing on the web is akin to this sort of witchhunt. Hordes of nameless (actually anonymous) trolls take to social media to defame, decry, and denounce the witchhunt victim.

In seventeenth-century English lore (custom) and law, the witch was a cunning woman (herbal healer), a beggar, or a nag gone wrong. They used powers given them though a pact with the Devil or his agent to do harm. They spoiled the milk, curdled the cheese, made children sick, and even caused those who offended them to die. The fear of witches always accompanied some natural disaster, for example an outbreak of epidemic disease, or a man-made crisis, like a war. At the same time, tales of witches fascinated English and New England readers, and books of extraordinary events were best sellers. A perfect setting for Zombies!

Were there women and men who practiced casting spells and mixing various potions for sale or for their own use? Almost certainly yes. The "eye of newt" and the rest of the recipe of the three witches in William Shakespeare's historical drama *Macbeth* is a little extreme, but folk remedies of dog's urine and other common items were part of the local culture in the villages of New England and the home country. How did communities of neighbors who lived and worked with one another for many years decide that someone among them was a witch? And what turned otherwise ordinary customs into a hanging offense (no one was burned at the stake for witchcraft in New England)? Historians have probed these issues since the early nineteenth century.

The Salem, Massachusetts outbreak was of course the best known, for in it some eighteen convicted witches were hanged, a nineteenth suspect was killed in the process of eliciting a plea from him, and hundreds were held in jail until the governor of the colony decided to bar "spectral evidence" from the trials. A group of tweens and teenaged girls had led the accusations, claiming that witches were afflicting them in the accuseds' spectral form (visible only to the girls). After the first sets of trials, in the spring and summer of 1692, leading ministers warned that the Devil could be behind false accusations as well as the witchcraft itself. The trials were resumed in January 1693, but, without the spectral evidence, nearly all of the suspects were acquitted or pardoned.

Some scholars believe that the root cause was a rivalry between the leaders of an older farming community in what is now Danvers, Massachusetts and the better off leaders of commercial Salem town. Other scholars blame the Salem crisis on the tales of men and women returning from the horrific Indian raids along the Maine coast (there was a war between the English and French, and French missionaries were among the Indians who struck at English settlements). Still other historians, looking at earlier witchcraft accusations and trials, suggest ways in which the accusation grew out of community problems. The alleged witch became the scapegoat for bad crop yields, or for outbreaks of diphtheria. A few historians have found in the witchcraft cases evidence of profound misogyny (woman hating) among the New England settlers, or acute psychological pressures resting on Puritan childrearing methods. We will return to these in a moment.

One fact is indisputable. At this distance, far from the clamor of accusations, it is hard not to see the shadowy figure of the Zombie moving through the contemporary accounts and into the scholarship. It is the Devil, old Nick himself. The people of New England truly believed that the Devil had singled them out for punishment because their piety had fallen away from the high standards of the founders of New England. Leading minister Cotton Mather warned his Boston congregation that worse was to come if they did not mend their ways. Fears of the Devil and His works pervaded the Salem courthouse, the streets, and the dark woods surrounding the villages. New Englanders knew he was near.

Most academic historians, I would venture, do not share this fear of an immanent evil presence, certainly not in the shape of a demon with horns, cleft feet, and a collection of dogs, cats, and other "familiars." So historians ignore the potency of the supernatural, invisible world for those who lived then. Modern historians immersed in modern ways of explaining are not satisfied that the Devil did it. Instead, they are skeptical about the motives of the accusers and the prosecutors. But modern skeptics are vulnerable to the same machinations of the Evil One as the weak women and men who made a pact with the Devil in 1692, according to the prosecution and the judges at Salem.

For many ordinary Americans, the Devil has never left our shores. He is still plotting evil, twisting the morals of the weak and the avaricious. The very same Devil that tempted the women (and men) of Salem is at work in the colleges and universities where the historians work. According to presidential candidate and former US senator Rick Santorum, in a speech at Ave Maria College in 2008, "The place where [the Devil] was, in my mind, the most successful and first—first successful was in academia. He understood pride of smart people. He attacked them at their weakest. They were in fact smarter than everybody else and could come up with something new and different—pursue new truths, deny the existence of truth, play with it because they're smart. And so academia a long time ago fell."

If the Bible is literal truth, as it is to millions of Americans, how can one doubt the continuing existence of the Devil? For "Satan disguises himself" in many ways and his followers are equally devious (2 Corinthians 11:14–15). One must then "Put on the whole armor of God, that ye may be able to stand against the schemes of the Devil" (Ephesians 6:11). Can one then say that the Beast was and is a Zombie? For indeed fear of deviltry concealed animus against Indians, women, and Catholics; it made bigotry into theology. It sanctified prejudice. That is what a Zombie does.

And skepticism—well, in 1692, there was little room for it. What if Old

Nick, a nickname for Satan, were to walk in the courthouse door, now visible to everyone? What would stop Him from hurling his malign power against the bench? One of the accused raised the question: If her powers came from the Devil, why did she not have the power to afflict the judges? They could not answer, but they did not think the question made any difference. They were devout, and that was their shield. The faithful today are right to this extent—the idea of the Devil still plays havoc with us. In modern courtrooms, prosecutors blame Devil worshippers for crimes, and the accused insist that the Devil made them do it. Able historians agree that it was people, not the Devil, who were responsible for the crisis, the trials, and the infamous witchcraft episode. But the Devil is the greatest of the first Zombies, and Zombies this powerful are very hard to kill.

The Zombies of the distant past, like those of the first years of European presence in the Americas, are often hard to spot. Contemporaries mistook them for real. We should not. Of course, the distant past is very different from our own times. For the students of the distant past, that translates into a relative paucity of reliable written sources. The ones that come down to us are riven with the prejudices of that past. Zombies love mist and shadow lent by distance and difference. We must discipline ourselves to penetrate that mist and shadow as best we can, lest we mistake the Zombie for the historical truth. Alas, this happens all the time, when hysteria leads to modern witchhunts, people uncertain of their old privileges discern figures of evil in the shadows, and defame one another for crimes no one has committed. Then Zombies rule the land.

CHAPTER TWO

Colonial and Revolutionary Zombies

The English settlers and the native peoples of the eighteenth-century British North American provinces were not the only inhabitants of colonial North America. There were mixed ancestry, African, French, Spanish, Portuguese, and even Russian traders, settlers, sailors, and soldiers all over North America. In the Caribbean Americas, Africans from the western rim of Africa joined with the Dutch, French, Spanish, and English colonizers, and the surviving native peoples. Not surprisingly, one can find among our idea of these people Zombie intruders.

Some of the Zombies are familiar to us because historians embraced them uncritically. Francis Parkman, a best-selling and certainly one of the most respected nineteenth-century American historians, filled the pages of his history of the French and British contest for North America with Zombies. Daniel Boorstin, who occupied a similar niche in the pantheon of American historians 100 years later, invented Zombies in his prize-winning *The Americans: The Colonial Experience.* Parkman's Indian Zombies left behind them in the wartime forests "the half consumed bodies of men and women, still bound fast to the trees, where they had perished in fiery torture." How exactly his savage Indian raiders managed to burn their victims and then eat them while they were still tied to trees is a puzzle, but no matter, it was surely the work of Zombies. After slaughtering the innocent pioneers, the Indian warrior/Zombie "smoked his pipe in haughty indolence." The same murderous Zombies stalked Boorstin's work, but he did not pay as much attention to them as did Parkman. Instead, they appeared, committed massacres, and left without further trace. If the haughty, indolent, and by turns savage Indian were not enough of a danger for the virtuous but perpetually unprepared colonial frontiersmen, there was the "vagrant" and yet potentially rebellious slave loitering on coastal plantations, about whom more in the next chapter.

Asylum for the Oppressed

"America you have it better" was an aphorism coined by the famous German poet Johann Wolfgang von Goethe in 1808, and many Germans did come to the colonies of New York, Pennsylvania, and Georgia hoping to escape hunger, violence, and intolerance in their homelands. The image grew even stronger in the nineteenth century, epitomized in Emma Lazarus's "New Colossus," written to raise funds for the State of Liberty in 1883, and in 1903 inscribed on a tablet at the foot of the statue. "Here at our sea-washed, sunset gates shall stand / A mighty woman with a torch, whose flame / Is the imprisoned lightning, and her name / Mother of Exiles. From her beacon-hand / Glows world-wide welcome; her mild eyes command / The air-bridged harbor that twin cities frame. / 'Keep, ancient lands, your storied pomp!' cries she / With silent lips. 'Give me your tired, your poor, / Your huddled masses yearning to breathe free, / The wretched refuse of your teeming shore. / Send these, the homeless, tempest-tost to me, / I lift my lamp beside the golden door!'"

The ideal of an asylum in the New World from the oppressions of the Old World was 250 years older than Goethe and 350 years earlier than the Lazarus inscription. From the time of Queen Elizabeth to her Hanoverian successors in the eighteenth century, the crown had sought to protect its American holdings by populating them with loyal immigrants. As Marilyn C. Baseler has summarized the process, "England's reputation as an asylum grew to its apogee in the decades following the Glorious Revolution." Not by chance, royal authorities also recognized the economic benefits to the home country of relatively cheap labor in the staple-producing colonies. To the mainland colonies went Welsh Quakers, French Huguenots, Palatine Germans, and a host of English Borderers, Scots farmers, and London poor. Wheat, corn, livestock, fish, timber, and, even more-important, tobacco, rice, sugar, and indigo cultivated in America made English and Scottish merchants wealthy and the empire the most prosperous commercial concern in the eighteenth-century Western world.

The ideal of asylum and self-betterment in a land of milk and honey was the invention of the royal lawyers, the promoters, jobbers, shipowners, merchants, and speculators who benefitted from gathering and sending poor people to work in the colonies. The promotional literature luring immigrants began with Sir Walter Raleigh, in the 1580s, and continued throughout the colonial era. Cheap land, plentiful food, timber for houses and warmth, drinkable water, all were supposedly waiting for the newcomers. First, however, they had to survive. Letters from these young men and women servants to their parents in the first years of settlement reveal that disease, near starvation, horrible working conditions, and insensitive masters made survival chancy. Life expectancy grew longer in the eighteenth century, but as Pulitzer Prize–winning historian Alan Taylor has written, "the new recruitment invented America as an Asylum from religious persecution and political oppression in Europe. . . . As a land of freedom and opportunity, British America had powerful limits." The ideal of asylum was a Zombie, created to further imperial policies in the years before the American Revolution.

True, for some who came, the British mainland colonies proved to be both a refuge and an opportunity to restart lives or create families. Not all the newcomers were so lucky or successful, however. Hundreds of thousands of immigrants, servants and slaves, soon learned that America was not an asylum for the oppressed. Most of those who actually made the voyage found debt and toil. The convict laborer, the indentured servant, and the slave—the most oppressed of all the newcomers—did not have it better in America.

The slaves' plight began with capture by other Africans, a "middle passage" from Africa to the Americas in which nearly 10 percent of "cargo" died, and finally sale and hard labor. In some of the colonies, particularly in the Caribbean, slave life expectancy was low and the death rate was high. In the Chesapeake, life expectancy for servants and convict laborers was longer, and by the eighteenth century, slaves' natural increase allowed African Americans to create their own communities on the plantation. Servants who did survive could become small farmers, but they had to compete with large landowners for wealth and status. A few slaves were freed by masters, and others successfully ran away, but the second-generation African American society was a slave society, that is, with a majority of slaves. Masters and slaves did negotiate for the slaves' time, space, and limited autonomy, but rarely did slaves prefer bondage to freedom. Nevertheless, defenders of slavery opined that slaves were better off working in their masters' fields and gardens than in their African homes. As one anonymous contributor to the *London Magazine* wrote in 1740, "The Inhabitants of Guinea are indeed in a most deplorable State of Slavery, under the arbitrary Powers of their

Princes both as to Life and Property. . . . [but] by purchasing, or rather ransoming the Negroes from their national Tyrants, and transplanting them under the benign Influences of the Law, and Gospel, they are advanced to much greater Degrees of Felicity, tho' not to absolute Liberty. That this is truly the Case cannot be doubted by any one acquainted with the Constitution of our Colonies, where the Negroes are governed by Laws, and suffer much less Punishment in Proportion to their Crimes, than the People in other Countries more refined in the Arts of Wickedness; and where Capital Punishment is inflicted only by the Civil Magistrates." (The idea of America as an asylum for slaves worked its way into antebellum defenses of slavery as a positive good. It's proof that Zombies can live for a long time.)

A small minority of immigrants occupied a relatively favored status. They were young men and women of the "better sort" who came to the colonies with some wealth in hand. They had connections in the home country, and these afforded them a head start in America. Here, they would become ministers, lawyers, doctors, merchants, shopkeepers, and planters—joining the elite already in the colony. Some, like Scotland's James Wilson, England's Thomas Paine, and St. Kitts-Nevis's Alexander Hamilton, would play a major part in the establishment of a new nation. It was that nation, not the colonies, that would be an asylum for the poor and oppressed. As one of the beneficiaries of American opportunity, Tom Paine, wrote in *Common Sense*, as England sank beneath its tyrannous overloads, America must keep open its doors, "O!, receive the fugitive, and prepare in time an asylum for mankind."

What explains the persistence of the colonial asylum Zombie? Paine's invocation offers a clue. The coming of the movement for American independence was as unplanned and, even for those who led it, unthinkable as late as the opening of 1776. How could such a momentous event for so many people with so little warning have come so quickly? After all, in 1763 Britain had won a great victory against French and allied Indian forces in North America, a victory in which the colonists had taken a major part and which they celebrated. Bear in mind that the Revolution was a violent and illegal overthrowing of a legitimate government. Whether that government had violated the liberties of the colonists (including their liberty to buy, sell, and inherit slaves) or not, there is no question that the revolutionaries ignored sworn oaths and carried out systematic violence against their loyalist neighbors and colonial officials. What could make this kind of conduct licit?

Follow the logic of the revolutionaries, as Paine had seen it and as political scientist Eric Nelson explains: it was Paine's *Common Sense* pamphlet that galvanized the nascent longing for independence. Paine said aloud what many were thinking. These included members of the Continental Congress who drafted the arguments for separation from Britain. At the center of those arguments was the idea that America was the asylum not just of people, but of liberty itself, fleeing from the corruptions of Britain. According to Thomas Jefferson, John Dickinson, and John Adams, among others, the colonies were built by those fleeing oppression, and the rights of their descendants did not rest on imperial gift, but on the world they built in America. To make this account work, the colonies had to be the refuge of liberty escaping from English tyranny. Hence the need for the Zombie of colonial asylum.

Roger Ekirch, a leading scholar of early immigration, recently carried on the Paine/Franklin tradition. In an op-ed for the *Guardian* online entitled "Asylum Once Defined America," he wrote, "Asylum is a defining element of America's national identity. The United States bears a special stake in the plight of refugees, which originated well before the Statue of Liberty famously urged foreign nations to send 'your tired, your poor, your huddled masses.' Indeed, it was on the eve of American independence in 1776 from Great Britain that Thomas Paine's Common Sense promised an 'asylum for mankind.'" Ignoring the purposive origins of these quotations, and giving weight to the title claim that asylum once defined America, he continued, "Today, opportunities for asylum in America stands imperiled on multiple fronts, not least owing to the priorities of President Trump. . . . Many applicants continue to languish in detention centers. Diverse reforms would help to improve the asylum process, including prioritizing the admission of families, especially women and children, the most common victims of abuse and the least prone to violent crime." It was this uplifting vision of America's unique role, supposedly widely shared by the founders, that Ekirch promotes: "In a world of tyrannical governments, the United States would welcome victims of oppression willing to forsake Old World allegiances. . . . Americans remain bound not by religion, ethnicity, race, or, for that matter, language, but by a set of political values embedded in the Constitution. It is those same principles on which the doctrine of political asylum is predicated in a world beset by intolerance and oppression." Much as one might agree with his views, they are not based on sound historical ground. In fact, the history of immigration law (as apart from the ability of people seeking to come here) is not as he suggests. The traditions of nativism and exclusion, although episodic, more often define immigration law than the ideal of asylum. Genuine asylum initiatives, apart from mere words, are few and far between. And that makes the claim that America is the world's asylum a Zombie.

Frontier

The classic works of early American history began with Europeans coming to a howling wilderness, the frontier of civilization, an invisible border beyond which there was nothing but impenetrable woods and fierce, nomadic savages. None of this, except for the European migration, was true. But the idea of the frontier was a powerful Zombie and especially hard to kill. The reason was simple. The frontier supposedly made the American unique and unconquerable.

The foremost spokesman of the frontier thesis was Frederick Jackson Turner. Born in Wisconsin in 1861, and educated at the University of Wisconsin and Johns Hopkins University in Baltimore, Turner loved to backpack, hunt, and fish in the Wisconsin woods. Even more, he loved the idea of the forest primeval, a place where men could express their masculinity. In an unpublished essay written in 1890, he glorified "the hunter type": "On the western outskirts of the Atlantic colonies, pressing continually toward the West, dwelt the American backwoodsmen. They found too little elbow-room in town-life. They loved to hear the crack of their long rifles and the blows of the ax in the forest," a somewhat limited sensory array, to be sure.

At the Chicago World's Fair, in 1893, he explained the "Significance of the Frontier in American History" to the members of the American Historical Association. The 1890 census had foretold the end of the frontier, defined by the increasing density of population in the West. Turner was frankly worried that this was a sign of an uncertain future for American character. His thesis was the America had been the leading edge of the advance of civilization: "In this advance, the frontier is the outer edge of the wave—the meeting point between savagery and civilization." The American was unique because of the frontier, a vast expanse of relatively free land that had to be conquered, and the midwife of Americans' fierce individualism and love of democracy. The frontier bade the American to cast off the superstitions and frailties of the Old World, and take on the challenges of the New: "The wilderness masters the colonist. It finds him a European in dress, industries, tools, modes of travel, and thought. It takes him from the railroad car and puts him in the birch canoe. It strips off the garments of civilization and arrays him in the hunting shirt and the moccasin."

Turner's thesis, repeated in countless textbooks and in his own essays and talks, had no room for class (everyone was the same), gender (women were there but invisible), victims (triumphalist history did not abide victims), or anything European. Later historians of the colonial settlements knew that the Turner thesis had problems. Europeans transplanted to the Americas seemed to want to retain their culture and material things—they clung to their old language, books, music, religion, and styles of dress. Had Turner looked over his shoulder, as it were, he would have seen a movement west of schoolmarms, piano teachers, lawyers' libraries, and everything but moccasin-clad hunters. But Turner did not much care for the flood of Europeans entering the country in his own day (he died in 1932 a committed nativist and anti-Semite).

Turner's frontier was a Zombie. In reality, the edges of English settlement were not empty. Indian villagers among and on the edges of colonial settlements had turned forests into a patchwork of clearings, brushland, and second-growth new forests. The glades that Indians left behind were filled with German newcomers to whom the Hanoverian kings of England had opened western lands. French trading posts and Spanish pueblos dotted the western landscape. Turner's frontiers were in reality borderlands of the British, French, and Spanish Empires, sometimes violently contested, sometimes crisscrossed peacefully by beaver fur and deerskin traders.

Nevertheless, the idea of the wild frontier continues to excite the American imagination. *Star Trek* begins with an invocation to space, the final frontier, where the men of the *Starship Enterprise* will journey. To these strange new worlds they bring the Federation's message of peace and prosperity. There, they will encounter the studio makeup designers' fantastical versions of other species, including Zombies—in the endless adventure that appeals to the "hunter type" in some of us.

A Minister of State and His King

In 1763, drunk (sometimes literally) with pride and relief over the signing of the peace treaty ending the French and Indian War, British colonists offered toasts to the young king George III. He was the first of the Hanoverians born in Britain, and the first to take special notice of the colonies. What he noticed, and perhaps many of the colonists did not, was that the colonies had paid only a small portion of the cost of victory. Tutored by John Stuart, Lord Bute, that the king must be the ruler of the empire in fact as well as in law, George III sought a prime minister with a plan to refill the treasury and make the colonists obey imperial laws on trade and tariffs. After some hesitation, he chose George Grenville, a lawyer, veteran politician, and imperial administrator. The rest was history—too often Zombie history.

From the beginning of the revolutionary crisis to our own day, public historians, classroom teachers, and Fourth of July orators, among others, turned two decent and able British leaders into Zombies. Blamed for corrupting British liberties and conspiring to enslave the (white) colonists, Grenville and George III were easy targets. Opponents of the Stamp Act, Grenville's final effort to force the colonists to do what the subjects of the crown in Britain already did (use stamped paper for official documents), marched through the streets of Boston, New York, Newport, Philadelphia, and Charles Town with effigies of Grenville. Disfigured in the anti-stamp-tax movement (and by Parliament when it repealed the Stamp Act), he soon died in disgrace.

The young king's personal and public writings, now open to the public, show a young man who was intensely patriotic, well intentioned, and frugal. He understood the importance of pomp in public, but loved to walk about the town of Windsor in comfortable clothes and say hello to everyone. He was bidden by his father to avoid war and debt, but his reign was mired in war in America and Europe. Above all, his father insisted that the young man do everything he could to reduce the interest the government had to pay on its indentures. In that, George III failed. Thus, of the Stamp Act, he wrote after its repeal: "Because any part remaining sufficiently ascertain'd the Right of the Mother Country to tax its Colonys & next that it would shew a desire to redress any just grievances; but if the unhappy Factions that divide this Country would not permit this in my opinion equitable plan to be follow'd I thought Repealing infinitely more eligible than Enforcing, which could only tend to widen the breach between this Country & America." This was a king who tried to maintain the rightful authority of the mother country in the empire while being aware of the legitimate complaints of his subjects abroad. He was hardly the monster that Jefferson portrayed. What then gave rise to the latter? It was the Boston Tea Party and the violence of resistance to the administration of Lord North, and finally Lexington and Concord.

In the final days before hostilities made compromise almost impossible, colonial leaders petitioned the king to reverse parliamentary punishment of the Tea Party. The petitions went unread, as George III issued a proclamation warning the colonists against rebellion. As the titular head of the empire, he was well within his legal rights to act. In response, the revolutionaries did to him what they had done to Grenville. In his 1774 *Summary View of the Rights of British Americans*, Thomas Jefferson accused the king of acts of "despotism to which no parallel can be produced in the most arbitrary ages of British history." Men like Jefferson blamed the king for the upheaval they themselves had caused, and in the Declaration of Independence laid all manner of grievances at his feet. As Jefferson wrote and the members of the Continental Congress agreed, "The history of the present King of Great Britain is a history of repeated injuries and usurpations, all having in direct object the establishment of an absolute Tyranny over these States."

George III did play a decisive role in the hostilities between British forces and revolutionary arms. He did not start the fray, however. General Thomas Gage's decision to remove cannon and powder from the arsenal at Concord, in April 1775, after a series of "gunpowder raids" on other eastern Massachusetts towns had mixed results, leading to the first major clash, at Lexington and Concord. Gage's next move, to drive colonial forces from Breed's Hill, was also taken without direct orders from the crown, although to be fair to everyone, Gage had portrayed himself to King George, a year earlier, as the man for the job of putting down colonial resistance to Britain. The king became a major player on August 23, 1775, with his proclamation that the colonies were in a state of rebellion:

> "WHEREAS Many of Our Subjects in divers Parts of Our Colonies and Plantations in North America, misled by dangerous and ill-designing Men, and forgetting the Allegiance which they owe to the Power that has protected and sustained them, after various disorderly Acts committed in Disturbance of the Public Peace, to the Obstruction of lawful Commerce, and to the Oppression of Our loyal Subjects carrying on the same, have at length proceeded to an open and avowed Rebellion, by arraying themselves in hostile Manner to withstand the Execution of the Law, and traitorously preparing, ordering, and levying War against Us. . . . We do accordingly strictly Charge and Command all Our Officers, as well Civil as Military, and all other Our obedient and loyal Subjects, to use their utmost Endeavours to withstand and suppress such Rebellion, and to disclose and make known all Treasons and traitorous Conspiracies which they shall know to be against Us, Our Crown and Dignity."

The last portion of the proclamation is significant for two reasons, first, because the king saw colonial resistance as a crime against the crown, not against Parliament. Second, the proclamation did not array the full force of British arms, in particular the Royal Navy, against the colonies, but only asked that loyal colonists report to crown officials all conspiracies against lawful authority. There is nothing in this of a tyrant. The crown instead called for vigilance and civil order.

Nevertheless, at least from the revolutionary perspective, one can understand why Grenville and George III would be demonized. There had to be some justification for men who had taken oaths of loyalty to crown and empire to raise rebellion. Conspiratorial thinking and finger-pointing were well established political themes in Britain and the colonies long before George III ascended the throne. Seen from a distance during the crisis and the war, the king appeared a tyrant, unfit to rule. Up close and personal, as John Adams discovered when he was the United States minister plenipotentiary to the Britain after the war, the king was "the essence of courtesy and poise," an avid reader, with a love of gardening. Adams found it hard to hate his former adversary. One could even pardon the next generation of American chroniclers for turning Grenville and George III into Zombies. A second war against Great Britain, the War of 1812, was fresh in the minds of men like George Bancroft, the best-selling and most respected American historian of the nineteenth century, when he wrote his history of the Revolution. "Acclamations welcomed the accession of George III," but victory and "the love of glory" had already turned his young head, Bancroft decided. "From the day of his accession, George III displayed an innate love of authority . . . which doomed him in an age of change to oppose reform." Jefferson had turned a patriot king into a Zombie king, just as critics of Grenville had turned a veteran imperial administrator into a Zombie.

One would imagine that the special relationship existing between Britain and the United States, an alliance stretching from the First World War to the present, would restore Grenville and his king to their human forms. In the process, they would become less important to the story we tell about the coming of the revolutionary crisis. Learned accounts of the crisis would regard the prime minister and the king as less movers of events than their prisoners, accounts in which nothing about them "fully explains" the coming of the crisis or its resolution. Restored to their more human dimensions, they become simply characters in a roomful of politicians and administrators dealing with unprecedented issues.

But the Zombies have survived even the mildest of rehabilitation efforts. One Scholastic Books best seller, subtitled "A Wicked History," has King George determined to defeat the "ungrateful traitors" of 1776, whatever the cost. (Other entries in the wicked history series are Napoleon Bonaparte, Adolph Hitler, and Genghis Khan). And Grenville, well, "too often" has the man been lost in the welter of criticism of the Stamp Act, clouding "the judgment" of historians and students of the American Revolution.

Indians, Slaves, and the War for Independence

Old Zombies can renew themselves by eating historical facts. The Old Zombie herein was that the Revolution was fought to free Americans from English enslavement. The leaders of the revolutionary movement created this Zombie to ensure unity among the very diverse interests in the colonies. It appeared in their pamphlets, their newspaper essays, and their public addresses. The Zombie seemed to do its job, eating away at English claims that Americans had all the rights and privileges of Englishmen.

Enter a young Zombie, fresh from the pages of a new history, well garbed in quotation and citation. He is the reverse argument—that the American Revolution was waged to protect slavery against English abolitionism and the revolutionaries at war were held together by a shared fear of the end of slavery or at least slave rebellion and Indian uprising. Simon Schama's *Rough Crossings: Britain, the Slaves, and the American Revolution* (2006) presses the former claim, while Robert Parkinson's *The Common Cause* (2014) is the home of the latter assertion. At the heart of both, according to Schama, was the patriot leaders "panic" at the thought of an "imminent slave insurrection" in regions where slaves outnumbered whites. Look at the first Naturalization Act of 1790 after the war, Parkinson tells the reader, and find that it conferred citizenship only on free white persons. The cat was out of the bag: citizenship was white and free—not black or red. Despite the freeing of slaves who fought the British, the end of slavery in much of the North, the barring of slavery from the newly won Northwest Territory, and treaties that guaranteed Indians a portion of their ancestral lands (despite their service to the British during the war), the victorious revolutionaries were racist to the core.

We are to conclude that racism was the glue that held the revolutionary cause together through seven years of warfare. The Zombie has a haven in the perturbed consciences of the sensitive academic. For example, Alan Taylor's *American Revolutions* (2016) concludes that "patriots defended Freedom for white men while asserting their domination over enslaved blacks." None of the southern states followed the logic of the Declaration to free their slaves. Their rhetoric of freedom from British enslavement was a glass half empty.

Not everyone agreed. After all, one result of the Revolution was the end of slavery in New England, provisions for gradual abolition in the Atlantic states, and a prohibition of slavery in the Northwest Territory. Alan Gilbert explained that racial discrimination remained a fact of life in the postrevolutionary North, but if abolition "lagged" behind and was "incomplete," it nevertheless would not have come without black agitation and revolutionary service made possible by the war. Robert Middlekauf's *The Glorious Cause* (1982) also read the evidence differently than Schama, Parkinson, and Taylor: "The irony of white Americans claiming liberty while they held slaves did not escape the revolutionary generation. . . . In one way or another all the northern states acted to provide for the gradual emancipation of slaves." A glass half full? Gordon Wood's *Radicalism of the American Revolution* (1991) filled the glass to the brim: "It is important to realize that the Revolution suddenly and effectively ended the cultural climate that had allowed black slavery . . . to exist throughout the colonial period without serious challenge." Slavery was now a "conspicuous" anomaly, albeit a historical judgment that did most of the slaves little good.

Slaves did better when they acted to free themselves, but there were relatively few occasions when slaves took up the British offer to run away from their masters, and fewer still of slaves who offered violence to their masters. From the many accounts of slave uprisings in the middle pages of the colonial newspapers that Parkinson collected in his *The Common Cause*, one would have expected a good deal more of the latter. In fact, few slaves rose up in rebellion. Some left their masters to enter British lines, as the British had promised freedom (a promise only sometimes kept). Others simply left their quarters on the plantations, but returned. Most stayed put.

The strength of the slaves and Indians Zombie is that the facts do not matter—the thesis is so impressive and so fitting our modern need to find fault with the founders that facts only get in the way. So long as the colonists thought that slave rebellion was imminent, the thesis works. Despite the newspaper coverage, however, there is no evidence that these accounts motivated the leaders or the followers of the revolutionary governments, at least not in Parkinson's account. There is concomitance—the newspaper reports and calls for unity—but no causal connection. One can conclude that the accounts of immanent slave uprisings were simply fillers, replacing missing advertisements for imported British goods (as there were no imports).

Indian raids on the frontier were real, and greatly concerned the set-tlers on the frontier and, at times, the revolutionary state and Continental Congress governments. In particular, warfare along the Mohawk River in New York called forth a brutal response from George Washington, com-mander in chief of the Continental Army. Fighting in the Ohio Valley and the frontier areas of the Southeast was sporadic but deadly. There is no evidence that this fear held together the revolutionary forces, or that it was a major concern of the Continental Congress, however.

So the slave rebel and the Indian marauder become Zombies. Who cre-ated them? The answer lies in the sources themselves. Revolutionary com-mittees of safety occupied newspapers offices, confiscated printing presses, and drove off loyal printers and editors to control means of distributing information. Patriot presses were allowed to continue publication, but like all businesses during the crisis, faced serious financial problems. One way to deal with the shortfall of information and of subscriptions was to fill the middle pages with inflammatory articles. In fact, these articles were not news; they were the same pieces that other papers had published already. Thus rumor circulated through the middle pages, replacing the advertise-ments for goods no longer coming into the ports and spreading through colonial shops. The ports were closed by the Royal Navy after 1775 any-how. Nothing was coming in, except where blockade runners could sneak it through.

The Zombies were the savage Indians and the rebellious slaves, news-worthy figures when real news was hard to get. Historians, by reviving a focus on these faux news items, were actually beckoning the Zombies to return.

An Age of Democratic Revolution

In our times of hacked elections, it is comforting to think that the Ameri-can Revolution was the avatar of an age of democratic experimentation. Even if we are currently plagued by domestic and foreign electoral high jinks, we can fall back on the belief that at least some among the founders of our nation always advocated free and fair democratic politics. That be-lief, so basic to our political identity, rests on a history Zombie. Our leading founding fathers were not democrats, did not espouse democratic electoral politics, and regarded the mass of the populace with suspicion. The period 1775–1800 was not, as one historian described it, an "Age of Democratic Revolution," not if democracy means a universal suffrage, the legitimacy of opposition political parties, a healthy respect for freedom of press, speech, and petition, and all the other accoutrements of a truly representative form of government.

Instead, in almost all of the new revolutionary states, the franchise was confined to white, Protestant adult men who paid taxes or owned property. Women could not vote. The laboring poor could not vote. With a few exceptions, Native Americans and free African Americans could not vote. Restrictions on office holding were even stricter. While the state constitutions, again with some exceptions, paid lip service to freedom of the press, speech, and petition, contempt of the assembly was severely punished, as was criticism of the government. Freedom of the press meant no prior censorship.

How then do we explain the remarkable persistence of the revolutionary democracy Zombie. We need to return not to the revolutionary era itself, but to the 1950s. It was then that Atlantic world historian Robert R. Palmer announced that the American revolutionary was not alone. He was part of and chronicler of an earlier Age of Democratic Revolutions: "It is argued that this whole [Atlantic] civilization was swept in the last four decades of the eighteenth century by a single revolutionary movement . . . that this movement was essentially democratic." Palmer was a member of the liberal intelligentsia of the post–World War II era, a student of eighteenth-century ideas, his whose career spanned much of the twentieth century, featuring professorships at Princeton and then Yale. His *History of the Modern World* (1950) was regarded as a model of its kind—part textbook, part extended essay—and is still around in its twenty-second edition. His *Age of Democratic Revolution: The Challenge* (1959), the first volume of two on the subject, won the Frederick Bancroft Prize, and was required reading for graduate students in my generation. Written with great learning and verve, it made the case for the democratic instincts of the revolutionary generation. It was a "groping toward" a new idea of the polity, not a fully established system of idea or practices, but its direction and its force could not be denied.

Palmer conceded that the term "democracy," although of very old vintage in Western thought, was not highly regarded by the American revolutionaries. They believed in the sovereignty of the people as a collective entity, and relied upon popular support to overturn imperial government and fight the British Army, but they did not embrace participatory democracy. They were republicans who believed in representation of the people by the better sort. The term "democracy" did not come into common currency until the 1790s, when friends of the French Revolution formed Democratic Republican societies, held rallies, and voted for candidates whom they thought shared their views.

Why then would Palmer, and others, embrace an anachronism? With the specter of world communism becoming more visible every day, and anticommunist politicians carrying on a campaign against suspected fellow travelers, liberal historians found refuge in notions like consensus. For some, like Boorstin, according to historian Peter Novick, the refuge was fortified by "strident conservatism, boosterism, and unabashed patriotic celebration." For others, like former radical thinker Sidney Hook, the postwar era brought a swift volte-face: "If the Stalinists and their international salon of fellow traveling literateurs and totalitarian liberal politicos" foisted their version of Marxist history on American students, then America's unique heritage of democracy would be lost. The consensus view of the Revolution, wherein just about everyone (who was important) supposedly agreed, was one of the central themes of the new history. Louis Hartz, a Harvard political scientist writing in 1955, explained that "we see in the very nature of the social forces which went into the personality of the American radical the non-feudal world from which he derived his strength." The revolutionary was "centrally a man of the land, a small capitalist in the American backwoods." Boorstin agreed: "There is, then, no paradox in the fact that the colonies were willing to revolt and yet were unwilling to unite. . . . These too were the very reasons why, in the long run, it was impossible for the British regular army to subdue that Americans." "Colonies" and "Americans" made the American Revolution. One should add that all of these thinkers rejected the label "consensus"; neither did they think highly of one another.

True, the language of the great Declaration seemed to imply that something profoundly democratic lay at the center of the drive for independence, but "All men are created equal" was not a new doctrine. One can trace it back to the Bible and to English seventeenth-century political writers. The "Levellers" of the 1640s certainly used similar language. The irony is that the author of these ringing words was himself a slave owner who never quite got around to freeing his hundreds of slaves except his slave mistress and their children. The Virginia state constitution to which he contributed his ideas did not free any slaves, nor did he when he was governor of Virginia, secretary of state of the United States, or president of country from 1801 to 1809. To the adherents of the consensus school, the American—free, white, armed, and looking West toward an empire of freedom—was already a democrat. Never mind that the economic backbone of this great enterprise would be that other, peculiar institution of human bondage. Some history Zombies, like the Age of Democratic Revolution Zombie, wear the raiment of hope—hope that a history of unity and aspiration can combat enemies of the free world. One should never trust Zombies, even those created with good intentions.

A Zombie is not a flawed interpretation. With new evidence or on reconsideration scholars can discard flawed points of view. Historians call that process revision. The impetus for the Age of Democratic Revolution Zombie is not susceptible to such revision, however, for it is rooted in geopolitical and ideological ground rather than scholarship, in retrojection rather than historical mindedness.

And the Zombie, like all Zombies, continues to live on, once again, like its original in the 1950s, energized by the best of motives. The American Revolution has to be part of an Age of Democratic Revolution because the founders of the nation have to be recast as the founders of democracy. Distinguished historians like Gary Nash and Tim Breen have in the later years of their careers returned to the American Revolution to remind a new generation of students and lay readers how democratic some of the revolutionaries were. In Nash's account of *The Unknown American Revolution: The Unruly Birth of Democracy*, democracy means moving ordinary people to the center stage, "men with little or no previous political status." At the time minions of their betters, they now become seeders of the democratic world to come. Breen's *American Insurgents, American Patriots: The Revolution of the People* (2010) recovers the stories of "ordinary people who flocked" to the defense of Boston after the Coercive Acts of 1774, a "huge percentage" of the revolutionaries, reappearing in a huge percentage of Breen's pages, some 148 pages out of 301 pages of text. It's not easy to do this against the weight of evidence, and as one sees in Alfred Young, Nash, and Ray Raphael's effort at the start of their collection, *Revolutionary Founders: Rebels, Radicals and Reformers in the Making of the Nation* (2012), bringing democracy back to 1776 requires some pretty convoluted prose: a "rich dialectic, in which men in power chose to accommodate or repress threats from below, was central to the forming of the nation. As radicals and reformers pushed their demands, they engaged with those who were trying to gain or keep power. Such is the stuff of history, but that history is lost when we fail to recognize the individuals and movements forcing the issue."

The Age of Democratic Revolution, like its alleged original in the eighteenth century, supposedly has a global reach. Today the Zombie is a useful reminder of the victory of democracy over its rivals after World War II. "A key issue of our times is the fracturing of nation-states by the twin pressures of globalization and resurgent ethnic solidarities," writes the University of Melbourne's Peter McPhee. "What is at stake here is not simply the tragic manifestation of animosities produced by a violent history and smothered for centuries by authoritarian states." At stake is democracy, a new and apparently fragile blossom of the Age of Democratic Revolution. McPhee believes that the higher duty of the historian is an "intelligible and engaging history" that ensures the continuation of the democratic turn.

The Constitution and Slavery

The next great achievement of the Americans was the framing of the federal Constitution. In that hot, humid, fly-infested Philadelphia summer, the framers could not avoid the question of slavery.

Can two history Zombies occupy the same space? The answer is yes. Zombies can do a lot that real women and men cannot. One of these Zombies is that the federal Constitution was a pact with the Devil for enabling and protecting slavery. Although Zombies cannot reproduce themselves, this view of the 1787 document is the grandchild of the antebellum slaveholders' own claim that the original compact (they called it that rather than a Union) promoted the slave interest, or slaveholding states would not have ratified it. As historian David Waldstreicher explained, by the time that the framers agreed to compromises on representation (and the notorious three-fifths clause), "the evils of the slave trade had already been pushed off the table" and by the time that the federalists had won the contest of ratification, "the proslavery aspects of the Constitution were strikingly absent" from their celebrations. The slave states had triumphed. Slavery was safe. This is a terrifying Zombie, meant no doubt to remind readers of the sins of their (historic) fathers.

Not so say other historians like Sean Wilentz, who have adopted the antebellum abolitionists' view that slavery was not mentioned in the Constitution (the word never appeared until the Thirteenth Amendment ended slavery) so the Constitution could not be proslavery. "Judging from what we now know about what happened in Philadelphia, though, the Constitution's proslavery features appear substantial but incomplete," Wilentz wrote. "Above all, the framers took care to prevent the convention from recognizing what had become slavery's main legal and political bulwark . . . the legitimacy of property in man." Instead, slavery's opponents in the convention and out of doors were already "preparing for a nation in which there was no slavery." This, Wilentz admits at the outset (but then ignores), is "hindsight," attractive to modern eyes, but the second Zombie, more aspiration than history.

A lot of this argument among historians turns on some pretty obscure or at least hard to follow doctrinal argument. The result is dueling Zombies in the shadows of constitutional history. In fact, although some of the delegates to the Constitutional Convention abhorred slavery, opponents of slavery at the Constitutional Convention focused on the overseas slave trade. Some members of delegations from southern states, like George Mason and James Madison of Virginia, abhorred the external slave trade, and did not care much for slavery in the US either, but recognized that other southern delegates, like Edward Rutledge of South Carolina, would bolt if the new document condemned slavery. Some northern delegates, led by Elbridge Gerry of Massachusetts, Rufus King of New York, and Gouverneur Morris of Pennsylvania, openly attacked the trade in human flesh, but other northern delegates, like James Wilson of Pennsylvania and Roger Sherman of Connecticut, were willing to compromise on slavery.

The result of these divisions was a series of compromises that left slavery to the states to vote up or down. In the Constitution itself, a compromise over the basis of representation in the House of Representatives (the three-fifths compromise), the delay in barring importation of slaves until 1808 (although Congress actually began the process soon after it met), and the rendition clause (Article IV, clause 2, section 2), laying the groundwork for later Fugitive Slave Acts, were clearly concessions to the slave states.

Perhaps the best interpretation of the Constitution's view of slavery is that the delegates as a whole refused to face the issue head on, instead working out a series of concessions that would, in time, bedevil the Union and become a basis for secession. The evil was slavery itself, lurking on the edges of the debate over the Atlantic slave trade. Only a few of the delegates dared directly attack slavery. Outside of the convention hall, a handful of Quakers, a few abolitionists in New England, England, and France, and of course the slaves themselves objected to the institution. In fact, as David Brion Davis demonstrated, until the end of the eighteenth century, most economic thinkers saw slavery as a progressive institution, leading to the full deployment of capital investment in new lands. Zombies love new lands—perfect places to do whatever Zombies do when the rest of us are not watching.

In truth, the full narrative of the founding of the new nation is filled with victims and villains as well as virtuous women and respectable men. It is a tale of self-interest and self-dealing as well as decency and self-sacrifice. Why do we fool ourselves by following paths into Zombieland, or more precisely, when do we embrace the Zombies rather than the messier truth? As the late historian Michael Kammen explained in his *A Season of Youth* (1978), a magnificent essay on the misuses of revolutionary history in poetry, drama, and the arts, "anxiety induced by national crises, particularly political ones" spurs bouts of unthinking patriotism and unconstrained finger-pointing. We change the past to "persuade the present"—or we would be mere antiquarians. But source-mining, scene setting, and treating opinion as if it were fact is an invitation to Zombies.

CHAPTER THREE

Zombies of the Early Nation

The new nation's cleverest Zombie was an uncritical view of the new nation's homogeneity. It concealed itself in the most banal and comforting of generalizations. Perhaps it was abetted by historians like Daniel Boorstin. After all, he welcomed this Zombie at the beginning of his *The Americans: The National Experience*: "America grew in the search for community. Between the Revolution and the Civil War, the young nation flourished not in discovery but in search. It prospered not from the perfection of its ways, but from their fluidity. It lived with the constant belief that something else or something better might turn up." The nation was a thing; it acted; it believed; it fulfilled itself. It was one.

Surely a historian as honored as Boorstin (Librarian of Congress and winner, for separate books, of the Parkman, Bancroft, and Pulitzer Prizes) can be excused some oversimplification and overgeneralization. Where is the harm in that? Alas, Zombies carry infections, and the one-nation Zombie had the potency to infect histories of the new nation with a loose and swollen tongue long after Boorstin was gone. Consider this crucial passage from a major new work on the federal Constitution: "Putting a [the federal] Constitution up for public debate was entirely novel, and the proposed instrument almost instantly consumed the nation's interest." Seriously? The public debate over the ratification of the Constitution from 1787 to 1788 was hardly novel. The Massachusetts Constitution caused a public debate that consumed the state's interest for nearly three years from 1776 to 1779. What was more, although the federalist-antifederalist newspaper and pamphlet exchange of 1787–88 was a major episode in the nation's political and legal history, it did not consume the attention of the nation. To argue in this manner assumes that there was a nationwide communications network much as there is today, and that, as today, a single issue or set of issues can galvanize public opinion across the nation—as if all Americans were part of a "public" whose opinion expressed itself in government formation. Or see Gordon Wood's Pulitzer-Prize winning invocation of the transformation of society and politics from deference to democracy in the westward movement: "This spectacular growth and movement of people further weakened tradition forms of social organization and intensified people's feelings of equality." Well—not for the slaves taken west by their masters, or for the womenfolk who lamented leaving family and familiar landscape behind; but the people "wanted independence"—all the people, all the time. The one-nation Zombie speaks for all of us.

America, meaning the United States, did grow in territory with the accession by treaty and by force of the Louisiana Territory, the Southwest, the far West, and the Oregon Territory. Boorstin and those who adopt his script of one people and one nation capture the yearning of some early national intellectuals for a truly American culture, but any homogenization of the American, and a far too easily characterized wholeness of experience, is a Zombie. Who else but a Zombie could have inspired lines like "when before had men put so much faith in the unexpected?" Look in vain in Boorstin's pages for women, black Americans (there is slavery but no slaves), and Indians who were not marauding. The one–nation Zombie had eaten them all, and left nothing behind.

In fact, when most people in the early national period identified themselves, they did not say that they were Americans. They said that they were from Virginia or from Massachusetts. America and Americans were divided by free and slave, Republican and Federalist (later Whig) affiliation, and North and South. Nationalism and national identity would come, but only after a terrible Civil War showed how a divided people could divide the land. The notion that one people and one nation moved west, embraced democracy and equality, and sought individual rights is an appealing one, and it persists in our idea of our history, but it is not true, and its ability to survive its patent falsity labels it a Zombie. But it is not the only Zombie that inhabits our conception of the early republic.

Free Markets

The antebellum free market is a history Zombie so well entrenched that it has eaten and digested living beings all around it. Looking from a distance at the free for all over land use, water use, right of way, and other features of property; the explosion of paper money emissions from banks (and counterfeiters); the canal and rail booms (and busts); all manner of get rich quick schemes that flourished in the antebellum period; and the "no-holds barred" competition for wealth—one could easily conclude that the markets were unregulated. Conservative legal and economic writers extol it. It is the basis for policy planning in both modern political parties. As history, however, the idea that a free market existed—free of government interference, free of regulation, run according to the immutable laws of supply and demand—is nonsense. The idea that a free market supposedly helped the antebellum US economy take off is also nonsense. There were free market advocates, but no part of the Zombie of a free market is true. As William J. Novak has written in his seminal article on the subject, early Americans understood that "the well ordered market" was part of a "well regulated society," and that "commerce, trade, and economics, like health and morals . . . were fundamentally public in nature, created, shaped, and *regulated* by the polity via public law" (emphasis in original).

Economic growth was intimately tied to regulation of the marketplace. First, the leading sector of the antebellum economy was staple exports, cotton and wheat primarily. In these enterprises government interfered (or assisted, if you prefer) all the time. Governments intervened in both promotional and regulatory ways. True, the federal government was not a major direct promoter of the overseas economy, but protective tariffs did enable home industries to compete with otherwise larger and more efficient foreign manufacturers. Equally important was the federal management of national lands. Regulations on these enabled speculators to make profits, farmers to bring land under cultivation, and, in a negative way, moved native peoples out of the way. The federal government promoted foreign investment in the economy. Money flowed from English and European sources into American industries. Foreign credit facilitated capital accumulation.

Even more important was the role of antebellum state and local government in financing economic growth. These bodies issued bonds and sold stocks in everything from railroads and canals to new industries. State courts also intervened directly to protect investments in the economy, by enforcing contracts and promoting commercial transactions. State legislatures passed laws against monopolies, unfair trading activity, and certain kinds of combinations. While the justification for some of these laws was fair competition, the means by which competition was protected was not laissez-faire, but government intervention.

Finally, one government-protected institution gave the new United States a tremendous economic advantage over its rivals in the Old World. It was the most regulated institution of all. That institution was chattel slavery. Slavery existed elsewhere and had for centuries, but only in the new nation did state governments ensure that slaves were property pure and simple. Although most state laws gave masters absolute control over their slaves, that control was nevertheless regulated. Slaves had no personhood, and no institution, neither the state nor the church, intervened to lessen their burdens. Again, although the primary beneficiary of the slave's labor was the master, the master did not control the larger parameters of that labor. The international slave trade was barred by act of Congress in 1808, and federal courts enforced the exclusion of slave imports with fines and imprisonment. State and federal restrictions prevented slavery from expanding into the Northwest and, for a time, north of the latitude line of 36° 30' (under the Missouri Compromise of 1820). Just as slavery could not exist without the active complicity of governments, so government action limited how far slavery could progress into the north and west of the nation.

What then was the antebellum free market? It was a moral paradigm, a model, whose roots lay in the protests against eighteenth-century imperial "mercantilism." The English Navigation Acts and similar provisions of the French and Spanish Empires ensured that trade remained within the empire and the home countries had favorable balances of trade. Economists like Scotland's Adam Smith and the French physiocrats objected to these laws, because they believed that free trade benefited the empire more than mercantilism. The French coined the term "laissez-faire" (let it be) to capture the idea that the free market rested on natural laws, and whoever tampered with free exchange of goods and services harmed everyone. The idea grew in the work of Scottish theorists like David Ricardo and American economists like Francis Wayland.

Wayland's reputation in the Baptist ministerial community, his credentials as an educator (he was the first president of Brown College), and his unshakeable faith in free market ideology made his views the more potent. For example, in his best-seller *Elements of Moral Science* (1835), he explained that all sales had to be fair to all parties, the seller to furnish goods or services to the best of his ability, the buyer to pay fair market price. Government intervention was "a violation of liberty." Science and morality together undergirded free market ideology.

We want to believe in the power of a free market, because we want to believe that individual will, effort, and inventiveness will bring individual profit and social progress. That ideal is a good one, but it is not a historical reality. In fact, the strongest correlative of personal economic success is not individual ability but family capital. If you want to be successful, try to be born into a family that is already successful, wealthy enough to provide the social and economic capital for you to succeed. In the meantime, this free market Zombie will continue to infiltrate our histories.

Angels of the Home

There may be no more powerful figure in Christian imagery than the angel. A combination of power and sanctity, the angel ties heaven to earth. Until well into the early modern period of Western cultural history, women were accused of being the source of men's temptation to sin. The biblical figures of Jezebel and Eve dominated this narrative of sexual temptation and misconduct. Then, something happened in the eighteenth century: a movement in literature, art, and domestic customs that cultural historians have called the arrival of the age of sentiment, literary historians have recognized as a Romantic turn, and family historians have seen as the rise of child-centered households and loving marriage. However characterized and however caused, this movement changed the image of wife and mother. She became the angel of the home in popular magazines and books.

At the same time, women were denied the full fruits of the American Revolution and the first age of constitution writing. The language of the new states' and federal constitutions was male—he was allowed to vote, he could hold office, he was a political actor. (He was also white and free.) Women were thus (supposed) to remain at home, care for the children, and set a moral example by staying out of the public arena. As Benjamin Rush wrote in what was probably the most read pamphlet on women's education, "From the numerous avocations to which a professional life exposes gentlemen in America from their families, a principal share of the instruction of children naturally devolves upon the women. It becomes us therefore to prepare them, by a suitable education, for the discharge of this most important duty of mothers. The equal share that every citizen has in the liberty and the possible share he may have in the government of our country make it necessary that our ladies should be qualified to a certain degree, by a peculiar and suitable education, to concur in instructing their sons in the principles of liberty and government." Otherwise, "I am not enthusiastic upon the subject of education. In the ordinary course of human affairs we shall probably too soon follow the footsteps of the nations of Europe in manners and vices. The first marks we shall perceive of our declension will appear among our women. Their idleness, ignorance, and profligacy will be the harbingers of our ruin."

For what it gave and what it took, the depiction of angel of the home was and is a Zombie. Early national women were many things inside and outside of the home, married with children and childless, but they were not angels. Angels have power; women did not. As a metaphor for the ideal women (in men's minds), the angel became something closer to a prisoner of domestic drudgery. As reformer Elizabeth Cady Stanton wrote in the "Declaration of Sentiments" at the 1848 Seneca Falls Convention, men have "created a false public sentiment by giving to the world a different code of morals for men and women, by which moral delinquencies which exclude women from society, are not only tolerated but deemed of little account in man . . . has endeavored, in every way that he could to destroy her confidence in her own powers, to lessen her self-respect, and to make her willing to lead a dependent and abject life."

As historians began to write about women's history, they had to grapple with the angel of the home Zombie. In 1928, a pioneer in the field, Arthur Meier Schlesinger, called on historians to track women's "actual contributions to progress in American national history." He did not think well of the "silence of the historians." It was the silence of the historians rather than the absence of contributions that explained why women did not take their rightful place in the narrative. With the rise of second-wave feminism in midcentury, women became even more visible, and more important in the larger story. To be sure, historians long noticed that the great white men of the antebellum period had helpmates at their sides, but historians did not think women's work was very important. Read the classic works of the post–World War II era, Arthur Meier Schlesinger Jr.'s *Age of Jackson*, Daniel Boorstin's *The Americans: The National Experience*, Perry Miller's *The Life of the Mind in America*, all major prize winners, and look in vain for women's work.

Historian Gerda Lerner offered a powerful corrective to this myopic worldview. In her writing and her support for other women entering the field of history, including the introduction of programs in women's history at Sarah Lawrence College and the flagship campus of the University of Wisconsin, she emboldened women to focus on the centrality of women's roles. The renaissance of women's history continued with Nancy Cott's work on women's roles in the domestic economy. In what for graduate students at the time was a must-read account of *The Bonds of Womanhood*

(1977), Cott argued that women were always central to our history, but men and women often occupied separate spheres of life in the antebellum middle-class family system. Women worked at home, and with children. Men went to work. By the end of the 1970s, women's history was an established subdiscipline. As Joan Wallach Scott, one of the foremost historians of women, wrote as early as 1983, "Historians have not only documented the lives of average women in various historical period but they have charted as well changes in the economic, educational, and political positions of women of various classes in city and country and in nation-states."

Soon gender studies joined women's history, the former the simultaneous invention of theorists in sexology, literature, and psychology. In gender studies, one did not view women separate from men. Instead, one saw the interactions of women and men. Gender was social and cultural rather than biological, performed rather than ingrained. This allowed scholars like Scott, Drew Gilpin Faust, Glenda Gilmore, and Catherine Clinton among others to bring women into the story of public events hitherto reserved for men. As Scott wrote after almost three decades of thinking about gender categories and categorization, "the articulation" of the relation between women and men, "of the meanings for sex and sexual difference" in different contexts, is itself a concept that is not fixed or easily explained. She "has never been entirely satisfied with my own formulations," and the complex and contested conversation over feminist history and gender goes on.

As more and more women entered the field of academic history (more than half the history PhD students at major universities now are women), more and more fine women's history appeared. Much of it retained the older focus on work and family, but Gilmore and others pioneered a field called new political history, an example of gender studies. In it, historians examine how the roles of women in what was once called the private sphere interacted with local and national politics. The domestic economy of the home and the family capital it generated was just as important to the family as the earnings of husbands, fathers, and male children outside the home. These historians also discovered a vital fact about women—they were beginning to control their reproductive careers. Antebellum family size grew smaller, even though women married earlier and should have borne more, rather than fewer, children. This was not only true of feminists, it was true in farm families, immigrant families, and poor families in the city.

But the angel of the home Zombie not only refused to die, it grew wings. In 1972, conservative, pro-life activist Phyllis Schlafly created the Eagle Forum. Although she was a practicing lawyer, something that all-male bar associations refused to allow in the nineteenth century, she opposed the Equal Rights Amendment and other feminist programs. The anti-ERA campaign was a pro-domesticity campaign, and it stressed that the proper role for proper women was in the home. Using the argument that history was on her side, she brought together traditional religious groups, conservative political activists, and pro-life lobbies and was able, narrowly, to prevent the ratification of the amendment. It was not so much that the amendment said much that was not already part of constitutional jurisprudence as it was the feminist support for the amendment that Schlafly and her coalition opposed.

The Eagle Forum is still flying, and in its beak is the motto "We support constitutional amendments and legislation to protect the institution of marriage and the important roles of father and mother. We honor the fulltime homemaker." It opposes abortion rights, same-sex marriage, and all other forms of social and economic activity that it argues undermine the angel of the home's role. Full-time homemaking, child care, and domestic laborer whether married or not is surely an honorable role for both women and men. But it is not and never was the only role that women performed, and it is not and was not, even in the early nineteenth century, the only role in which women were well regarded. Using fake history to deny women the many roles they have played and do play is a near perfect example of Zombie history in the popular mind.

Sambos and Rebels

There are two Zombies here, both well entrenched in the popular culture of the day and later historical writing. Although slavery is long gone, Zombies live forever, and both continue to roam the southland where I teach. The first is Sambo, the happy darky, the slave who loved his master. The second is the slave rebel, fiercely independent and willing to die for his and others' liberty. Both were deeply embedded in the mind of the antebellum South, and both survived the end of slavery. Although there were slaves who bore affection for their masters and there were slaves who rebelled against their bondage, the depiction of slaves as essentially one or the other is the way that real people are turned into Zombies.

The sambo Zombie sang and danced through the pages of antebellum southern writers and intellectuals like Thomas R. Dew, George Fitzhugh, and other purveyors of the Moon and Magnolias school. Sambo was featured in Virginia lawyer and professor Fitzhugh's *Cannibals All* (1857). Of slavery, Fitzhugh gushed, "The negro slaves of the South are the happiest, and, in some sense, the freest people in the world. The children and the aged and infirm work not at all, and yet have all the comforts and necessaries of life provided for them. They enjoy liberty, because they are oppressed neither by care nor labor." By contrast, the northern laborer was a wage slave, disposed of by the factory owner when he or she could no longer work; paid wages far lower than the equivalent food, clothing, and other in kind remuneration given the slave; and allowed far less time to rest. Mary Schoolcraft's *The Black Gauntlet, a Tale of Plantation Life in South Carolina* (1860) was typical of the novelization of these Zombies, in which "for these sympathizing negroes lived to see this loving [white planter] couple rejoicing in a beautiful family of nine children all of whom they loved with a fealty known only in this cold world by the old homestead servants of the South."

The same argument, somewhat differently phrased in the early twentieth century (after all, slavery was gone), was the centerpiece of Ulrich Bonnell Phillips's *American Negro Slavery* (1918). The only sources he quoted were those of the masters, for example from one manual for religious instruction of the slaves, "a zealous and vehement style, both in doctrine and manner, is best adapted their temperament." Phillips then added, "It is clear that [this author] had observed plantation negroes long and well." Slaves were happy darkies, well cared for by white folks, like perpetual children. Phillips, like Fitzhugh, did not credit the individuality of slaves, for example that they might have individual views of God and salvation, because neither man heard, or sought to hear, the voices of slaves or ex-slaves. Phillips's view of slavery was something of an orthodoxy among white historians, even in the North. For example, Harvard's Samuel Eliot Morison's *Oxford History of the United States* (1928) repeated much of Phillips's claims uncritically—never bothering to consult evidence that his own forebears, abolitionists, had assembled. "Although brought to America by force, the incurably optimistic Negro soon became attached to the country and devoted to his 'white folks," Morison wrote. Slave rebellions planned by the disaffected were "invariably" disclosed to the master by "some faithful darky."

The Zombies were once again feted in former Marxist Eugene Genovese's later books on the mind of the South. Reconceptualized as conservatism rather than racism, as a deeply religious rather than a crassly materialist worldview, and then set in the conservative intellectual tradition that attacked capitalism, industrialization, and urbanization, the old defense of slavery looks almost reputable—a Zombie in frock coat and clerical collar. As Genovese wrote in a series of lectures published shortly before he died, "Southerners grounded the proslavery argument in an appeal to scripture and denounced the abolitionists as infidels who were abandoning the plain words of the Bible. The southern divines, relying on the Word, forged a strong scriptural case." Note that here and after "southerners" means white southerners. The fact that this is understood in both the antebellum and the modern literature is a reminder that blacks were not considered southerners by these writers, even though blacks toiled under the southern sun, made the southern soil profitable, and brought forth many generations there. But absent from this writing, both contemporary and modern, is any attempt to see the world through the slaves' eyes, something that a younger Genovese had attempted.

When slaves gave testimony from firsthand knowledge, they revealed that slavery was inherently a brutal and brutalizing institution. In law, it reduced human beings to chattel—pieces of property that could be bought and sold, inherited and gifted away, at the will of the owner (or his creditors). In practice, it allowed all manner of physical and psychological abuse so long as the owner, his agent, or any free white person called it "correction." In law the slave could offer no resistance to such punishment, as in law the slave was not a person with any rights.

Defenders of slavery then and later offered the following response—in practice, slavery was far gentler than it was in law. Violent punishment was rare, in part because of the value of the slaves as laborers, in part because of the humanity of masters and overseers. Many masters knew slaves personally, sometimes throughout both their lives. Slaves could negotiate with masters for time and space of their own, in effect owning gardens, tools, pets, and even their own houses. Some historians have argued that slaves were better fed, clothed, and housed than day laborers in the North.

In response, abolitionists then and observers now demonstrate that free persons never wanted to change places with slaves, denouncing more onerous callings as slavery. For example, female household help in the antebellum North rejected the term "servant" and wanted to be called "maid" because servant was a code word for slave. Slaves wanted to be free. The constraints on acting on this desire were familial—slaves did not want to be parted from their children, parents, or other relatives. In fact, while few slave families were intentionally severed, at auction and in wills mothers were separated from children. Every slave family would have known or seen such separations, and the threat of them, perhaps more terrifying than physical correction, hung over every slave family. In particular, the expansion of slavery from coastal regions farther to the south and west broke up families. When slaves could run away from bondage safely, for example during the Civil War, they did so in the hundreds of thousands.

The second Zombie is the slave rebel. There were few actual slave revolts, but later evidence suggests that the watch and warn system of patrols, and the arming of white militias, was a sufficient disincentive. Law also made "conspiracy," any two or more slaves even discussing rebellion, a capital offense and more than once slaves who had done nothing more than grouse about their bondage were rounded up and executed. The law made the Zombie—the fear of slave rebellion that lay in every free person's mind.

The 1820 Vesey Rebellion in Charleston, South Carolina, which involved only words, was one such instance. Gabriel's Rebellion in Richmond, Virginia (1800) may have involved the gathering of arms, though no act of rebellion occurred. The ringleaders were put to death. In the national period, only Nat Turner's Rebellion south of the James River, in Virginia (1831) and the German Coast, Louisiana, Rebellion of 1811 included white casualties. One must conclude that the means of repression of rebellion were effective, although defenders of slavery argued that the nature of the African was docile, and the institution was so gentle, that only a few maladjusted slaves even considered rebellion. The masters and overseers still slept with loaded pistols under their pillows and took firearms to church, lest the dreaded slave rebel Zombie became real.

For various reasons of their own, historians have given new life to the slave rebel. For some scholars, the slave rebel was a hero, a fighter against economic or racial oppression. In 1939, historian Herbert Aptheker published the first of what would become a multivolume collection of slave rebellions. Aptheker's pamphlet-sized *Negro Slave Revolts in the United States, 1526–1850* (1939), though oddly titled (there was no United States until 1776) was a seventy-two-page answer to U. B. Phillips and others who preferred white supremacy and moonlight and magnolias to the raw truth. Instead, Aptheker argued, slaves engaged in a persistent and desperate struggle against their bondage, and nothing in American history, he believed, had been more neglected or distorted than slave rebellions.

Aptheker, an unapologetic Communist, saw history as a struggle, labor history in particular, and the slave rebel fit the model of the labor radical. In other words, Apthetker needed slaves to rebel. He filled in the paucity of actual rebellions in North America with more frequent rebellions in the Caribbean and Brazil, as if all of the New World were one, and covered the period from the introduction of African slavery at the beginning of the sixteenth century through the end of slavery in North America, some 350 plus years, as if it were a far shorter period. He lumped alleged conspiracies, in which the slave rebel was a creature of white fear, with prosecutions of slaves for talking about rebellion, and with evidence of slaves' discontent with slavery, as if they were all of a piece. When slave rebellions did erupt, the horror felt by their victims was real enough. So was the horror at outbreaks of the plague, shipwrecks, and other natural catastrophes.

Aptheker's pioneering work spurred a small cottage industry in finding and exploiting slave revolts. So Gabriel's Rebellion in Virginia, a nonevent that frightened Governor James Monroe down to his socks, became a way to "conceive of the state 'as Gabriel's'" rather than Monroe's or Jefferson's or Madison's. Virginians were more occupied with the prospect of slave rebellion than with banks, tariffs, and national roads according to James Sidbury's *Ploughshares into Swords: Race, Rebellion, and Identity in Gabriel's Virginia, 1730–1810* (1997). Denmark Vesey's was a similar nonrevolt in Charleston, South Carolina, where a rumor of a freedman's plotting led to widespread panic, arrests, and executions of slaves and free blacks. For the take on the events as far north, according to Douglas Egerton's *He Shall Go Out Free: The Lives of Denmark Vesey* (1999), was that Vesey, whose only real crime was preaching to slaves, was instead guilty of abominable cruelties. To whom did not matter. The event was a watershed in both abolitionist thinking and proslavery politics. A Zombie had taken control of antebellum history, then and now. A real rebellion, resulting in the deaths of dozens of whites and hundreds of slaves, came in Southside (south of the James River) Virginia in 1831. The most recent and compelling retelling of those events conceded that "readers may choose to cheer a heroic figure such as Nat Turner." Seriously? Not readers who are upset by the killing of women and children in their beds. One of the authors of this book recalls Vietnam atrocities with the very same results. The new, new, new history of slave revolts has made a Zombie into a heroic figure, the antitype of the lurking, savage rebel so feared by whites in the antebellum South.

The Agrarian South and Industrial North

An interpretation of historical events can be a Zombie when it runs so counter to the evidence and is so boldly asserted that it kills all rivals. Charles Beard, an otherwise superb historian, treated the agrarian South–industrial North Zombie to dinner. Eugene Genovese, another fine historian, served him breakfast. Marc Egnal, a superb economic historian, kept the kettle warm for him. In between meals, this Zombie walked through a dark period in American historical writing. Beard wrote that the Civil War was waged between an agricultural South and an industrial North. The ethos of the South was preindustrial. The ethos of the North was capitalist. Eugene Genovese insisted that the South was in but not of the market—more like a medieval baronial patchwork than a capitalist system producing staple crops. Egnal argued that the diverging focus of the North and South was not based on slavery, but on "the evolution of northern and southern economies."

In fact, although the plantation ideal of the South was leisured gentility, hospitality, and noblesse oblige (be nice to your inferiors), the reality of the plantation South was successful, sometimes ruthless agrobusiness. The wealth of the South depended on production for distant markets. Good management of that wealth was a capitalistic enterprise. It was also necessary to attract foreign capital, primarily from England. Without the aid of northern banking, warehousing, and industrial goods, the plantation complex that produced the cotton, sugar, rice, and tobacco would fail. Without slave labor to clear the land, plant and harvest the crops, and provide the extra profits of the internal slave trade, the South's economic miracle would have been stillborn.

The Northeast had many more factories than the South, but most northerners worked in agricultural pursuits. The North did produce and sell industrial goods, but its cash crops of wheat and other comestibles outweighed its industrial productivity. The northern industrialists, merchants, and entrepreneurs were capitalists, but the vast majority of northerners were shopkeepers or farmers who sold a very small portion of their produce to local markets. They were no more capitalists than the upland white yeoman farmers of the South. In fact, there were as many farms and farm boys and girls in the North as in the South. When the Civil War came, soldiers on both sides were very similar in outlook, background, and ethnicity. The differences were real—many northern formations were composed of immigrant Germans, Irish, and Scandinavians, African Americans, and many came from cities. Nearly 150,000 Union troops were people of color. But in the main, it was not a war of northern industrial workers versus southern farm boys and planters' sons.

What was more, the two regions were economically integrated into a national market. Northern textiles and shoes went South. Southern raw cotton went north to be spun into shirts and pants, socks and blankets. Northern bankers handled southern finances. Northerners married southerners. Southerners went to northern schools. Rails, canals, and roads generally went east to west, and river traffic was sectional, but the Mississippi and the Ohio connected both regions.

Senator John C. Calhoun of South Carolina, an astute economic observer, saw all this. His argument against abolitionism was rooted in an economic analysis of the Mississippi River traffic as well as a defense of the humanity of slavery and the inferiority of the African American. What he told the Senate was strikingly modern: the nation was held together by farm and factory, and neither could survive if slavery were eliminated. He was wrong, as the aftermath of the Civil War proved, but that does not mean that Calhoun's political economy was a Zombie. It would be if it were all fakery.

Deranged Abolitionists

The fanatical abolitionist was a Zombie created in the 1830s in the minds of frightened southern slaveholders and periodically thereafter reanimated by scholars and writers who fear that zealotry will once again destroy the peace of the republic. Thus one Stephen Foster of Lynn, Massachusetts, who in 1842 would not stop lecturing religious gatherings on the evils of slavery, though he was manhandled and thrown from churches (twice from second story windows), became a zealot and a fanatic. Others of his ilk, followers of William Lloyd Garrison's radical brand of uncompromising antislavery, were dismissed as "crackpots." Garrison himself, as Manisha Sinha reports, "provoked outrage as a madman, a fanatic" among his Boston neighbors.

Some leading historians have fallen victim to this too-easy dismissal of the abolitionists' commitment to pull down what seemed to them the towering edifice of slave power. Thus Pulitzer Prize-winning biographer David Donald judged Massachusetts senator Charles Sumner a neurotic, Smith College historian Stanley Elkins castigated the abolitionists as "guilt ridden fanatics," and James H. Hutson decried the paranoia of the antislavery advocates. In fact, the abolitionists were largely nonviolent, using words and their own bodies to press for change; more often than not, a lot more often than not, they were the victims of proslavery or antiblack mobs and assassins. It was the secessionists who burned abolitionist literature, mobbed abolitionist speakers, and drove anyone who expressed abolitionist sentiments out of town. Thus the abolitionist became a Zombie, driven mad by his own fanaticism.

Only one among the actual, as opposed to the Zombie, abolitionists, John Brown of Kansas, might be called unbalanced in mind, and that because of his belief that only violence could overcome the slave power. The rest of the abolitionists were not insane, but intensely moralistic reformers in an age of intense moral reform. That they were vocal is not in question. Some of their rhetoric was incendiary, as when Wendell Phillips called the slave South one great brothel. They held meetings, edited newspapers, engaged campaigns to petition Congress, and faced threats to their lives, but they never dominated a political party or dictated a platform. The Free Soil Party of the 1840s was not given to abolitionism. In the 1850s, abolitionist societies did elect some of their number to Congress and state office as Republicans, but even these abolitionists, like William Henry Seward, Salmon P. Chase, and John P. Hale, did not control the Republican Party.

Among themselves, the abolitionists were long divided between those who wanted a gradual end to slavery through persuasion of slaveowners to manumit their slaves and those who wanted immediate abolition through law. A handful of the abolitionists supported John Brown's plan to lead a general slave revolt. An even smaller group believed that blacks should have full social equality, though most abolitionists supported legal and political equality only.

True, when Lincoln was elected, some of the "fire-eaters" who wanted secession misread him as an abolitionist and mischaracterized the Republican Party as an abolitionist party, but it was not committed to abolitionism at all. The "radicals" in his party could not even persuade Lincoln to free slaves in the early years of the war, so concerned was he that it would alienate slaveholders in the border states of Missouri, Maryland, and Kentucky.

When South Carolina, followed by the rest of the soon to be Confederate States of America, seceded, they blamed the abolitionists for all manner of crimes. The worst was planning domestic insurrection among the slaves, ironic in the light of the fact that secession was domestic insurrection in the Union. The abolitionists did support the war effort, with one of two exceptions who thought that the slaveholding lands were so besotted with sin that they could not be saved. These were just words, however.

Why did historians of the quality and repute of David Donald and Stanley Elkins join with advocates of Jim Crow to denigrate the abolitionists? The answer may lie not in the 1850s, but in the 1950s. In the 1950s, some historians given to a species of academic retrenchment created another Zombie, the abolitionist who was so upset that he had lost social and cultural status that he turned to radical reform. This "status revolu-

tion" theory ignored the moral and religious background of the abolitionists themselves, replacing biography with theory. The idea that reformers
compensated for feelings of lost potency neatly fit the intellectual malaise
of the 1950s (when "eggheads" were under attack from all directions—see
chapter 7), but it did not fit the moral fervor of the 1850s, when reformers
really believed in their various causes, or the 1960s, when historians again
recognized the moral fervor of reform for what it was. Not by chance in
this turnaround of historical perspective, the 1960s saw the flowering of
the civil rights movement, a movement whose roots lay in abolitionism.

Today, "as in Foster's time," Joel Olson relates, "zealotry is held in low
esteem." The mainstream mind is frightened by nonviolent courage and
does not really understand the roots of moral outrage. Thus the advocates
of free speech at UC Berkeley, in 1964, were actually children rebelling
against their (surrogate) parents, and the young people who, fifty years
later, similarly risked their future prospects in the Occupy movement, were
said to be wandering about in a leaderless herd—obviously, a new generation of Zombies.

Politicians and intellectuals in the antebellum America nation faced two
intertwined problems of leadership. The first was to explain away the violence of the revolutionary era, convincing their countrymen and visitors
from abroad that the United States was here to stay. The second was to
demonstrate that they were entitled to wear the mantle once worn by the
revolutionary generation. Answers lay in many places—making and spending money, catering to the voice of the people, moving and moving again.
But the energy in all these activities had a frenetic quality, as if something
was chasing these men and women, and something was. For as historian
Gordon Wood wrote in his Pulitzer Prize-winning *The Radicalism of the
American Revolution*, "no one was really in charge." Self-interest, the very
enemy of the revolutionary leaders, was now the force driving their children to seize more territory, build cities, and bring more land under cultivation. And unregulated, uncompromising self-interest was tearing the
nation into two—free and slave.

CHAPTER FOUR

Civil War and Reconstruction Zombies

The literature on the Civil War and Reconstruction is the most volumi-nous in all of American historical writing. We tell the story of the Civil War and its aftermath in endless variations. Civil War buffs jam the battlefield parks and the bookstore Civil War shelves. We cannot get enough of the Civil War and Reconstruction in works of fiction and nonfiction.

It would be little short of a miracle if a field so littered with the dead did not have its Zombies. And it does. There are almost more Zombies in Margaret Mitchell's *Gone with the Wind* (1936) than there were real people. There are sambo Zombies, southern belle Zombies, noble Confederate Zombies, and evil carpetbagger Zombies. True, it's only a novel, and novel-ists like Mitchell were free to weave memory, imagination, and idealiza-tion into a historical narrative, but what made it such a best seller was the way that it seemed to capture a moment in American history. Even the nomenclature of the "War Between the States" and the "War of Southern Independence" in the South and the "War of the Great Rebellion" in the North suggests the way that we need turn to these Zombies to ease our horror at the losses and destruction of what was, in fact, a civil insurrection on a momentous scale. (Of course, had the Confederacy won, it would have been a War for Independence in some sense.). Zombies also walk through might-have-been novels like Newt Gingrich's *Gettysburg* and John Jakes's *North and South Trilogy*.

Even the best fictional accounts sometimes prefer the Zombie to the man. Michael Shaara was a New Jersey journalist and science fiction writer, whose *Killer Angels* (1974), a novel about the three days of Gettyburg fea-turing the heroism of the 20th Maine Infantry regiment and Colonel

Joshua Chamberlain, is one of the best-selling works of historical fiction in America. It has been made into a movie, *Gettysburg* (1993), that is often shown in history classrooms. The novel has been assigned to West Point students. College essays on the war routinely cite it as though it were a work of nonfiction scholarship. It won the Pulitzer Prize in fiction and Pulitzer Prize-winning historian James McPherson called it "my favorite historical novel." In classrooms and home libraries *Killer Angels* replaced but did not supplant Stephen Crane's novella, *The Red Badge of Courage* (1895), still on some Civil War reading lists at colleges. By focusing on individuals who survived the fighting, and units that neither ran nor were annihilated, the books give the impression that the war was somehow different from other wars. It was not. Indeed, most of the death was due to camp fevers and most wounds led to deadly infections. In the end, the student greets columns and lines of Zombies disguised as the men who actually suffered and died in the war.

In some of the most popular histories of earlier days, the Civil War soldier assumes a Zombie–like solemnity. As Bell Wiley wrote in the introduction to his account of Billy Yank, "For the common soldiers of both sides the qualities that stand out were pride in themselves and their families, a strong sense of duty, courage; a capacity for suffering, a will and strength to endure, and, for most, a devotion to country and cause that exceeded that of the folks at home." In these accounts, the Civil War soldier wears a ragged, bloodstained uniform and lifts aloft a tattered flag. When peace comes, he will be truly represented by the "bloody shirt" of the postwar GOP or the lost cause of the defeated Confederacy. This Zombie soldier cannot be killed by ordinary means because so many Americans are Civil War buffs, and they prefer the Zombie to the real men.

Missing from these popular histories are people of color. If a Zombie is an undead being, how can the absence of something be a Zombie? Actually, people of color are not missing, they are simply not regarded as people. Free and freed black men served in the Union Army, but not in these accounts. When slaves are mentioned, they are a group or submerged in the general term "slavery." There are former slaves, and there is slave country, in which (white) southerners loudly proclaim that they are not slaves. Slaves were nearly 20 percent of the Confederacy's population, but they appear in no more than a handful of places in these books. With a very few exceptions, they do not have speaking roles. They do not have names. In effect, the slaves have already become the invisible men and women of Ralph Ellison's novel, *The Invisible Man* (1952): "A walking zombie! Already he's learned to repress not only his emotions but his humanity. He's invisible, a walking personification of the Negative." They are Zombies who shamble through the narrative, running away from their masters, acting in inappropriate gratitude to the Union troops and their former masters both, sometimes seen working on fortifications, cooking, or washing in the Union camps. They are always part of the scenery, and never actors in front of it. Apparently they were too frightened, too ignorant, too undisciplined, and too childlike to take an adult part in their own emancipation. Well-meaning patriotic historians had turned flesh and blood into Zombies. (So, yes, the invisible man can be a Zombie.)

Why? Perhaps, writing during or after World War II, influenced by the sacrifices of millions of American soldiers, sailors, and marines on foreign soil and distant seas, the authors of these histories believed that the soldiers and officers on both sides of the Civil War had to be honorable. Americans could be no less. To bring slavery into the account would be to introduce a moral blemish and demean the sacrifice.

Stories are not enough to satisfy our gnawing curiosity about the Civil War and its aftermath. Causation is the most important and the most vexing task of the historian. We all celebrate the good story and honor the able storyteller, but the most important contribution of the historian may be the explanation of why things happened. No episode in American history has been so controverted among historians than the causes of the Civil War. Surely the corruption of politics in the era played a role, but did it betoken so venal and oblivious a generation of political leaders that they blundered into the war? Was slavery more than just a sectional division between the North and the South, but a worm at the very core of the Union?

"States' Rights"

An idea can be a Zombie if it fits the description of Zombie—fake history that refuses to die. That a quarrel over the doctrine of states' rights caused the Civil War is such an idea. The doctrine of states' rights itself was not the Zombie. It was an arguable, if (I believe) historically and jurisprudentially mistaken, interpretation of the federal Constitution. This would put it in the category of false fact rather than fake fact. But for many years the states' rights causation thesis was classroom orthodoxy. Textbooks routinely insisted that the South seceded and fought to preserve its view of the Constitution, particularly the Tenth Amendment. As David B. Scott's popular *Smaller School History of the United States to 1876* (1878) summarized the matter, the Civil War was a test of states' rights.

In fact, the Constitution established a dual sovereignty, in which the states retained the powers (reserved) of self-government in certain areas and the new federal government had exclusive authority in other (delegated or enumerated) areas of governance. The boundary between these reserved and delegated powers might be contested, but the larger outlines of the Union and final federal authority were explained by the federalists in the ratification debates. A strong states' rights argument was offered by opponents (so-called antifederalists) of the Constitution, but they lost.

States' rights was still a relatively new doctrine when, in 1798, Thomas Jefferson, in his secretly authored Kentucky Resolves, and James Madison, in his openly proposed Virginia Resolutions, explored it. Jefferson's draft began by resolving that "the several states composing the US. of America are not united on the principle of unlimited submission to their general government; but that, by a compact under the style & title of a Constitution for the US. and of Amendments thereto, they constituted a general government for special purposes, delegated to that government certain definite powers, reserving, each state to itself, the residuary mass of right to their own self-government; and that whensoever the General government assumes undelegated powers, it's acts are unauthoritative, void, & of no force." Jefferson had no part in writing or ratifying the federal Constitution. Madison, by contrast, was a key figure in both. His resolution for the Virginia House of Delegates read, in part, "That this Assembly doth explicitly and peremptorily declare, that it views the powers of the federal government, as resulting from the compact, to which the states are parties; as limited by the plain sense and intention of the instrument constituting the compact; as no further valid that they are authorized by the grants enumerated in that compact; and that in case of a deliberate, palpable, and dangerous exercise of other powers, not granted by the said compact, the states who are parties thereto, have the right, and are in duty bound, to interpose for arresting the progress of the evil, and for maintaining within their respective limits, the authorities, rights and liberties appertaining to them." Both documents were partisan special pleading (the two men were the leaders of the Republican opposition to the Federalists' Alien and Sedition Acts). In time, both men recanted their notions of nullification and interposition, respectively.

States' rights thus was already a controversial view of the federal Constitution when Senator William Smith of South Carolina openly defended it in the presidential campaign of 1820, and again secretly, when Smith's longtime foe, Vice President John C. Calhoun, used it to defend South Carolina's opposition to the tariff of 1828. During the controversy, Vice President Calhoun offered a theoretical defense of states' rights, based on the idea that the Constitution was a compact among the states, and any state had the right to withdraw from the Union as they might from a contract when one of the parties (in this case the federal government) had failed to perform its duties. South Carolina had argued states' rights against federal land policy in 1830, and against the admission of California as a free state in 1850. At the same time, South Carolina politicians had argued against states' rights when it came to the Fugitive Slave Acts of 1793 and 1850, and against the Pennsylvania anti-kidnapping law in 1841. Thus, the states' rights position was a flexible one, to say the least, when it came to the interests of South Carolina. But there is no question that South Carolina based its secession declaration of December 1860 in part on states' rights doctrine.

Supposedly, by electing a Republican president on a platform of free soil, the federal government had violated the rights of the slave states. In the mind of South Carolina's secessionists, the Republican-led Congress would soon interfere with slavery where it existed, or allow abolitionists to bring their agitation against slavery into its heartland. They believed too that the Union was not perpetual or indissoluble. Six more states adopted this view and withdrew from the Union, agreeing to form a new Confederate States of America. After fighting began, the states of Virginia, North Carolina, Tennessee, and Arkansas joined the Confederacy. The idea outlived the Confederacy. As former Confederate vice president Alexander H. Stephens wrote in 1868, "the conflict in principle arose from different and opposing ideas, as to the nature of what was known as the General Government. The contest was between those who held it to be strictly federal in character, and those who held it was thoroughly national."

President Lincoln and the majority of Congress took the opposite view—not of states' rights (many of the Republicans, including Lincoln, believed in the "old Constitution" of limited federal powers)—but of secession. Lincoln thought that the Union was perpetual and no state could leave it without the permission of all the other states. Any attempt to use force against the federal government or its officials was simply the crime of insurrection, as defined in federal law.

But that is not to say that states' rights doctrines caused secession, much less the Civil War. When it suited their interests, states in the North offered states' rights arguments akin to those that southern states proffered, for example in opposition to congressional fugitive slave legislation in the 1850s. There was no necessary sectional component to insisting that state power trumped an act of Congress or a presidential decision or an order of the US Supreme Court. Instead, South Carolina's "Declaration of the Immediate Causes Which Induce and Justify the Secession of South Carolina from the Federal Union," adopted on December 24, 1860, made clear that the real reason for its secession was its fear that Lincoln's Republican Party would impair slavery in South Carolina. "They have denounced as sinful the institution of slavery; they have permitted open establishment among them of societies, whose avowed object is to disturb the peace and to eloign the property of the citizens of other States. They have encouraged and assisted thousands of our slaves to leave their homes; and those who remain, have been incited by emissaries, books and pictures to servile insurrection." South Carolina visitors to the Georgia, Virginia, and other secession conventions in the fall and winter of 1860–61 made the same point.

Whether the fear was based on a genuine threat to slavery where it already existed (the Republicans and Lincoln denied any such threat), it was clear that the new Republican majority in Congress and its president were determined not to let slavery expand beyond its present borders. That was the real threat to slaveholding interests, for if slavery could not expand into new territories, the second and third economically most profitable aspects of slavery, beyond the worth of slave labor itself, would be harmed. The internal slave trade thrived on the expansion of slavery to the West, and the value of new crops of slaves—literally the next generation of slave boys and girls—would suffer if the demand for slaves in those new territories was curtailed. States' rights theories are wrong, but they are not Zombies. The idea that a disagreement over states' rights caused the Civil War is a Zombie.

States' rights did not die with the Confederacy. In March 1956, 99 members of Congress issued a virtual overruling of *Brown v. Board of Education*. The so-called Southern Manifesto was the work of segregationist southern lawyers in the Senate, and its arguments encapsulated the long tradition of states' rights lawyering. Senator Strom Thurmond of South Carolina circulated a mimeographed draft of the Manifesto to his southern colleagues on February 2, 1956. A second version followed a week later. This was assigned by Senator Walter George of Georgia, the senior member of the Southern Caucus, to a drafting committee headed by his Georgia colleague Richard Russell. A third draft was the work of

Russell, with help from Senators John Stennis of Mississippi and Sam Ervin of North Carolina.

Thurmond's first draft used the term nullification, relying on the precedent of Thomas Jefferson's secretly drafted Kentucky Resolves of 1798. Interposition claimed the power of a sovereign state to interpose itself between its citizens and an unconstitutional act of Congress. Although some southern defenders of segregation, notably *Richmond News Leader* editor James J. Kirkpatrick, beat the drum for interposition, most of his editorial peers in the South thought the idea a nonstarter. Neither interposition nor nullification was accepted constitutional law in 1956, the supremacy clause of the Constitution having said and the Civil War having demonstrated graphically that states could not refuse to obey federal law.

The Southern Caucus's "Declaration of Constitutional Principles," styled after the Declaration of Independence, aka the Southern Manifesto, was introduced on the Senate floor on March 12 by Senator George. In Russell's final version, incorporating comments and amendments from Ervin and Stennis, the Manifesto took the form of a brief of the sort that amicus curiae (friends of the court) may offer when the Court hears a case rather than a decision of the court, Thurmond's original format. And at the center of the document was a fulsome version of states' rights. Education was left to the states by the founding fathers, and nothing in the Reconstruction amendments changed that fact, according to the Manifesto. The Manifesto, like the Kentucky and Virginia Resolutions, Calhoun's "Exposition" of 1828, and the South Carolina declaration of causes of secession, changed nothing because, like all the other states' rights proposals, it was not an accurate reading of the Constitution. States' rights rhetoric did not cause anything.

Slavery Caused the Civil War

If the quarrel over states' rights did not cause the Civil War, perhaps it was the sectional debate over slavery? This is a second-generation Zombie. Its parent, the first Zombie, still shambling through some classrooms, denied that slavery had anything to do with the Civil War. After all, racism was rife in both the North and South's free white population. Except for a relative handful of immediatist abolitionists, few in the North wanted to free slaves. White northerners simply preferred free labor to slave labor, did not want to compete with slave laborers, and thus wanted to prevent the expansion of slavery into the western territories and, even more, into existing free states.

This said, slavery did not cause the Civil War. There are two kinds of historical causes, the necessary, or without-which-not, and the sufficient. Slavery divided the nation for a long time before the war came. Without that division, there would never have been secession or a war. But slavery was not a sufficient cause of war. It was a root cause of secession, as the constitution of the Confederacy, drafted in February 1861, revealed. That constitution stated outright that no state could free its slaves, something that the federal Constitution never said. Ordinances of secession also stated that major reasons for secession were fear of slave rebellion spurred by northern abolitionists and concern that the federal government would interfere with slavery.

Slavery caused the severing of the Union, but secession was not the same as civil war. In fact, both President Jefferson Davis and Vice President Alexander Stephens of the Confederacy hoped that the federal government would allow its former southern states to depart in peace. Lincoln, Secretary of State William Seward, and other Republicans hoped that the governments of the seceding states would see reason and rescind their declarations of secession, and return in peace to the Union. Full-fledged military action came only after Confederate forces fired on Ft. Sumter, a federal military base in Charleston, South Carolina, harbor months after the Confederate government formed. As Lincoln told the nation in his second Inaugural Address, in March 1865, no one wanted war, but the war came.

What had then caused it? A recent and ill-considered statement by President Donald Trump's chief of staff, John Kelly, offered that the war came because both sides would not compromise. This too reanimated an older Zombie, one of a small crowd of them walking this hallowed ground. The Zombie was in part the work of historian James G. Randall, who wrote in the 1930s that the war was the work of a "blundering generation" of politicians. Randall may have been influenced by the way that the US seemed to stumble into World War I, and the ineptitude of American diplomacy in the years after that war. In both Kelly's and Randall's formulations, it was the ambition, greed, and shortsightedness of Lincoln's generation that failed to find a compromise short of war. There may be some truth to those accusations. The 1850s was a decade of graft and greed among politicians.

But nothing of that big barbeque was cause for war. In fact, a group of politicians gathered in a peace conference in winter of 1861 proposed grounds for compromise, but states that had seceded refused to send delegates to the conference. The conference drafted an amendment to the

Constitution that would have allowed slavery in the western territories, but the Republicans could not accede to this, and the secessionists wanted slavery national—the right to take their slaves anywhere in the country. So compromise after secession was too late.

Would compromise before South Carolina seceded have worked? Assuming this came after the election of Lincoln, there seems no basis for this. No sooner did the news reach South Carolina that Lincoln had won than its "fire-eaters" pressed for the reassembly of the secession convention that had adjourned, without being dissolved, in 1850, during the congressional debates over the Fugitive Slave Act. The delegates gathered in Columbia, South Carolina, and when they saw that there was some Unionist sentiment in the capital, they adjourned, and reassembled in Charleston, where no Unionist dared show his face. Compromise was never mentioned. Again, slavery, or the fear that the free states would somehow interfere with slavery, was behind the secessionist agitation.

Perhaps compromise was possible before Lincoln was elected? After all, compromises occurred in 1820, when Missouri wished to enter the Union as a slave state; in 1846, when free soilers tried to bar slavery from any territory ceded by Mexico; after the Mexican-American War in 1850, when California wished to enter the Union as a free state; and in 1854, when Kansas Territory sought admission to the Union. Why not compromise in 1860? The answer lay in the presidential conventions for the Republican and Democratic Parties. Congress had already proved itself unable to compromise over the admission of Kansas. The federal courts found that compromise was impossible when it came to slavery, as the reaction to the *Dred Scott v. Sandford* (1857) case demonstrated.

So, compromise was left to the electoral process. But there, the old compromises that had made the two-party system so effective had ended. The Whig Party that brought conservatives in the North and the South together had collapsed over the issue of slavery. In 1860, the Democratic Party, the other great national institution, nominated two candidates, Stephen Douglas and John Breckinridge, dividing itself over the slavery issue. Douglas favored the policy that he had introduced with the 1854 Kansas-Nebraska Act—letting the settlers of a territory decide for themselves. The result was "Bleeding Kansas," but Douglas stuck to his formula. Breckinridge favored the decision in *Dred Scott*, in which Chief Justice Roger Taney had written that slavery was a form of property protected by the Fifth Amendment and Congress could not bar it from a territory without giving due compensation to the master. His views were merely dicta (he could not get a majority of the justices to sign on to his opinion), but they sent a chill through the free states.

Neither Democratic candidate gained a majority of the popular vote or the electoral college. Had the electoral votes of both candidates been added up, they still would have fallen short of the electoral vote of the Republican candidate, Abraham Lincoln. The Republicans, running on a platform of free soil, won all their votes in the free states and none in the slave states. Slavery, not a blundering generation or the failure to compromise, had brought on the crisis.

But here appears the second Zombie: slavery did not cause the Civil War. Slavery was a necessary condition but not a sufficient one. Slavery caused secession. Slavery was a necessary condition; without it there would be no secession. But slavery was not a sufficient condition. Slavery had not caused secession in 1850. It was the election of Lincoln and South Carolina's decision to secede that caused the Civil War, for secession was, wearing its other face, civil insurrection. In violation of federal law, secessionists seized federal armories, destroyed federal post offices, and occupied federal forts. When secessionists fired on one of these, Ft. Sumter in Charleston Harbor, Lincoln had little choice but to call for volunteers to put down the civil insurrection. The war that no one really wanted had come. Its cause was widespread criminal activity in the South masquerading as the creation of a new slave nation.

"War Between the States"

A war between the states is the most misleading of all the Civil War–related Zombies. It refuses to die, making it the most resilient of all the history Zombies. In 2007, Cindy Hyde Smith, a Mississippi senator, wanted her state to honor its Confederate soldiers by passing a resolution on the "War Between the States." Apparently, Mississippi had engaged in a war against other states. The Sons of Confederate Veterans and the League of the South (founded by historians Michael Hill, Forrest McDonald, Grady McWhiney, and Clyde Wilson, among others, at the University of Alabama campus in Tuscaloosa in 1994) continues to refer to the conflict as the War Between the States.

The first appearance of the term was in a group of lawsuits to regain property taken during the Union blockade of the Confederate coastline, in the form "war between the Confederate states of America and the United

States of America." The argument, made by counsel for the plaintiff ship-owners and cargo masters, was that the conflict was a war between two sovereign nations, or "states." Ironically, this would mean that it could not be regarded as a war between any or all of the states that made up the two federal systems. At the end of the nineteenth century, lobbying groups representing the veterans of the Confederacy pushed for "war between the states," and were practically (but not officially) successful. School systems throughout the former Confederate states adopted the war between the states as the official title, but schools in the North did not. The original *Harvard Guide to American History* (1954) featured articles and books with that title, but the revised edition, in 1974, discarded those items in favor of the Civil War.

Whether adopted or rejected for classroom use, the "war between the states" makes no sense grammatically, unless there was a war between only two states. It should be the war *among* the states. In fact, no state declared war on any other state. States did not declare war at all. Under the federal Constitution, only Congress could declare war. No state could do it and no state did it. The constitution of the Confederate States of America similarly barred individual states from declaring or carrying on war (Article I, section 8, clause 11). But the semantic and legal difficulty of a war between the states was only the beginning of the term's Zombie character.

The federal government never declared war on the Confederate states, because as far as the federal government was concerned, the conflict was not a war at all. It was the suppression of a domestic insurrection. The federal government never recognized the existence of the Confederacy, or that any state had a right to secede, or that any state had sovereignty as a separate nation. When the war was over, the former Confederate states were readmitted to the Union as if they were still part of the United States, not by treaty or annexation, as though they had been foreign nations.

The Confederacy never declared war on any of the states in the Union, or on the federal Union itself. Instead, the Confederate Congress declared that it was defending itself against northern aggression. Self-defense did not entail a declaration of war. When the fighting was over, former Confederate officials and officers were, for a time, barred from voting, holding office, and the like, until a general pardon in 1871 returned them to full citizenship.

Why then did the textbooks call the conflict a war between the states? That was a concession to southern schools and the doctrine of states' rights. According to that idea, the war was fought to defend the rights of southern states, another Zombie we have already encountered. Remember that Zombies are only comfortable with other Zombies.

President Abraham Lincoln Frees the Slaves

This is a Zombie that many want to believe, but it is not true. In times of crisis, we look to heroes to save us. For many after his assassination, Lincoln became Father Abraham. Part of his apotheosis was the notion that he stretched out his hand and freed the slaves. "We are coming, Father Abraham," read recruiting posters during the war to attract free blacks to Union service.

Most slaves simply freed themselves. They walked to the Union lines. They rowed across bays and rivers to freedom. They acted as if they had never been slaves. General Benjamin Butler in Virginia and General John C. Fremont in Missouri, in different ways, accepted this verdict. Butler decided that the slaves who came to him had been working on Confederate fortifications. He treated the men as contraband of war. Fremont simply treated them as free. Lincoln, concerned about the loyalty of slaveowners in the border states of Missouri, Maryland, and Kentucky, was wary about these policies, but the three men, all lawyers, had to concede that the slaves were the first to free themselves.

As Secretary of State Seward conceded and Lincoln recognized, slavery was the most comprehensive and difficult to resolve legal question that secession and the Civil War raised. Slavery was not mentioned by name in the federal Constitution, and before the war abolitionists insisted that omission meant that slavery was unconstitutional. Seward was an abolitionist, but when he joined Lincoln's cabinet he moderated his views. Lincoln was not an abolitionist, but he hated slavery and did not want it to expand outside the South. In *Dred Scott*, the Supreme Court rejected that view. Slavery was a matter of domestic (state) law, and would remain so, according to Chief Justice Roger Taney's opinion. It could even be read as implying that Congress could not bar slaveholders from bringing their slaves into the territories. Although candidate Lincoln had little good to say about that decision or about slavery itself, he understood that it was the law of the land.

There followed President Lincoln's first efforts with regard to slavery, his inaugural address promising that slavery would not be touched where it already existed. Then, when the war had begun, he agreed that slaves who contributed to the Confederate war effort were contraband of war. Next, he offered federal compensation to slaveowners who freed their bondmen and women. None of this addressed the general emancipation of slaves.

The war was not going well when his Cabinet met on August 3, 1862. Lincoln was leaning toward emancipation as a wartime expedient to induce Confederate slaveowners to reverse course or lose their slaves. Announced on September 22, 1862, and applying only to those portions of the country still in rebellion on January 1, 1863, the Emancipation Proclamation did not free many slaves. For example, it did not apply to slavery in the loyal border states, or even to those parts of Confederate states by then in federal hands, like New Orleans. Yet even in New Orleans, according to page 1 of the *New York Times* on February 2, 1863, it was assumed by many that "by the Emancipation Proclamation of the President, Slavery is everywhere abolished—the institution is legally extinct—the title is defective, and cannot be made good. To such an extent is this the case, the acknowledgment of the independence of the Confederate States to-day would not restore the negro to slavery, for the still acknowledged supreme law of the land has declared that such an institution does not exist."

Former Supreme Court justice Benjamin Curtis, no friend to slavery himself, also saw it as a first and giant step toward ending slavery, but condemned it because he thought that Lincoln's wartime powers did not include the legal authority to take private property from noncombatants (for example, white women who owned slaves). The legality of the Proclamation remains controversial to this day. Lincoln's own views were evolving, and it is possible that the president intended the abolition of slavery—that is, whether freeing the slaves of a wartime enemy—would become a wider and permanent freeing of all slaves when the war was over.

Why do we want a Lincoln who planned to free the slaves all along? And why do we want to credit him with doing exactly that? One reason is because we do not want to consider for more than a moment the alternative. Could slavery have survived the Civil War? Our repugnance to slavery today makes that possibility abhorrent. Even more startling is the fact that the federal government had taken from private citizens more of their property than all of the income taxes so repellant to many today. The taking violated the Fifth Amendment to the Constitution, which barred the federal government from taking private property without due process and compensation. Not every slaveholder in the Confederacy was waging war against the United States, but every slave in the Confederacy was included in this Emancipation.

Consider also the impact of the emancipation on the wealth of the

South. For example, in the year before the war, according to historian Edward Ayers, "about one fifth of the white families owned fifty-five hundred slaves in Augusta Country, Virginia. Slaves were worth about six million dollars in the county, making its farmsteads the most valuable, per capita, in the state. Slavery lay at the heart of Augusta County's economy." The prospect that emancipation was permanent, that is, that slaveholders in the Confederacy would never regain ownership of property worth nearly three billion dollars, and that three million men and women, and their progeny, would be freed, profoundly changed the economic character of the nation. Before secession, the slaveholding South was considerably richer than the largely agricultural North. With emancipation, the per capita wealth distribution of the two sections changed dramatically, as the prospective freedmen and women would have little property, while the slaveholder would lose about twenty thousand dollars (in modern figures) per slave.

Seen in these terms, emancipation was a government-mandated redistribution of wealth unparalleled in the nation's experience. The funds raised by the excise taxes under the Internal Revenue Act of 1862 and the brief experiment with an income tax in the United States during the war paled by comparison. The excise taxes were regressive, but were limited to luxury items, and the income tax only applied to those whose incomes exceeded six hundred dollars. Rising from three percent across the board to 7 percent, the income taxes raised a maximum of nearly seventy million dollars in the final year of the war.

The idea that law could effectuate such a redistribution of wealth was, like emancipation itself, a wartime expediency. The Union simply needed the funds to carry out its military operations. But the constitutional implications of such expediencies outlived their implementation. Slavery existed, or did not exist, as a function of state law. By supervening state law in this most important legal area, emancipation hinted at a profound shift in federal-state relations. Northern Democrats' opposition to emancipation rested precisely on this ground—the federal government's enumerated powers, the defining limits of strict construction of the Constitution and states' rights federalism, did not include emancipation. Lincoln did not refer to Alexander Hamilton's idea of loose construction of the Constitution, but Lincoln's program furthered the goals of a strong national government that the Hamiltonians had pursued in the 1790s. At that time the Jeffersonian Republicans had opposed Hamilton on states' rights grounds. Lincoln's Republicans reversed those polarities. Emancipation was the opening wedge of this reversal.

The Emancipation Proclamation began the process of ending slavery as an American institution, because shortly after it went into effect Republicans in Congress, who had previously refrained from calling for the end of slavery, now presented bills to end it. These did not pass, but the next year Senator Wade Wilson and Representative John Ashby drafted and proposed an amendment to the Constitution ending slavery. The Senate passed the draft amendment in the spring of 1864, and after a year of debate and the election of 1864, returning Lincoln and the Republican majority to Congress, the amendment was passed in the House of Representatives. Its ratification was required of states that had joined the Confederacy and wanted, after the surrender of its forces, to rejoin the Union. The Thirteenth Amendment became law in 1865.

Zombies who walk through our accounts of slavery take all shapes and forms. Some of them masquerade as the owners of slaves. Others as abolitionists. Some act like slaves themselves. We have to be wary of all of them, but make no mistake, we cannot write or teach a history of our country without examining slavery.

The Lost Cause

One reads all the time that the South lost the Civil War. That war was thus a lost cause forever haunting the southern mind. If only the South had won. The lost cause is a Zombie. In the first place, the South was a not a contestant in the Civil War. That was the Confederate States of America. The difference is that between a region (the South) and a political and legal entity (the Confederacy). True, all of the states that joined in the Confederacy were in the southern region, but other southern states, including Maryland and Kentucky, were not in the Confederacy. Southerners fought on both sides, including a Virginian who played a crucial role in winning the war for the Union—George Thomas of Virginia. Northern sympathy for the southern cause was rife among the Democratic Party in Ohio, Illinois, Indiana, Maryland, and Kentucky. Unionist sympathies in parts of Georgia, North Carolina, and Tennessee led significant numbers of people there to a kind of informal secession of these parts of Confederate states from their new government.

Was it nevertheless a lost cause from the start? The Confederacy did not lose the war because it ran out of arms and ammunition. The home-front suffered severe deprivations, often because slaves ran away from their servitude, but the troops did not starve. The armies of the Confederacy were smaller by one-third than the armies of the United States, but the difference in troop numbers was countered by the Confederacy's efficient use of the railroads to concentrate its forces, by the Confederacy's fighting on home soil, and by effective defensive tactics. There were desertions from Confederate lines, particularly late in the war, but nearly 80 percent of white adult males served. There was no lack of morale among the troops.

The Confederacy lost the war because it lost key battles, because the Union strategy of never losing contact with the enemy eventually prevailed, and because when the Confederacy did go on the offensive, as at Shiloh, Sharpsburg, Gettysburg, and Nashville, Union generalship and superior manpower proved their worth. Lee finally recognized that his losses could not be replaced and that his mobility was fatally limited when he surrendered at Appomattox. The Confederacy did not lose the war. The Union won it in a series of battles that, at first, could have gone either way, and then, had the cumulative effect of driving smaller and smaller southern forces further and further into the Deep South.

The US naval blockade of the southern coastline, preventing the Confederacy from trading with foreign powers, was the first of these victories. Urged by Winfield Scott, declared somewhat precipitously by Abraham Lincoln, subsequently confirmed by Congress, the blockade was not clearly legal if the conflict was a civil war (in international law, one nation can only blockade the ports of its enemies if they are also sovereign nations), but it was effective. A handful of Confederate blockade runners slipped through the net, and the converted ironclad *Merrimack* for a time threatened the Union Navy, but the blockade strangled southern cotton exports. The US Navy was also able to invest Mobile, Alabama, New Orleans, Louisiana, and much of the Sea Islands and coast of North Carolina and Georgia. Only Charleston held out.

Was the defeat then proof that the Confederacy itself was a "lost cause"? That Zombie, which wanders over the battlefields of 1861–65, celebrates the honor and heroism of the fallen Confederate forces and the moral superiority of the prewar (antebellum) southern way of life that fell to the heartless industry of the North. The term itself, though not the feeling, was the invention of Richmond journalist Edward Pollard, and the title of his history of the Civil War, *The Lost Cause* (1866). In it, he offered the "lessons" of the war. Glorious and unprecedented as it was, it ended with a whimper. The cause was the "demoralization of the armies and people of the Confederacy." They had lost the will to fight. They had exhausted their store of endurance. The North did not win. The South simply conceded the prize. Worse, the South had left the war unrepentant, believing that they were still "the better men." But Pollard himself still believed, and made no secret of it, that the white race was the ruling race, and that the South had been betrayed by its own leaders, principally Jefferson Davis. In any case, the idea of a lost cause of white supremacy and racial harmony based on the subordination of the freed peoples gained a life of its own when he died, at age forty, in 1872.

There was honor and courage in abundance on both sides, but one should not glorify the carnage. More than two-thirds of the dead were victims of camp fevers, including diseases like measles and mumps to which farm boys had no immunity and camp doctors had no cures. Another large proportion of the dead were victims not of mortal wounds, but of sepsis (infection) resulting from nonfatal wounds. Finally, letters, diaries, and official reports agree that the soldiers in battle did not fight for honor and glory, they fought because their comrades fought, because they had been trained to fight, and because they had learned how to hate the soldiers on the other side.

In the meantime, the lost cause staggered on in textbooks, public lectures, and private societies like the Daughters of the Confederacy and the Confederate Veterans Society. The latter's history committee prepared a series of reports spanning the Gilded Age and the turn of the century, for as Fred Arthur Bailey wrote about the persistence of the lost cause, "far more than sectional honor" the defenders of the lost cause regarded it as a proof of the "southern aristocracy's legitimate authority" despite the failure of secession. The history committee reports were two pronged: first, counter every suggestion that the southern elite bore responsibility for the defeat in northern "perverted history," and second, ensure that southern teachers taught southern students "in such a way as to promote southern self-respect and manhood."

Carpetbaggers and Scalawags

The carpetbagger Zombie was a northern corruptionist come south after the Civil War to take from the good (white) people of the defeated Confederacy those few possessions that the evil bluecoats left behind. He carried with him a capacious piece of luggage made of carpet in which to place his stolen items. The scalawag Zombie was his southern helper, a white scamp who voted Republican and abetted the newly freed people. The scalawag was likely to have been born outside the South, was never a planter, and had some formal education. Together they despoiled the Reconstruction South until Redeemers chased them away. Or such is the tale that explains why Reconstruction failed. They are Zombies of course, caricatures of men whose purpose was otherwise.

One of the most visible and troubling themes in American history is the supposed failure in the great experiment in civil rights following the Civil War. The end of slavery was just a start in this, but what a start! The freeing of over three million men, women, and children held in chattel bondage was an administrative and legal challenge to government, unused to such sweeping social tasks, especially when much of the land occupied by the freedmen had been until very recently in the hands of their owners.

If the so-called Radical Republicans envisioned a transformation of the former slaves into free farmers and laborers—that is, free to bargain for their services—that would have been a rather tame project. In effect, the idea was to turn former slaves into replicas of northern farm folk. In practical terms this meant that they had to be guaranteed civil rights, and Congress acted to define those rights in a series of enactments. Would these enactments be proof against the animosity of former Confederate soldiers and civilians and any government institutions they came to control? It was no easy task that the Republicans in Congress assayed, especially as the Democrats in Congress, although they may have supported the war effort (though many did not), were opposed to any kind of legal equality for the freedmen. The great experiment did not end with the removal of troops from the former Confederate states in 1877, because the ideal of civil equality never died in the hearts of many whites and blacks, but the decade of Reconstruction would shortly be recounted in an entirely different light.

In 1966, Kenneth Stampp told the story of the Zombies of Reconstruction in his *Era of Reconstruction*. The titles of the Zombie histories hinted at their disguise: tragic, dreadful, hate, blackout when "honest government" failed, as if honest government had been the hallmark of earlier eras in the South, or anywhere else in the nation for that matter. There was an anger in these accounts of the betrayal of the whites of the South by a cabal of vindictive northern Republicans and witless southern blacks. "Most American historians" bought into some version of this account in the period from 1890 to 1930.

Zombie northerners walked through Reconstruction histories by former Confederates, supposedly perpetrators of schemes of unparalleled political ambition and personal greed. Hordes of these Zombies allegedly descended on the South bearing carpetbag luggage. They stole with both hands what remained of personal property, and turned once obedient and trustworthy bondsmen into Zombies. That version of the carpetbagger and his ally, the southern scalawag, gulling the childlike sambo, was a central theme of the lost cause—the South's explanation of why the war was waged and why it was lost.

Following the war, northern publishers offered readers accounts by Confederate leaders like Jefferson Davis and Alexander Stephens of how the honorable southern white man fought for liberty, and the dishonorable northern white man sought only political and financial advantage. Those images were not only popularized in political speeches and newspaper pieces, they became a staple of literature and movies. Scholars listened, and agreed that northern desire to despoil a supine white South led to widespread corruption.

The Zombies of Reconstruction era history reappeared in the university-sponsored essays of William A. Dunning and his graduate students at Columbia University, from 1900 to 1930. This included Dunning's own work, *Reconstruction, Political and Economic, 1865–1877* (1907), a volume in the distinguished American Nation Series. His students, William Watson Davis, Walter L. Fleming, James W. Garner, J. G. De Rouhac Hamilton, C. W. Ramsdell, J. S. Reynolds, Thomas Staples, and C. Mildred Thompson, argued that freedmen voters in the South were easily manipulated against their own interests, which lay with their former masters rather than with the Republican invaders; that the Republicans' primary motive was to use southern votes to retain control of the national government; and that the Reconstruction governments in the South were marred by corruption. The undergirding of their work was racism, and its superstructure was Jim Crow. Dunning summarized his message as being "about the struggle through which the southern whites, subjugated by adversaries of their own race, thwarted the scheme which threatened subjugation by another race" (that is, by the exercise of civil rights by freedmen). These were not simply southern extremists without academic credentials. Dunning was born and raised in New Jersey and earned a doctorate at Columbia University, at the time arguably the premier graduate institution in the country. His students went on to occupy distinguished teaching posts.

Their views were echoed by popularizers like Democratic politician and diplomat Claude Bowers, whose *The Tragic Era: The Revolution after Lincoln* (1929) supposedly revealed that "the Southern people" (meaning southern white people) were "put to the torture" after the Civil War by "the despotic policies" of unscrupulous and "brutal" Republican politicians and their allies. Although World War II brought greater insight into the horrors of racism to most Americans, the Zombies of Reconstruction still stalked the South. At the University of Georgia, department of history head E. Merton Coulter opened his *The South during Reconstruction* (1947) with the sweeping conclusion that the Civil War and Reconstruction "riveted tighter upon the South a colonial status under which it had long suffered."

Why such perverted and perverse accounts? The authors were eminent in their fields. Dunning was one of the first great graduate mentors at the university that could claim to be the foremost trainer of historians at the time. Bowers was a prolific author, reform advocate, and power in the Democratic Party. Coulter was arguably the foremost southern historian of the South in his time and the editor of the prestigious Louisiana State University Press history of the South series. The answer is that all three men did not credit the words of the former slaves. They did not figure in their history, except as objects in the landscape. They thus were treated as though they were Zombies.

Once the words of the freedmen were added to the account, it changed profoundly. As John Hope Franklin noted in his *Reconstruction after the Civil War* (1961), "no group has attracted more attention or has had its role more misrepresented by contemporaries and by posterity than Southern Negroes during Radical Reconstruction." Using their own words, and observing their contributions without the distorting lens of racism, revealed that Reconstruction carpetbaggers and their freedmen allies notched a number of remarkable achievements. Reconstruction succeeded in expanding the first public school systems in the South, including schools for the freedmen. Many of the carpetbaggers were women who came to teach in those schools. Reconstruction aided in rebuilding the region's infrastructure after the Civil War, particularly the railroads. Reconstruction brought African Americans into government as well as other fields previously denied to them because of slavery. It was only after 1876 that white supremacists succeeded in destroying the Reconstruction state governments, the US Supreme Court limited legal redress, and, even then, many of Reconstruction's achievements remained. The freedmen were not Zombies. The Zombie was the image of the freedmen and their allies that defenders of the Old South proffered.

Second, in light of the new, or newly incorporated, evidence, it became clear that what brought Reconstruction in the South down was not northern moral weakness or even northerners becoming fed up with corruption. Corruption was a part of northern politics for a long time—the 1850s were, in particular, an era of "good stealings." True, northern capital was eager to make a profit from rebuilding the South. What caused the failure of northern attempts to rebuild the infrastructure and the commerce of the South was not northern rapaciousness, but the great Depression of 1873. It undermined all sorts of capital ventures in the South, bankrupting northerners who had invested in railroads and other businesses in the South.

The Zombies called the "carpetbagger," the "scalawag," and the ignorant freedman continue to stalk history books, particularly when they are coupled with the lost cause. And in the North, as Mark Summers has demonstrated, the fever for reform receded. A few old abolitionists like Charles Sumner carried on the fight, and the Republicans still had a majority to pass the Civil Rights Act of 1875, but the relatively new alliance of conservative and radical Republicans (after all, the party was only a little over twenty years old) was fracturing, and the Democrats were gathering strength. Summers recounted that "time stood with the conservatives" who wanted peace and prosperity, and hoped the freedman could make it on his own, but did not really care if he did.

Unlike northern commitment to racial reform in the years of "redemption" of the South, the Civil War Zombies thrive, perhaps because they offer a semblance of truth, assembling their tattered costumes from bits and pieces of contemporary political and legal creeds. Such creeds, in the context of their own times, may have swayed some, but as historical arguments about motive and rationale, they are Zombies. Or perhaps the Civil War remains so horrific in our national memory that we seek Zombies to provide a degree of comfort. When Zombies offer to ease your pain, however, you need to be suspicious. Most likely, the Civil War Zombies are a form of psychological defense mechanism—among some who still believe that slavery was not as severe as industrial labor, a defense against the charge of immorality; and among some who cannot accept that war was the only way to scourge the nation of immorality, an explanation why the search for an alternative to war failed. When history is used as a psychological palliative rather than a realistic analysis, the Zombie finds a home.

CHAPTER FIVE

Gilded Age Zombies

Mark Twain and Charles Dudley Warner's coauthored novel *The Gilded Age, A Tale of Today* (1873) coined the phrase "Gilded Age." The central theme of the book was that corruption had infiltrated everyday life, from poor farmers in the Southwest to rich senators in Washington, DC. The coinage caught on, as it seemed to describe not the aspirations of the poor but the excesses of the wealthy. Urban mansions occupying entire city blocks, with marble facades and ornate interiors, were the visible evidence of a growing disparity between the very wealthy and the wretched masses of the city. Novelists like Stephen Crane, reformers like Jacob Riis, and artists like John Sloan focused on the contrasts.

Students of the Gilded Age have continued to dine at that table, with Zombie wait staff. Dessert is the "declension narrative," a story of how bad everything became. Take, for example, Richard White's *The Republic for Which It Stands* (2017), whose beautifully crafted pages are replete with Zombies—literally in this one case: "Nineteenth-Century Americans were a sickly people. The decline of virtually every measure of physical well-being was at the heart of a largely urban Gilded Age environmental crisis that people recognized but could neither name nor fully understand." The sickly American is a Zombie. In fact, compared to medieval and early modern life span, life expectancy of children, and body weight and size, the nineteenth-century American was longer lived, bigger, and healthier. Immigrants noted with delight the introduction of meat in their diets. By focusing on the industrial city rather than the surrounding hinterlands, or rural areas, White cherry-picked data for his declension narrative. By focusing on a narrow stretch of time rather than the longer span, he embraced the Zombie. He knew this, and followed the dire opening passage of the book's chapter with the admission, "In the Gilded Age people living in mostly rural areas outside the South were comparatively healthier and lived longer lives," then immediately returned to his theme, like Twain, "but in the cities the crisis intensified." White ignored the fact that most Americans did not live in cities until the end of the nineteenth century, and that the cholera and other urban disease epidemics of the nineteenth century occurred before the Civil War.

Travel next if you will with White to the Centennial Exposition of 1876, in Philadelphia. Its giant pavilions were the wonder of the world, and thousands thronged them. But White saw that "continuing racial and sectional conflict, along with class conflict and the gendered exclusion of women from voting, all formed fault lines visible at the Exposition." Divisions there were, and real harms, but White applied the standards of the twenty-first-century's social geology to highlight the social and economic fault lines at the exposition. Actually, women and men, northerners and southerners, and folks of African and Asian ancestry all roamed the grounds. There was a women's pavilion, and black painting and statuary were also present, along with tributes to Robert E. Lee and Stonewall Jackson. The promoters of the exposition, albeit in halting and, to modern eyes, not always successful fashion, tried to show progress in racial, sectional, and gendered debilities. By reading modern antipathy to racism and sexism back to 1876, and judging its character by our own values, no good-intentioned effort at racial equality is ever good enough. White invited the Gilded Age Zombie of nothing is good enough for me to the table. There it greeted older members of the same ragged clan.

Jim Crow

From its inception, Jim Crow was always a pernicious Zombie. It wore many faces, none of them attractive. Before the Civil War, Jim Crow was a white man in a minstrel show who bootblacked his face so he could sing dirty songs and tell lewd jokes. After the war, Jim Crow was the symbol of racial prejudice that allowed whites to denigrate blacks. Above all, Jim Crow was the name of a legal regime that demoted people of color to second-class citizenship, the back of the bus, the substandard schoolhouse, and the "colored" part of town that had unpaved streets and no running water. Under Jim Crow laws, people of color could not eat in segregated restaurants, spend the night in hotels on main streets, or go to "white" hospitals. Sometimes Jim Crow was present by its absence, a shadow on the wall, for example in the paucity of references to the black experience at the Centennial Exposition, even though black laborers had done much of the drudgery of setting up the pavilions.

One may be surprised to find disapproval of Jim Crow absent from the first Progressive era journalism and scholarship. Consider Thorstein Veblen, whose many works slammed ostentation and elevated class consciousness. Though not a racist himself, he never mentioned racism or Jim Crow, though he was surrounded by it. In other works that condemned poverty, obscene displays of wealth, and just about everything in between, look in vain for Jim Crow. In Lincoln Steffens's *Shame of the Cities*, an account of corruption in New York, Philadelphia, St. Louis, and Chicago, among other cities, there were no people of color. The census tells us that these cities were home to thousands of African American workers. Steffens was a perceptive journalist. Did he not see color? The same was true of Ida Tarbell's history of Standard Oil—a shellacking of John D. Rockefeller, although Rockefeller was a financial supporter of black schools, colleges, churches, and other charities.

When the Progressives did speak of race, Jim Crow reappeared, but not as an evil. Progressive Woodrow Wilson's five-volume *History of the American People* (1901) concluded with a study of reunion after the Civil War. The work had a good deal to say about blacks in Reconstruction, and Jim Crow turned the pages. During the war, Wilson offered, "how devoted in the service of their masters the great mass of the Negro people remained." Well, not when they had the chance to flee to freedom—when blue coats were near by. And when they did flee to Union lines, "how every federal commander had had to lead in his train as he moved a dusky host of pitiful refugees." No mention of the blacks who fled by the thousands to wear the same blue coats and die alongside white Union troops. The Jim Crow Zombie had hidden his true nature.

Populist reformers in the South and West preached the rights and needs of the family farmer, but these egalitarian thoughts never crossed "the color line," according to Charles Postel, a historian of the Populists. Urban, professional Progressives' commitments to science, expertise, and state regulation actually furthered the institution of Jim Crow. Contrary to their reputation and even their own rhetoric, the Progressives were most effective segregationists. In the words of historian Michael McGerr, these reformers "seldom contested the increasing division of Americans into separate enclaves." The boundaries of these divisions were drawn by race, and the Progressives' "support for segregation" was indistinguishable whether the Progressives lived in the North or the South.

Segregation thrived during the Great Depression. "During his long term in office, Franklin Roosevelt never pushed civil rights legislation." He needed the support of southern segregationists in Congress. Jim Crow reached out into the distant corners of recovery efforts. Take, for example, the Works Progress Administration, which, among other programs, employed six thousand professional and amateur chroniclers to document America's past in a series of forty-eight state handbooks called the American Guide Series. The purpose was "to make history seem alive," and celebrate the national achievement as well as the resources, landscapes, and peoples of each of the states. In other words, manufacture Zombie histories.

One of the last of these to be published was *Alabama: A Guide to the Deep South* (1941). The WPA acknowledged the assistance of librarians, historians, curators, state officials, and one historian, Clanton Williams, at the University of Alabama. Williams, Alabama born and educated (except for his PhD, at Vanderbilt), taught at the university from 1929 to 1955, and wrote histories of the state. He wrote the history section of the WPA guide. In the welter of information on everything from deer hunting licenses to living accommodations and the dates of flower shows, there was an almost grudging nod to Jim Crow, "everywhere enforced," but not always appreciated, a feature central to life in the state. For the fear Zombie stalked the Deep South in the form of racism.

Williams conceded what every Alabaman knew: the blacks of the cities did not accept the Jim Crow laws "with humility." But perhaps readers from other states would swallow fake history: away from the mines and the mills, one found "a leisurely and friendly land. Many of its families still live on ancestral plantations. . . . relations between the two races remain pretty much what they were in the old plantation days . . . and most of [the Negroes] depend upon some white man or white family for advice and guidance in everything they do." "Vehemently," Alabamans struggled to find a way between the past and the present, the old South of cotton and the New South of industry.

Race relations, here muted, were powder kegs, and memories of the Lost Cause are still very much alive. "At the end of the war, Alabama, sadly stripped of men, money, and property—was in the hands of Northern Troops." Northern, not federal or Union, but invaders from a place far off. For the newly freed black folks, "standards soon became such as one might expect among an illiterate people suddenly thrown upon their own resources," as if the mountain folk were any more literate, and the blacks had never before farmed the land or fed themselves and their families. No mention of Jim Crow, segregation, lynching, or other unpleasantries followed in the rest of the history section.

But surely the civil rights revolution, with the end of state-sponsored Jim Crow and the passage of various new civil rights acts, scourged the Jim Crow Zombie from the land? Surely after the rise of black history, with Black History Month every February, young black and white historians have corrected the nonsense that earlier generations spewed? Not so. The Jim Crow Zombie lives in every southern monument erected to spite civil rights and promote Jim Crow, every statute that honors secessionist leaders and Confederate generals, and in every white supremacy blog post and rally. For the monuments were not erected immediately after the war, but during two periods of Jim Crow enthusiasm—the 1910s and the 1950s. They were white marble and granite memorials not to southern suffering, in which whites and blacks shared, but to defiance of the federal government and resistance to desegregation. And the white supremacy rallies that have reappeared with the election of President Trump are the direct descendants of the Klan rallies, minus the robes and dunce caps.

Once more we face the task of killing a Zombie that refuses to die. As James Grossman, director of the American Historical Association, wrote in 2016, "That which is memorialized and that which is left to popular memory are not accidental. Choices are made about what gets built, displayed, and given plaques. Memorials are public commemorations that legitimate what comes to be called 'heritage.'" What was that heritage? If it is the sacrifice of the white South during the Civil War, there can be little objection. But those monuments are more than that, because of their own history. Everything has a history, including the decision to finance, design, and place monuments. My purpose here is not to accuse, but to remind readers of the persistence of the Jim Crow Zombie.

Machines

Despite the pre–Civil War industrialization of commodities like canned foods, handguns, machine tools, steam engines, and construction-grade cast iron, most American manufacturing was by hand, using the power of animals, water, or the workers' own efforts. After the war, heavy industry began to turn to machines to make machines. The best example came after the turn of the century, with carmaker Henry Ford's assembly line churning out Model T Fords. Charlie Chaplin's iconic silent movie *Modern Times* demonstrated how depersonalizing the assembly line could be.

To advocates of workers' rights, defenders of the environment, and critics of the sooty and sickly city, these machines were the enemy. They shrieked with the terror of a thousand animals in the slaughterhouse. Mindlessly, they roared through the countryside, leaving havoc in their wake. Upton Sinclair's *The Jungle* (1906) protested the mechanized slaughterhouse: "It was all so very businesslike that one watched it fascinated. It was porkmaking by machinery, porkmaking by applied mathematics. And yet somehow the most matter-of-fact person could not help thinking of the hogs; they were so innocent, they came so very trustingly; and they were so very human in their protests—and so perfectly within their rights! They had done nothing to deserve it; and it was adding insult to injury, as the thing was done here, swinging them up in this cold-blooded, impersonal way, without a pretense of apology, without the homage of a tear. Now and then a visitor wept, to be sure; but this slaughtering machine ran on, visitors or no visitors. It was like some horrible crime committed in a dungeon, all unseen and unheeded, buried out of sight and of memory."

Or the butchery of the pastoral landscape and its innocent denizens? The locomotive, in Frank Norris's *The Octopus* (1901) is a Zombie: "In some way, the herd of sheep—Vanamee's herd—had found a breach in the wire fence by the right of way and had wandered out upon the tracks. A band had been crossing just at the moment of the engine's passage. The pathos of it was beyond expression. It was a slaughter, a massacre of innocents. The iron monster had charged full into the midst, merciless, inexorable. To the right and left, all the width of the right of way, the little bodies had been flung; backs were snapped against the fence posts; brains knocked out. Caught in the barbs of the wire, wedged in, the bodies hung suspended. Under foot it was terrible. The black blood, winking in the starlight, seeped down into the clinkers between the ties with a prolonged sucking murmur."

The idea that the Zombie could be a machine, a locomotive or an automated factory line, was part of the anti-industrial literature of the turn of the century. In fact, at the same time, the slaughterhouse and the railroad were undergoing reforms that made them safer. The "shambles," the open air, unregulated, filthy slaughterhouse, was being replaced by pens and chutes to minimize the danger to workers and the terror of the animals. Meat inspectors, created by law in America in 1906, were to ensure, in theory at least, that the product was safely produced. Slaughterhouses were moved away from cities and provided with their own water and waste removal provisions. Railroad turnstiles and right of ways were inspected, and efforts made to make grade crossings safer. State and the federal law provided for worker compensation for injuries. Tracks, signals, and other technological improvements, including the standardization of track gauges, the Westinghouse brake, and the four standard time zones introduced in 1883, made rail travel safer.

None of this banished the machine Zombie from the histories. Indeed, a Czech playwright named Karel ▢apek gave the Zombies a new name in a 1920 play titled *R.U.R.* The Robots of the play (more like the Replicants of *Blade Runner* fame) take over the planet. So historians worry about mindless technological innovation replacing inefficient people with superior machines, as they should. We cannot live without refrigeration, according to historian Jonathan Rees, and that's just the tip of the iceberg of our dependence on machines.

Like the creature hiding in the story of the Indian atrocities, the Zombie is not a person, it is a persuasion. Most historians of my acquaintance are intellectual Luddites. They like to break machines. The machine in the garden is the Zombie—mechanical in its movements, a prejudice made into metal and fiber optics. Historians of technology are among the most sophisticated observers, and the worst offenders, sensitive to the way that technology can run out of control, quick to blame the machine. Historical critics of weapons production may be the leading edge of this criticism. In these and other stories, the machine soon drives the man. Historian of technology Merritt Roe Smith explained: "Decade by decade the pace of technological change quickened" in America, and soon the new heroes were not the framers of ideas but the "men of progress," the inventors and their machines. The individual good gave way to the economic good. In effect, the nation was itself becoming a machine, grinding people on the assembly line as it ground out products and profits. Progress was a technocrat whose ideal was a machine that would run of itself.

That vision of a world of machines that drove other machines finally came to fruition in World War II. Other nations committed time and manpower to the struggle. Coming relatively late to the war with a huge reserve of underutilized factories and vast supplies of natural resources, it was relatively easy for the United States to become, in Franklin D. Roosevelt's words, the "arsenal of democracy." Auto plants became armored vehicle plants; aviation plants turned from civilian to military uses; ordnance plants drew on new sources of workers—women. The machine was roaring. In the words of historian David Kennedy, the United States had chosen to fight a war of machines. But some of those machines had frightening agendas of their own, as the makers of the atomic bombs began to suspect. Machines, once invented, could not be prevented from being used. They had become real, the goal of all Zombies, and possessed the power to end the world.

Robber Barons

In commerce, the "Gilded Age" was a time of striking transitions and highly visible contradictions. A largely rural nation was becoming increasingly urbanized and a few accumulated great wealth and displayed it conspicuously while many labored in soot-covered cities and ill-lit factories. Metropolises like New York City and Chicago warehoused millions of immigrants from foreign lands (over thirteen million entered the country during the Gilded Age) and nearby rural areas seeking jobs and hosted giant corporations whose headquarters filled new "skysrcaper" office buildings. Unrest and violence in the city pit newcomer against native-born, rich against poor, and labor against capital in a witches' brew of poverty, illness, crime, and corruption, but a few men obtained almost unimaginable wealth.

Their secret was not only to think big, but to embrace bigness. In 1860, the largest business enterprises employed thousands, were capitalized at one million dollars, and served a national market. In the Gilded Age, behemoths like Standard Oil employed tens of thousands, were capitalized in the tens of millions, and reached global markets. The new middle-management corporation, with layers of "general managers" between different divisions of the corporation, and squadrons of middle managers reporting to the general managers, abetted by investment bankers and aided by corporate lawyers, came to dominate the country's economic development. The value of manufactured exports rose from $205 million in 1895 to $485 million in 1900, increasing its share of total exports from 25.8 percent to 35.3 percent. By the end of the Gilded Age in the mid-1890s, American heavy industry stood alongside food production and staple crop enterprises as the leading sectors in the national economy, exceeding them in terms of capital investment and market value.

The Gilded Age "robber baron" was supposedly an unscrupulous, self-dealing, corrupt capitalist. Of course the term was hardly factual. The federal Constitution banned titles of aristocracy, and the individuals were robbers only in a fictive sense. First associated with the railroad moguls of the 1870s, notably Jay Gould, of the Erie and later the Union Pacific Railroad, then with industrialists like John D. Rockefeller of Standard Oil of New

Jersey, the term was part accusation, part accolade, and all Zombie. These men were complex individuals, certainly capable of robbing one another, but rarely of robbing anyone else, and never barons.

Historians nevertheless found the robber barons easy targets. Matthew Josephson, in *The Robber Barons* (1934), blasted the "cut-throat competition, secret rebates, blackmail" that he believed were the weapons of the robber barons. The barons thought nothing of imposing their "wild fraud" on Americans—anything to make money. But that image has changed. By the end of the next century, many historians decided that the robber barons were "entrepreneurs" and "business revolutionaries" introducing efficiencies in management and scale impossible to achieve under earlier constraints. They understood that they could "walk away with millions" even if their businesses failed, and it was that realization, with its attendant impact on the economy as a whole, the lives of their workers, and the fortunes of their investors, that made them so odious to their countrymen. They were men in octopus suits according to historian Richard White.

Back to reality: Jay Gould was something of a Horatio Alger character come to life. From humble beginnings he grasped at opportunities to improve himself and his fortunes. He served the Union and himself in the Civil War by buying and selling stocks, and when the war ended he allied himself with the Democratic political machine in New York and amassed (and spent) a fortune in railroad stocks. He took risks, winning sometimes, but losing as often, with the Erie Railroad, the Union Pacific Railroad, the Western Union Telegraph Company, and the *New York World* newspaper. At one time one of the richest and most powerful men in America, he was also one of the most maligned. Maury Klein, who has written Gould's biography, brings to life the sickly child, a veritable scarecrow raised in the shadow of tuberculosis, who young learned perseverance, a love of learning, an attachment to family, and a secretive manner, and carried these through a life of risk in a world of uncertain fortunes. Hardly a robber baron, he was instead the consummate trickster, loving the game of business as much as its profits, and literally working himself to death.

A few of these enterprisers stood out—attacked at the turn of the century, but a few years later they were extolled as modern and efficient. Their rehabilitation in the history books began with the biography of John D. Rockefeller by journalist and Columbia University historian Allan Nevins. According to Nevins's *John D. Rockefeller: The Heroic Age of American Enterprise* (1940), written at a dark time in Western history, when Americans needed heroes, captains of industry like Rockefeller could fill that bill.

Rockefeller was a keen manager and organizer, a master talent spotter and delegator of responsibility. Rockefeller brought order out of chaos, just as Americans had to bring order out of the chaos of world war. Although critics called the work a house production, meaning that Nevins worked for the Rockefeller family, in fact it was only the access the family gave Nevins to Rockefeller's papers that allowed Nevins to write the volumes. Most biographers fall in love with their subjects anyhow.

Written in the last hours before the United States entered World War II, the work had an impact on politics. Nevins was never an isolationist, according to Gerald L. Fetner: "One of the goals that Nevins hoped to achieve in the books and articles he wrote on foreign policy in the 1930s was to persuade Americans that the United States could no longer avoid its responsibilities as a world power." Historians have come to believe that enterprises like Standard Oil had "signaled a new era in American life, that had both inspired and alarmed the populace." John D. Rockefeller's stewardship of the corporation both "chartered the way" to the multinationals and "exposed the abuses" to which he and they were and are still prone. Biographer Ron Chernow concludes that Rockefeller's legacy was marked by both "brilliance and rapacity." The businessmen their critics called robber barons were nothing of the kind.

The robber baron Zombie is a scapegoat for our sins of greed and indifference to the needs of our neighbors. We send the robber baron, like the Old Testament scapegoat, out into the wilderness carrying our sins, unwilling ourselves to recognize or admit to them. Blaming, one of our favorite cultural devices, here clothes and feeds a history Zombie.

If, in the last analysis, the so-called Robber Baron, not a Zombie of the same name, was not quite as influential as some journalists and political reformers believed, these men were successful because they earned it. Some were capable of genuine acts of charity and social justice. While unscrupulous and manipulative, they built substantial businesses, created a great deal of wealth, employed many workers, and innovated many of the corporate and financial devices present in our economy today. It was their very creativeness that caused them to run afoul of traditional notions of how to run corporations. Their practices are not only commonplace today, but accepted. Still, the robber baron Zombie waddles across the historians' pages, in part, we suspect, because he is so easy to spot. He appears something like the character in the Monopoly game, Rich Uncle Pennybags, who was drawn to look like J. P. Morgan.

CHAPTER SIX

Turn of the Century Zombies

The end of the nineteenth and the beginning of the twentieth century has a name far more evocative than "turn of the century"—fin de siècle. Contemporary observers thought it a time of technical advances and immoral decadence. It was the age of absinthe, a period driven to excess by a mixture of exultant imperialism (all those good things, so cheaply had, from the far corners of empire) and machine-like progress, combined with a widening gap between an opulent few and masses living in poverty. It was a time when fascination with the macabre—freaks, monsters, and death—pervaded both high-brow and low-brow culture. It was a time when hitherto hidden sexual excess and desire was revealed in the shape-shifting creatures of Art Nouveau illustrators like Aubrey Beardsley and the swirling postimpressionism of Henri de Toulouse-Lautrec.

For intellectuals, the lurid depictions of opium dens in the turn of the century cities like New York and San Francisco, and the ghetto photography of Jacob Riis and others, hinted at the coming collapse of Western civilization. As Henry Adams, president of the American Historical Association, wrote to its board, explaining his absence from the annual meeting in 1894, "No one who has watched the course of history during the last generation can have felt doubt of its [decadent] tendency. . . . Year after year passed and little progress has been made." Critics derided German fabulist Oswald Spengler's *Decline of the West*, first published in the last year of the Great War, as too pessimistic. In a second edition, Spengler retorted that he had seen the future, and it was grim. It took over a thousand pages to reach that conclusion, by which time only the strong were still reading. It was a time that seemed especially ripe for Zombies.

Spengler could have found evidence for his dour predictions in the disparities in wealth and power so evident in the Gilded Age. These had become an established part of American history. Photography, a somewhat exotic hobby in the Gilded Age, gained new power at the turn of the century to reveal these disparities. It was joined by the first motion pictures. Thomas Alva Edison's company specialized in movies of disaster scenes like the Baltimore Fire of 1904, the Galveston, Texas hurricane of 1900 that nearly swallowed the city in water, and the San Francisco Earthquake and fire of 1906.

Edison's movies, along with other visual reproductions of real life (or posed versions of reality), appeared in a grainy black and white. The absence of color gave a chiaroscuro appearance to the films, an ominous starkness that, when viewed today, still strikes the eye. One can almost spot the Zombies hidden in dimly lit shapes. The films thus reinforced the fin de siècle mood of harshness and danger. The Zombies of the turn of the century were thus especially frightening, harbingers of the decline and fall of a culture riddled with corruption.

Filthy, Dangerous Immigrants

In 2018, the president of the United States, aided and abetted by Fox News Network, announced that an invasion of the United States by dangerous and criminal elements was imminent. The reality behind this election-eve panic was a northward march of Central American men, women and children who were fleeing the violence of their homelands and hoping for legal asylum in the United States. As they approached the Mexican-US border, the tone of warnings from the White House grew more hysterical. It was as though a Martian invasion, à la the 1938 broadcast of "The War of the Worlds," was repeating itself. Like that Orson Welles radio dramatization, few saw anything like an invasion (few actually heard the broadcast). The latter was fake, and so was the former. Still, the panicky racist rhetoric had a lot more precedent that a radio broadcast.

From the closing decades of the nineteenth century through the first two decades of the twentieth century, the rhetoric of "restriction" and "nativism" sounded in the newspapers and the halls of Congress. According to Texas district attorney Martin Dies Sr. (later a member of Congress) in 1898, an invasion was coming of people who did not look or sound "like us" and would soon overflow the land. "The dangerous tendencies" of the newcomers were all too apparent to those who yearned for a pure Anglo-Saxon America, endangered by the arrival of "the beaten races of the earth."

In fact, millions of men and women entered the United States between 1877 and 1924. They came from far, like China, and near, like Mexico, but primarily from the south and east of Europe. They were Jews from the Pale, Italians, Slavs, and Poles. A few, largely from Northern Europe, were well to do, but most came for jobs and a better life. Still, those immigrants who preceded them, British, Welsh, German, Scottish, even the Scandinavians, often regarded the newest of the newcomers as dirty, disease ridden, and dangerous. The fear of the newcomers was a Zombie, made so by something akin to the racialist prejudice that fueled Jim Crow.

Most of the new immigrants did not have enough capital to buy land, and only those with farming experience sought to avail themselves of the 1862 Homestead Act's provisions for settling the land, improving it, and then gaining title. Most found homes and jobs in the cities of the Northeast and along the Ohio River. By 1890, according to the census of that year, over 60 percent of the foreign born lived in the cities. There, they worked in sweatshops sewing garments, rolling cigars, and loading and unloading cargos from the docks of New York, Boston, Philadelphia, and Baltimore. A few moved inland to the iron mills and factories along the Allegheny and Monongahela Rivers that bordered Pittsburgh. Some found jobs in the coal mines of West Virginia and Kentucky or in the oil fields of Pennsylvania and Ohio among the Irish and Welsh already there. A few went west to work in the copper and silver mines. Their backs were the backbone of the new industrial capitalism and their labor its fuel.

In the city, they lived in tightly knit communities of immigrants from the old country, focused around churches and synagogues whose worship services were carried on in the immigrants' native languages. The newcomers did not speak English. Not all were literate. Most of them were apolitical (they could not vote or hold office until they became citizens), but a few held radical political opinions and expressed them publicly. Others were drawn to the organized labor movement or to craft unions, as the leaders of these organizations spoke for these laborers.

The Zombie was not harmless. To those already here, the newcomers were "a hopeless burden" on the nation's economy. They were criminals or radicals whose views posed threats to order and decency. Italian immigrants were accused of being anarchists or criminals. Jewish immigrants were seen as clannish and greedy. Fear of the caricature Ching Chong Chop Chop—the Chinese immigrants who built the transcontinental railroads and settled in cities like San Francisco and Los Angeles—led to the Chinese Exclusion Act of 1882. Quotas for immigrants based on unreasonable census figures in 1920 and 1924 limited immigration from Southern and Eastern Europe. Jews and others fleeing Nazi persecution in the 1930s were turned away for similar reasons. A "gentleman's agreement" between US and Japanese leaders in 1904 ended Japanese migration to America. In defense of the relocation of thousands of hard-working and patriotic Japanese Americans during World War II, one US Supreme Court justice commented that a "non-Jap could not tell one Jap from another."

Historians accepted some of these Zombie notions and discarded others. The foremost historian of immigration in the twentieth century was Harvard's Oscar Handlin. The scion of New York immigrants himself, Handlin wrote learnedly of the immigrant experience. For him, "immigrants *were* American history." His Pulitzer Prize–winning *The Uprooted* followed the emigration experience, as it "took these people out of traditional, accustomed environments and replanted them in strange ground, among strangers, where strange manners prevailed." Handlin somewhat romanticized the struggles of the newcomers, for many of them were not from peasant backgrounds, as he suggested, but from Euroepan cities, and were not poor, but middling or middle class, and were not unaccustomed to novelty, but had been exposed to the diversity of urban culture in Budapest, Warsaw, Vienna, Berlin, Rome, and Milan, and . . . well, you get the picture. Nor, looking at their experience in America, did immigration always "strip away the veneer" of old ways, for well into the new generation the immigrants retained Yiddish, or Italian, or Polish, and published newspapers in the old tongue, carried on food ways, dress ways, and worship ways in the old manner, and passed these on to the next generation. Culture has a stickiness to it that even the transplantation of peoples cannot remove. Finally, it was not always true that "the old folk knew then they would not come to belong, not through their own experience nor through their offspring." Nor were they always "separate," nor did they suffer "from the consciousness that they were strangers." The prose is beautiful, unmarred on the page by raised footnote or endnote markers (like Boorstin's *The Americans* trilogy, Handlin did not have any notes, only a brief bibliographical essay). But Handlin's immigrant is a Zombie—more sympathetic than the Zombies of the immigration restrictionists and the America Firsters, but still a Zombie.

After World War II, bit by bit, the gates of restriction were opened a crack, and Chinese, Korean, and Japanese immigrants joined those from southern Asia and Vietnam. Immigrants from Latin America came as well.

New laws seemed to welcome the newcomers. Then, in the presidential election of 2016, the Zombie immigrant returned. A presidential candidate vowed to drive Latin American newcomers from the land because they were all animals, rapists, and worse. Fears of the decline of a white nation and white privilege fueled the electoral support for Donald Trump, and echoed the same fears expressed by politicians who favored immigration restriction at the turn of the century. One can hear in Trump's tweets the distant voice of Theodore Roosevelt's 1894 "True Americanism" essay in the *Forum* magazine: "It is not only necessary to Americanize the immigrants of foreign birth who settle among us, but it is even more necessary for those among us who are by birth and descent already Americans not to throw away our birthright. . . . The third sense in which the word Americanism may be employed is with reference to the Americanizing of the newcomers to our shores. We must Americanize them in every way, in speech, in political ideas and principles. . . . The mighty tide of immigration to our shores has brought in its train much of good and much of evil; and whether the good or the evil shall predominate depends mainly on whether these newcomers do or do not throw themselves heartily into our national life."

Hopefully, the Zombie Immigrant will join the other Zombies in quarantine, but so long as some Americans whose ancestors came here many years ago regard more recent newcomers as inherently inferior and dangerous, the Zombie Immigrant will walk the land. The program initiated in 2018 to separate undocumented immigrant children from their parents and the role of Immigration and Customs Enforcement in rounding up newcomers on the assumption that anyone who speaks Spanish must be illegal suggest that the Zombies' thralls are running the show.

Scabs

The "scab" is a term in labor history for a replacement worker recruited to break unions. As the term itself suggests, the scab is unwelcome. Used as an insult in early modern English, it implied that an individual was afflicted with some unwholesome skin disease—thus a base and unworthy comrade. By the eighteenth century, the term had gained usage as someone employers hired to threaten their own workers. By the next century, it was someone hired to cross a picket line or break a strike. The scab allegedly betrayed his fellow workers. He betrayed the union movement. He betrayed his class. The word conjures up all these connotations, but they are simplistic and misleading. The scab is a Zombie.

The scab Zombie first appears in American labor newspapers and oratory before the Civil War as a shadowy but fearsome creature. With the growth of the industrial sector of the economy, and industrial union-ism alongside it, the scab appeared even more threatening. It was as the strikebreaker that the scab entered the historical literature of turn of the century labor. Melvyn Dubofsky, a leading labor historian, found the scab at the 1892 strike against Andrew Carnegie's Homestead steel works on the Monongahela River. The Amalgamated Association of Iron and Steel Workers (a craft union, not an industrial union, whose membership was more diverse) had won earlier strikes, in part by preventing strikebreak-ers from entering the works. Locked out of the mill grounds in 1892, the union took physical control of the periphery of the mill. Pinkerton detec-tives were prevented from entering.

Then Henry Clay Frick (Carnegie was away, and though he seemed supportive of the union movement, he secretly wanted the Homestead union broken) asked for and got the governor to order out the militia to escort thousands of "black sheep" workers, the term the union men used for scabs, to enter and work the forges. Note the color of the scabs—for many were in fact African Americans kept out of the mills by the unions, and even those who were not black were tarred with the term. Note also that the scabs offered no violence to the union men. The union had, in ef-fect, a monopoly on the jobs that the scabs were trying to break. In another context, the union men would be the first to condemn railroads or other corporations from creating monopolies.

In miners' strikes, for example the Cripple Creek, Colorado, walkout of 1904, both union men and replacement workers died. The standard ac-count, for example Katherine Studevants', mentions the strikebreakers' deaths (an unknown bomber set off explosives in the pit where the men were working) in passing, but dwells on the systematic oppression of the union men. Nelson Lichtenstein is kinder: he accurately calls the new hires replacement workers.

The histories of labor that portray the scab rarely recognize that he was from a class that the union had excluded. He did not fit. He was the wrong color, or ethnicity, or did not come from the neighborhood. He was often an immigrant or black. He was the victim of union violence. He was just as deprived as the union men, perhaps even more so, and when the strike was settled, he was the first to go. Movies like John Sayles's much-praised *Matewan* (1987) showed the uneasy relationship between union men, com-pany men, and replacement workers (who in this case join the union), and graphically demonstrated the conditions of labor and violence in the coal mines of West Virginia in 1920. The use of private "detective" agencies (actually mercenaries), here the Baldwin-Felts Detective Agency, elevated the level of violence. In the end result, it was the insinuation that a "Red" had infiltrated the union that brings on a final orgy of killing—the aim of the Zombie all along.

Ignoring the individuality of blue-collar workers, lumping them into a debased category or denying their agency by calling them a derogatory name is how to make people into Zombies. Whether this is done by the bosses or by the unions, it demeans those who sought work and could not find it except as replacements. And it is very poor history.

Metal Zombies

Two metal Zombies clanked around the turn of the century landscape. One was made of gold, the other of silver. Bimetallism was a political and economic conflict over the change from a gold standard of federal money (paper money supposedly represented gold bullion in federal reserves) to a free coinage of silver, as well as backing the circulation of new paper money, or emission, on silver production. The shift would have expanded the currency and worked a controlled inflation. The silver emission would allow farmers hard hit by the depression of 1893 to pay their debts, and loosen the control of banks and other financial institutions on the commerce of the country.

The question of currency reform was genuine if complex, but the Zombies were not. Instead, Populists denounced the gold standard of currency as plutocratic excess and control by the bankers, while more conservative political leaders claimed that introduction of silver coins and certificates as legal tender was radical, unstable, and foreign—akin to the currency of Latin America and China. In short, the two complicated economic stances gave way to wild exaggerations of who and what the two metals represented. The election of 1896, bitterly fought over the bimetallic issue after the Populist and Democratic Parties' nominee William Jennings Bryan warned that the common people would be crucified on a cross of gold, ended in a smashing victory for Republican conservative William McKinley.

But the debate was not over, not when Zombies were abroad. Silver advocates would continue to insist that the currency must be expanded to provide a decent standard of living for the farmers and the city workers. Conservatives, at first buoyed by the recovery of 1896 and the apparent victory of the gold standard, were again driven to cover by the recession of 1903. Reformer Theodore Roosevelt, who became president when McKinley was assassinated, pushed for reforms that some Democrats long wanted, but not the minting of silver. The silverites would eventually win the end of the gold standard in 1933, during another Great Depression.

Historians are not, as a rule, particularly astute on economic questions. The exception are economists who do history and a handful of historians who are trained in econometrics. Zombies love to make complex subjects appear simple, and bimetallism is no exception. Rutgers economic historian Hugh Rackoff explained: it was all about the currency supply. "The crime of 1873" was the battle cry of the silverites. Congress demonetized silver in that year. (Actually, Congress simply left the silver coin off the list of legal tender.) You might as well have demonized the currency, wailed the Populists. Bring back silver, they demanded, so that the currency supply would expand, and farmers hit by the depression of 1873 could pay off their mortgages. But conservatives were worried that silver mining, taking off in the Southwest, would flood the nation with silver coins, cause inflation, and undermine the stability of prices (and the stability of the mortgage industry) under the existing gold standard.

Seventeen years passed, and the controversy over silver and gold became the centerpiece of national politics. In these same years, economics was becoming an academic profession, and contemporary economist Earnest Bogart explained that the issuance of silver coins under the Sherman Silver Purchase Act of 1890 had led to ruinous inflation, and subsequently the recession of 1893. Stability only returned after the repeal of the act in 1893—a curious argument given the timing of the recession and the repeal of the act. Bogart was one of the nation's first professors of economic history and became president of the American Economic Association. In short, he was no slouch in the opinion of his fellow economists. From his account, one would assume that the repeal was the cause of the crash, as purchases and credit based on the new currency were left hanging in the air when the government ceased buying silver and issuing notes based on it. "The uncertainty as to the ability of the government to redeem the greenbacks (issued during the Civil War and made legal tender) and treasury notes in gold prolonged the business unrest," he concluded. Faced with the problem of timing, the economist had a ready answer—it was the flow of gold out of the country because gold was no longer needed to back the currency, as if the government's gold reserves ever matched the supply of currency.

Another three decades passed and defenders of the western farmers had not forgotten the bimetallic Zombies. "We need to do something for silver" was the cry of the western silver mining states early in the Great Depression era, as if silver were a living being. The gold standard defenders again protested—more silver would drive gold out of the country, again, as if gold had a will of its own. Gold and silver, instead of mere soft metals, were acting like Zombies, with the power to rebuild or to ruin the economy. Little Zombies running around all through these explanations made the Scarecrow in *The Wonderful Wizard of Oz* look like a chaired professor by comparison.

The metallic Zombies are now part of our popular literary history, or so say some students of Populism. In 1900, L. Frank Baum published the first of a series of children's novels, *The Wonderful Wizard of Oz*. He did not class his work as political allegory, although, as we have seen, works by Upton Sinclair and Frank Norris would soon fill that niche. A play based on the book toured the country in 1902, and the book became a part of American fantasy on many levels. A movie adaptation in 1939 once again took the nation by storm. The Zombies had become familiar faces—a tin man, a scarecrow, and a cowardly lion. The only warning that danger was nearby was the Wicked Witch of the East, a favorite Zombie meme.

In *The Wonderful Wizard of Oz*, Little Dorothy, a Kansas school girl who stood in for the American people, is carried away to the land of Oz by a cyclone, actually a political storm over bimetallism. In the land of Oz, she encountered a good witch, who gave her magical silver slippers; munchkins, who represented the little people of the country; a tin man, who represented industrial workers; a scarecrow, who represented the farmers; and a cowardly lion, who represented William Jennings Bryan. They travel along the yellow brick road, the path of gold, to the emerald city (Washington, DC) and what is supposed to be the home of the all-powerful Wizard of Oz. He turns out to be a humbug, possibly McKinley's henchman, Ohio senator Mark Hanna.

Lurking evilly in the shadows is the Wicked Witch of the East, who can turn silver into dust—no doubt the Northeast banks. She is killed in the book when Dorothy's farmhouse falls on her. "Who was she?" asked Dorothy. "She was the Wicked Witch of the East, as I said," answered a little woman. "She has held all the Munchkins in bondage for many years, making them slave for her night and day. Now they are all set free, and are grateful to you for the favor." The farmhouse, perhaps symbolic of foreclosure, was itself a symbol of the nation's longing for an earlier, more bucolic time, when yeomen worked the land and from their sweat gained title to it, and family farmers built and lived in their own homes. The book's political allegory did not reduce its popularity, and it sold over a quarter of million copies. Sequels did almost as well. The gold and silver Zombies, transformed into tin, straw, and lion skin figures, were taken to America's heart—a dangerous thing to do with Zombies.

The metallic Zombies still stalk the labyrinthine corridors of the Treasury Building in Washington, DC, and reappear whenever monetarists and welfare staters do battle over fiscal policy. The federal reserve note is the basis of US currency, and much more money is in circulation electronically than all the bills and all the gold and silver in the world. But the Zombies of fiscal chaos can still swallow sensible government policy when entire governments threaten to devalue their currencies, or worse, default entirely on loans.

Marxist Zombies

This subchapter should begin "actung minen," warning, beware, this is a minefield. Thousands of intellectuals all over the world study and apply Marxist theory. Perhaps even more intellectuals derogate it. An analogy may help to explain the sharp disagreement. For millions, the Bible is the revealed Word of God, holy scripture that exists outside of time and space, or perhaps more accurately in all time and everywhere. For some of the students of Karl Marx's thinking, Marxism explains historical phenomena generally, again outside of particular times and places. It is universally true. For other students of the Bible, it is a document written by men of a certain time and place, and should be understood in its historical context. Similarly, for many students of Marxism, it is inseparable from Marx's own world and his view of it. However one regards Marxism, it is a tribute to the intellectual power of an individual when his or her name is attached to a theory of history. Few can claim this distinction. Alas, some who want the cache of Marxism have turned his views inside out. The Marx who walks through their work is a Zombie. No American historian has matched their fame in their own time or ours. But the Marxist theory of history is so commonly cited as to be part of every student's and scholar's lexicon.

In his own time, Karl Marx was not particularly famous. Born in Germany in 1818 to a wealthy family, trained there in law and philosophy, he moved to London and a career as an author, journalist, and social observer until his death in 1883. His chief contributions to Western thought, a short *Communist Manifesto*, in 1848, and the three-volume *Das Kapital*, finished after Marx's death by his long-time collaborator Friedrich Engels, rested upon a materialistic theory of human interaction. Influential in the thinking of later radicals, particularly Vladimir Lenin and Mao Zedong, the Marxist critique of capitalism, and his prediction that capitalism was doomed, became almost synonymous with communism.

Any attempt to reduce the complexity of Marx's own thinking to a sub-chapter is a fool's errand, but obviously that will not stop this author. The idea that all history moves through well-defined, predefined stages was not unique to Marx. Nor was his emphasis on hidden, subterranean forces moving people and events in predetermined ways. Nor was his particular insistence that the driving force behind all history was the struggle for control of the means of production. Cultural and intellectual institutions were best understood as expressions of that struggle. In the preface to *A Contribution to the Critique of Political Economy*, Marx wrote: "The totality of these relations of production constitutes the economic structure of society, the real foundation, on which arises a legal and political superstructure and to which correspond definite forms of consciousness. The mode of produc-tion of material life conditions the general process of social, political and intellectual life. It is not the consciousness of men that determines their existence, but their social existence that determines their consciousness." Ideologies of individualism, democracy, and Christianity were illusory ref-uges from material forces. The state weighed in on the side of the ruling classes. When the state and the ruling class can no longer impose their will on the masses, revolution must occur, and the result of the revolution will be the rise of a classless state and society.

In his own time, the second half of the nineteenth century, the strug-gle appeared between the industrial proletariat, the laboring classes, and the bourgeoisie, which controlled capital. This made sense as a descrip-tion of industrial centers like England and Germany, with which Marx was familiar. Thus, in its setting, Marxist historical thinking had a genuine explanatory power. As Marx's later defender, philosopher Gerald Cohen, wrote in 1978, "production relations profoundly affect productive forces," that is, workers and bosses. In this sense, Marx was part of a much larger group of political economists who saw that the Industrial Revolution was profoundly reshaping society. Working people's sense of themselves, that is, working class self-consciousness, was one striking result of this trans-formation of production relations. As E. P. Thompson, a modern Marxist, explained, "There was a consciousness of the identity of the interests of the working class, or productive classes, as against those of other classes." This rising self-consciousness rested on the struggle between labor and capital; it did not stand apart from the larger materialist process of history.

As Marx wrote in the opening passage of *The Communist Manifesto*, "The history of all hitherto existing society is the history of class struggles. Freeman and slave, patrician and plebeian, lord and serf, guild-master and journeyman, in a word, oppressor and oppressed, stood in constant opposition to one another, carried on an uninterrupted, now hidden, now open fight, a fight that each time ended, either in a revolutionary reconstitution of society at large, or in the common ruin of the contending classes." That the struggle Marx saw about him, in London, could be projected back into a preindustrial time, was far more speculative, for then capital was not the source of economic power; it was land. To equate feudalism with class struggle ignores the essential military nature of land ownership in medieval societies. Still, one can try to analogize serfdom and peasantry to a proletariat. Slavery does not quite fit, in part because it was not a major source of labor in medieval Europe, but one cannot fault Marxists for trying to fit it into their schema.

Marxist historical theory seemed to apply to the open warfare between radical labor unionism and capital in America at the turn of the century. The leading radicals of the era included Marxists like Daniel DeLeon. In 1900, his Socialist Labor Party platform was clearly Marxist. Its presidential platform averred: "The obvious fact that our despotic system of economics is the direct opposite of our democratic system of politics, can plainly be traced the existence of a privileged class, the corruption of government by this class, the alienation of public property, public franchises and public functions to this class and the abject dependence of the mightiest of nations upon that class. Again, through the perversion of democracy to the ends of plutocracy, labor is robbed of the wealth which it alone produces, is denied the means of self-employment, and by compulsory idleness in wage slavery, is even deprived of the necessities of life." Like Marx, DeLeon was a trained lawyer, and like Marx, he saw the coming end of capitalism in almost lawful terms: "The time is fast coming, when, in the natural course of social evolution, this system, through the destructive action of its failures and crises . . . shall have worked out its own downfall."

DeLeon's party did not win the election, but with the coming of the First World War, it appeared that his prediction would soon come to pass. As it happened, capitalism not only survived the war, the war brought a federal legal campaign against the radicals reminiscent of Lincoln's assault on the Copperheads in the Civil War. If many of the leading Marxists were jailed or expatriated, Marxism did not die. In 1919, the Communist Party of the United States split from other radical groups. Like just about every other American club, association, and party, the CPUSA framed a constitution: "The name of this organization shall be THE COMMUNIST PARTY of America. Its purpose shall be the education and organization of the working class for the establishment of the Dictatorship of the Proletariat, the abolition of the capitalist system, and the establishment of the Communist Society." The high-water mark of Marxism in America was the era between 1929 and 1939. The crash of the New York Stock Exchange in October 1929, and the halting efforts of banks, corporations, manufacturers, and finally government to deal with soaring unemployment and poverty, convinced many young Americans that communism was a viable course. Even at its height, in the 1930s, the CPUSA never numbered more than 55,000 men and women (although its leadership insisted that it had ten times that many members). It never had a major influence on American politics though it did gain adherents in organized labor (unions) and gained what was probably disproportionate attention from the FBI.

Whatever its actual influence on American history, whatever its close accord with labor versus capital in the real marketplace, Marxism detached from the historical Marx and from the central tenets of Marxist theory is a Zombie. Applied to history, the Marxism Zombie is overly general, hard to apply, often ill fitting, maddeningly vague, and smugly prescriptive, but it nevertheless refuses to die. The Zombie thrives when Marxism is stretched to cover postindustrial societies like our own. Nevertheless, it keeps on appearing among us, wearing a variety of disguises. Its adherents insist that everything about capitalism is bad, and thus anything one can call capitalism must be morally wrong. It is a rallying cry for groups that need a convenient radical ideology, even if their logic is wholly different from Marx's and DeLeon's.

The Marxism Zombie did what all Zombies do—sow confusion and start fights. For example, in the 1960s and after, even a sympathetic observer could see that "New Left historians" were divided over adherence to strict Marxist historical principles. Some labored to resuscitate the Marxist historical formula, at least in piecemeal form. Rather than engage in megahistorical forays, they deployed Marxist insights into microhistorical settings of "exploitation, domination, and oppression." They were the founders of MARHO (the Marxist historical society affiliated with the American Historical Association) and edited the *Radical History Review*. Jonathan

Wiener, writing in 1989, recounted the "fierce battles" between Marxist historians and rivals in the radical camp. In the midst of these battles, the "neo-Marxist revival," in the words of historian T. J. Jackson Lears, focused on the "the relation of culture to power relationships." The problem for the Marxists was still the "naïve empiricism" of the non-Marxists. Instead, the Marxists argued, historians should always see class struggle behind historical events, in which individuals were subject to larger forces. People in historical time just did not get it—their consciousness is just not raised enough to see how history makes them puppets.

E. P. Thompson, writing ten years later, had an answer. Stop thinking about strict Marxism and start thinking about "historical materialism," how "ideas and values are situated in a material context." On the one hand, that aphorism is obviously true: ideas and values in history are always situated in people's material existence. We are, to borrow from Madonna, material girls and boys. But Thompson meant something a little more slippery: "Marxism has given us a universal vocabulary." One could pick and choose from Marxist historical and philosophical writings what one needed to explain anything. The caution: avoid reductionism if one can, though it is not always possible, and there are times when we need to generalize.

Worse still are the scraps that advocates for radical reform in other academic disciplines leave for the Zombie when they show a lack of fidelity to Marx's basic formulations. They cite Marx in the way that preachers cite Bible passages, but get him wrong. Although in Marx's original formulation, the individual case meant little compared to class analysis, the modern Marxist Zombie is all about identity politics, virtue signaling, and other forms of the first person pronoun in what advocates have called "standpoint theory." Standpoint theory is an exercise in subjectivity, in which all knowledge is socially located, and the supposedly oppressed person is best suited to determine the nature and extent of her or his oppression. Applied to the study of history, it empowers the user to pick and choose bits and pieces, out of context (for what is context but one person's standpoint), and reassemble them to prove that capitalism in all its forms, and in all times and places, is evil. Marx wanted the working people of the world to unite. Today, the Marxism Zombie pits workers against one another on the basis of gender, sexual orientation, race, and ethnicity. Marx thought that all forms of oppression ultimately reduce to the oppression of the producing classes. The Marxism Zombie finds that economic oppression cannot be examined (much less be regarded) as the foundation of all other forms of oppression. Instead, all forms of oppression—economic, sexual, racial, and gender orientation—are fundamentally inseparable and cannot be examined apart from one another. Like those who see the Bible as teaching truth for all, all the time, and see those who denigrate the Bible as tools of the Devil, so those who embrace the Zombie Marxism believe that history is on their side and those who disagree with them must be, overtly or covertly, agents of oppression.

Turn of the century Zombies were combative. They sensed that Americans were angry and afraid of changes in life and work that individuals could not control. That attracted Zombies, who feed on human anxiety and frustration. Social contacts, once dominated by rural, face-to-face meetings, had become anonymous and alienating. The dark and polluted city of the 1900s and 1910s, whose streets seemed overrun by strange-sounding newcomers, was for many Americans a disquieting omen. The spread of radical ideologies did not quiet these fears—quite the contrary. The coming of war and the Spanish influenza epidemic that followed suggested that the end of days was near. No wonder Zombies found the turn of the century so appealing.

CHAPTER SEVEN

Modern Zombies

Post–World War I culture called itself modern. The idea of modernism turned a catastrophic world event, and withal, themes of rupture, irony, and discordance, into their opposites, an almost arrogant self-confidence in progress and improvement. Science and technology would rule. It was the age of new inventions like radio and motion pictures. But modernism could not escape the war's horrors. A "lost generation" of writers and architects gave us poetry and drama without conventional chronologies, and Bauhaus, the hyperfunctionalist blockhouse style of official buildings that looked like prison blocks. In the shadow of the war, fiction featured hard-boiled detectives like Los Angeles's Philip Marlowe, New York City's Philo Vance, and San Francisco's Sam Spade, and fighting faceless villains in dark streets of dangerous cities.

In fact, expressive modernism found a home in the early twentieth-century city. The city welcomed museum and gallery exhibits, filled with works of art formerly owned by European aristocrats. These included examples of cubism, futurism, and expressionism, whose common theme was the inadequacy of traditional ways of depicting the world. The wealth from an American upper class almost unscathed by the ravishing of Europe fueled a building spree in art deco office buildings like the Chrysler, American Radiator, and Empire State in New York City, the French Renaissance towers of the Wrigley Building in Chicago and its neighbor, the neo-gothic Tribune Building, all monuments to America's newfound world leadership and evidence of the technological advances in structural steel. When in 1932 architects wanted to introduce a wider public to the "international style," with its modernist facades and minimalist decoration, the natural choice was the new Museum of Modern Art, then housed in the 1921 Heckscher Building in New York City.

Along with capital investment, people flowed into the American metropole. For example, the consolidation of the five boroughs of New York City brought its population in 1900 to almost 3.5 million people. A decade later, that number had risen to 4.7 million. War did not depopulate Gotham. Instead, it brought internal migrants and refugees from war-torn Europe to the city, raising its population to 5.6 million in 1920. The population was diverse, with African Americans, Latin Americans, Asian Americans, Europeans from the North and South and East of the continent all piled into the city's housing. The shift from a wooden two-story construction to a multistory brick tenement apartment house block was necessary to contain the newcomers, and the overflow spilled out into South Brooklyn, eastern Queens, the northern portion of Manhattan Island, and the Bronx. Gotham's experience in various forms was repeated in Philadelphia, Chicago, Detroit, and as far west as San Francisco and Los Angeles. Overflowing, never sleeping, the city was the pulsating heart of modernity.

Zombies love urban haunts, as they offer a kind of anonymity that the Zombie can exploit. Turn of the century French cultural anthropologist Émile Durkheim called it "anomie"—wherein the person is detached from the norms and morality of the group. Zombies thrive on it, for they have no attachment to human morality. Zombies found their way into modern era histories, drawn there by real and imagined fears of criminals, the masses, and radicals.

The Ghetto

Can a Zombie be a place? Yes—if the place becomes something more than a physical space. If it has a face and reaches out to terrify us. One of these places was the ghetto Zombie. There was a real ghetto, of course—Zombies love disguises. The real ghetto was a Venetian island, where a foundry became, in 1517, the designated home district for Jews. It was a neighborhood of sorts, though hardly the same as the mansion district of San Marco. W. E. B. DuBois, traveling in Europe, saw the old Jewish quarters and was told that these were the remnants of the restrictions on Jewish habitation. In 1917, he applied the term to the black neighborhoods of the northeastern cities. The word was widely adopted by journalists and social scientists to describe how black migrants from the South were crowded in northern cities by real estate redlining and other segregationist devices. In short, it became a self-defining epithet. From a real place with real people living in it, the Zombie ghetto emerged. Ironically, its midwives were reformers who argued that the ghetto was merely a form of social control of minorities. According to Mitchell Duneier's *Ghetto: The Invention of a Place, The History of an Idea* (2016), the ghetto became synonymous with one ethnic group and the accompanying images. In television series like *Homicide: Life on the Streets*, the image of East Baltimore was so compelling that one could not see anything but crime, drugs, and ineffective policing in the ghetto.

The real ghetto is a neighborhood full of life. The Zombie ghetto is a dark and dangerous place in the imagination of historians and writers who do not live there. It is a "slum." Although the term originated in England, it was already captured in the photography of New York City reformer Jacob Riis. As Bonnie Yochelson and Danial Czitrom document in *Rediscovering Jacob Riis*, he actually posed many of his most striking images of urban housing decay and childhood poverty in front of studio backdrops. The effect was electrifying, identifying the urban core with rot. The men, women, and children who posed for him actually looked like Zombies. Whether the actual city resembled his widely circulated images, the movement to wipe out the slums had begun. As Riis wrote in 1902, the slum was the place where "in the back streets multitudes huddled in ignorance and want." The slum was the enemy, and slum dwellers, according to Frederick Lewis Allen's history of the 1920s, were especially susceptible to dangerous radical ideologies.

The ghetto Zombie strutted through the history of "urban renewal." From the early 1940s, urban planners, government policy makers, and real estate interests combined to tackle "blighted and slum neighborhoods." According to historians of the programs that became urban renewal, the emphasis was on clearance, as though the real enemy was structural dilapidation rather than economic need. This meant tearing down older low-rise housing, displacing families, destroying neighborhoods, and building high-rise apartment buildings. These, like Pruitt-Igoe in St. Louis, were high-rise failures. Where one "bulldozes" an area, the established older residents have to leave, and then with no neighborhood regulars to promote interactions among families and generations (vertical human dwellings cannot turn stairwells into streets), the renewed area truly was a hotbed of crime. As Alexander von Hoffman explained in a seminal history of the program, renewal became synonymous with "demolition" and "it failed." The ghetto Zombie, however, refused to die. It still lived on in the patronizing pages of histories like *The American Promise* and *A People and a Nation*, where the less fortunate of the early twentieth-century cities were "huddled together in dense ghettos" and "in impoverished and often hopeless inner-city neighborhoods" where they faced unrelenting "violent crime."

Muggers and Fear

The mugger is a violent criminal, technically (in law) a robber (as opposed to a thief, who takes by stealth). Robbery in the city is surely as old as cities. With the arrival of modern police forces in the mid- to late nineteenth century replacing untrained watchmen, rates of robbery dropped off sharply. According to crime historians Roger Lane, Eric Monkkonen, and others, property crime rates declined, albeit erratically, over the long course of the modern era. When robbery did occur, it was usually within a neighborhood and the victims had the same demographic characteristics as the perpetrators. When times were hard and jobs harder to obtain, robbery rates increased.

So, if muggers are real, where's the Zombie? How did it enter our histories? The mugger Zombie is a shadowy figure, hiding in the shadows. He's the fear we all have of places where we cannot see, and our fear makes him even more real. (I know this sounds like one of the Sphinx's aphorisms from the movie *Mystery Men*, with a nod to the great character actor Wes Studi, but it's true.) The city's sight lines are blocked by buildings, and it's hard enough to see around them, much less what's going on in them. Thus the commercial structure is the center of fears of financial fraud. The apartment house is the site of suspected rape and murder. Playgrounds become homes of gangs. The alleyways are filled with muggers.

The mugger Zombie is a refraction of white racism. Internal migration from farm to city had been a feature of American life from the beginning of the nineteenth century. For example, farm girls from rural New England were the first textile factory workers in America. From the 1840s through the 1920s, immigrants from Europe took low-paying jobs in factories throughout the Northeast. There was prejudice against the newcomers, but it was not based on racial profiling—until large numbers of blacks moved into Chicago, Detroit, New York City, Kansas City, Newark, New Jersey, and other metropolitan areas in the first years of the twentieth century. They posed an economic threat to blue-collar white workers, arousing fears similar to those of white antiabolitionist mobs in the North prior to the Civil War. Economic rivalry abetted by racist stereotyping turned the actual African American laborer into the mugger Zombie.

The mugger Zombie is one spawn of the fear Zombie. The United States has also been far more violent, for example in its embrace of handguns and its periodic foreign wars, than other modern nations. Fear is, in a phrase, as American as apple pie. Such fear is natural when danger presents itself to us. Fear is psychological and physiological, hard wired into human beings. Our pulse rate and respiration accelerate, our blood vessels constrict, and our neurological functions go into overdrive. How can such a normal response be a Zombie?

Primal fear becomes the fear Zombie when it changes our larger perception of the world. When we see danger all around us that is not there, the fear Zombie multiplies. It thrives in times of stress, when the effective response is to look to the past to find solutions to present problems. That is why newly elected president Franklin D. Roosevelt told the audience of his Inaugural Address, on March 3, 1933, that "first of all, let me assert my firm belief that the only thing we have to fear is fear itself—nameless, unreasoning, unjustified terror which paralyzes needed efforts to convert retreat into advance." Roosevelt had distinguished the fear Zombie from the legitimate emotion, and warned of mistaking the one for the other.

Roosevelt offered an explanation of the difference between genuine fear and illusion, for information and understanding is the first and final answer to the fear Zombie: "Our distress comes from no failure of substance. We are stricken by no plague of locusts. Compared with the perils which our forefathers conquered because they believed and were not afraid, we have still much to be thankful for. Nature still offers her bounty and human efforts have multiplied it. Plenty is at our doorstep, but a generous use of it languishes in the very sight of the supply. Primarily this is because the rulers of the exchange of mankind's goods have failed, through their own stubbornness and their own incompetence, have admitted their failure, and abdicated." What perhaps was new in his program was a commitment of the federal government to take a direct and sustained part in this recovery. The result was the New Deal "safety net" of Social Security, Federal Deposit Insurance, federal works programs to upgrade the quality of life like rural electrification, and protection of union members.

The context of that address was the third year of the Great Depression. Serious economic crises were nothing new in American history when Roosevelt spoke. From the very first years of the new nation, in the 1780s, then again for periods of years after 1819, 1837, 1857, 1873, 1893, and 1904, cycles of "busts" left many Americans unemployed and caused banks and businesses to collapse. The nation's economy had always recovered, and Roosevelt promised that his administration would do everything in its power to spur another recovery. History was on his side, but not if the fear Zombie ranged the land uncontested.

Roosevelt's invocation of earlier ages' confidence called on the nation's thinkers to place the current crisis in its proper context. Many did. But the fear Zombie was a resistant creature. It implanted itself like a parasite in the very means Roosevelt assayed to combat it—historical accounts. The Zombie lured some intellectuals into a fantasy world of lost past innocence. Frederick Lewis Allen, perhaps the most read and the most popular of the chroniclers of the 1930s, captured the edgy nostalgia in his *Since Yesterday: The 1930s in America* (1940): "During the latter nineteen-thirties there appeared a crop of autobiographies full of nostalgic memories of the Bohemian Greenwich Village of the early nineteen-hundreds, when young intellectuals were manning the silk strikers' picket lines, seeing Big Bill Haywood plain, cheering for the Armory Show of independent art, and experimenting with free verse and free love."

False history was a tempting but wrong-headed defense against fear. Fake history was worse. Withdrawal from a world once again spiraling into war was another of the victories of the fear Zombie. American historians Carl Becker and Charles Beard were among the foremost academic practitioners of their day, both presidents of the American Historical Association, and, in the 1930s, both advocates of isolationism. The fear Zombie had so clouded their minds that they could not distinguish the German threat to peace in 1914, and the war that followed, from the threat the Nazis posed in the 1930s. In "What Is a Liberal?" Becker wrote with a lofty and amused disdain of how liberals had fooled themselves into believing in progress and reason after the first world conflagration. "The Indian Summer of liberal content proved nevertheless to be a brief season." Liberal was no "magic word," and the "Punch and Judy" politicians who bandied it about were not to be believed. Americans were foolish to be led into a second round of world war.

Beard, writing and lecturing against the New Deal, was even more emphatic in his isolationist rhetoric than Becker. In the second volume of his revised survey of American history, titled *America in Midpassage* (1939), he mistook Zombies for realities and realities for Zombies. It was a time when nothing could be trusted as fact: "Into this ferment of facts and opinions, professional propagandists, known as public relations counsels, and more openly, radio announcers, flung their agitations. Seeing an opportunity to fish in troubled waters, many Communists thrust their activities into industrial unionism." "Inflammatory elements" had taken over the public discourse, and "heads were cracked and bodies broken" when strikers and thugs for "the worried upper classes clashed." Unfazed by the bloodletting, historians ignored current affairs, and continued to believe in universal truths waiting to be discovered. "They crowded their work with details, avoided colorful phrases, and aimed at a severity of style" akin to the sciences. (Beard, of course, exempted his own work from these limitations.) If any historians were to be singled out and praised for refusing to accept the orthodoxy, it was the southern historian, who rejected industrial capitalism in favor of an elegiac pastoralism. (Again, there is no mention of the racialist proclivities of this new, brave generation of southern rebels.)

Reds

Among those, according to Allen, who offered the most blind-eyed answer to the fear Zombie were the radicals. In the 1930s, "at the heart of the literary revolt against the America that had been stood the communist intellectuals. Numerically they were hardly important, but from them the revolt caught the fire of burning conviction." In fact, the zeal of the American Communist Party was self-destructive, for rather than incorporate communist ideas of equality and redistributive justice, the right turned communism into a Zombie. If "nothing short of revolution would serve," then nothing would serve, and Americans were not given to such absolutism.

Enter the Red. The "Red" is a Zombie, a soulless (because she or he abjures religion) enemy of the capitalist state. The "Red" is a communist, a socialist, or a syndicalist, or, if not actually a member of a subversive cadre espousing these views, a sympathizer, usually called a "pinko." To be sure, there were Communists, Socialists, Trotskyites, and all manner of other far left-wing radical groups in modern America. Some were "card carrying," openly admitting their membership. Others attended meetings, voted for candidates, or otherwise supported at least some part of the political mission of these groups. Twice, in 1919–20, and 1949–57, there were "Red Scares" in which real and suspected members of these organizations were harassed, arrested, deported, tried, deprived of jobs and careers, or otherwise hounded by state and federal authorities. These roundups were widely publicized events, the latter of which, led by the House of Representatives UnAmerican Activities Committee and by Senator Joseph McCarthy's Committee on Government Operations, did uncover Communist and Communist sympathizers in the federal government. In the end, the Supreme Court, which had been compliant in the blacklisting of such individuals and gave broad discretion to the government in prosecuting Communists, decided in *Yates v. U.S.* (1957) that espousing radical political positions, absent any violent action, was protected by the First Amendment. Nonetheless, such campaigns against internal enemies and enemy aliens based on their political opinions continue to roil American politics.

So much for the history. Now for the Zombie. On February 5, 1950, Senator McCarthy told a women's group in Wheeling, West Virginia, that "I have here in my hand a list of 205 . . . a list of names that were made known to the Secretary of State as being members of the Communist Party and who nevertheless are still working and shaping policy in the State Department." The number of these supposed Soviet infiltrators varied each time he gave the speech. The essence of the speech, that there was a well-organized conspiracy of Reds aimed at the violent overthrow of the government, never varied. Later evidence, evidence not available to McCarthy, showed that there were no more than a handful of Soviet spies and sympathizers in the federal government. The rest of the 205 were Zombies.

In the context of the rapidly heating Cold War, particularly during the Korean conflict, such charges frightened many Americans. They echoed through higher education administrations and local school boards, Hollywood movie studios and the American stage. Loyalty oaths, once a feature of the American Revolution and the Civil War, reappeared. Those who could not or would not sign were fired from jobs and blacklisted from future employment. Liberal thinkers like Arthur Schlesinger Jr., Daniel Boorstin, and Sidney Hook, who had heretofore been sympathetic to some of the far left reform projects, for example civil rights, now moved to the right to protect themselves. Zombies were abroad, and though few could see them, their work was everywhere apparent. A few notables refused to be panicked. Led by historian Richard Hofstadter, playwright Arthur Miller, journalist Edward R. Morrow, and actors Humphrey Bogart and Lauren Bacall, they called out McCarthy, FBI director J. Edgar Hoover, and the other "red baiters."

Where were the Zombies? Is it just our present-mindedness, our rejection of much of the supernatural, the fashions Zombies? Do we fail to credit the belief systems of the men and women who lived then and there? Were this our fault and not theirs, then the Zombies would vanish. But the same fears exist today. In the Salem witchcraft crisis, every stray dog or cat might become the Devil's familiars, and His spies wore the garb of one's neighbors. In the Red Scare, fears of subversives everywhere plotting mischief tapped into latent (and not so latent) anti-Semitism and racism. Every foreigner and civil rights advocate who criticized the status quo allegedly plotted against democracy, capitalism, and the American Way. They were the shadowy figures of the television show based on the autobiographical tell-all *I Led Three Lives*. The US attorney general, Tom Clark, compiled a list of suspected enemies and suspect organizations. A network of informants supplied tips, most of which were either entirely imaginary or meant to divert attention from genuine threats. As in the witchcraft scare, accusers thought themselves safe from accusations.

Eventually the tide turned. In 1954, Democratic presidential candidate Adlai Stevenson strongly condemned McCarthy's slash and burn methods. In a series of televised hearings, with America watching as McCarthy made reckless accusations about Communists in the US Army, attorney Joseph Welsh lambasted McCarthy: "At long last, sir, have you no sense of decency?" By the end of the year, even the Senate had had enough. On December 2, the Senate voted 67 to 22 to censure McCarthy for acting contrary to senatorial traditions. It was a rare rebuke for the senior chamber, and it signaled the end of McCarthy's reign of terror. The Zombies that he allowed to patrol the corridors of the Capitol once more receded into the shadows. There they remain, waiting for another demagogue to turn them loose on the nation.

Eggheads

Adlai Stevenson was a marvelous public speaker, in part because he prepared his remarks meticulously, in part because he valued his image as a thoughtful public figure. As governor of Illinois he attracted the support of other intellectuals like Arthur Schlesinger Jr., and together they managed to convince the Democratic Party to nominate him for president in 1952 and 1956. Stevenson was bald, with an oval shaped head, which gave rise to a derisive eponym for him and his bright liberal supporters. They were eggheads, first named and condemned in editorial pundit Joseph Alsop's editorial for abandoning the Republican Party for Stevenson's campaign. Historian James T. Patterson reported that Stevenson "ran a dignified issues-centered campaign," but Republicans snidely countered that "'eggheads' were the core of his support."

The effectiveness of the Republicans' rhetoric rested in part on fears that inside the egghead was a Red, but also on a deeper theme—anti-intellectualism in American culture. Throughout our history, according to the late historian Richard Hofstadter, the term "intellect" has been an epithet. Intelligence has always been prized as a vital component of problem solving. We love intelligence tests, and use them to place students in advanced courses. But intellect, associated with high-brow cultural tastes and expertise in subjects that the ordinary American cannot understand, is somehow resented. "Say that again in English" the tough police detective tells the egghead criminalist. Intellect is never respected separate from intelligence, a divide between the practical and useful, and the creative and theoretical. The intellectual offers that the life of the mind, with interests that may have little or no immediate practical application, is a higher principle than mere technique. The intellectual thus challenges, implicitly if not explicitly, the value of "common sense." The intellectual questions the common sense of things, and that is upsetting to those whose view of the world is fixed. The fear that the egghead is a subversive in a tweed jacket smoking a pipe drove contemporary cultural memes. Eggheads were by no means all Democrats, much less radicals, but the political label and the cultural image crisscrossed.

As the mantra of college for everyone became the creed of most American educators, and polls in the 1960s showed that the university professor's rating was rising in the public estimation, the egghead Zombie had to find a new disguise. When rich men who did not finish college started funding initiatives to persuade bright young people to forgo college, the egghead Zombie had found new clothing—the professor. Otherworldly, but vaguely sinister (on television crime shows the professor is often the culprit), the flashpoint was the decline of the liberal arts, in particular the humanistic studies of literature, history, language (other than English), philosophy, and the classics. All of these require brainpower, but none of them led to jobs in business, according to the new gurus of the new business model of higher education.

This new model welcomed the egghead Zombie in a clever inversion of the growing presence of professors among the professions. The notion that the purpose of higher education was not to train the mind in critical thinking (the mantra of the traditional intellectual), but to provide clinical training for future employment, was just what the egghead Zombie needed to walk among us. The Zombie is always on the lookout for a disguise that allows him to pass unnoticed, and under the new regime of distance learning and online courses, for profit degree mills and useless diplomas, the Zombie could do what he wanted, unafraid of being exposed for what he was—a fake.

The modern Zombie was a clever monster, preying on the living through fear and ignorance. The period, encompassing two world wars and the Great Depression, was congenial to Zombies of course. The modern Zombie learned our weaknesses and how to exploit them. Had we believed that there was nothing to fear but fear itself, the modern Zombie would vanish from our midst. Histories that propelled those fears, however, empowered the postmodern Zombie.

CHAPTER EIGHT

Postmodern Zombies

This concluding chapter is the most problematic in argument. It was the hardest to compose. It is a chapter about our world, and many of the examples in it are taken from today's social media, journalism, and scholarship. Some of its Zombies walk about in the light of day, unafraid. Others we barely glimpse. Searching for these Zombies is a form of painful self-criticism. In these days of identity scholarship, the long and agonizing demise of civility among academics, and social-media mobbing, one critic's Zombie may be another reader's avatar. After reading this chapter, a skeptical colleague concluded that Zombies were anything I did not like. There was more than a little truth in that harsh judgment. I do not like Zombies.

The post–World War II era needed a name. Historians are notorious for periodizing. Postmodern seemed appropriate. ("Avant-garde" would be another, but every novelty falls under this rubric and every age has its avant-garde.) Rebelling against modernism's geometric austerity, the postmodern is fragmented and questions convention, in fact, all traditional intellectual authority. It is both playful and critical. It gives readers intricate explanatory theories like deconstruction, in a vocabulary borrowed largely from French sources. Philosopher Stephen R. C. Hicks has authored a primer on the subject, proposing that postmodernism is antiphilosophical. It does not begin with first principles or statements of value. It is antirealist, in that its language does not match real objects or events, but is a set of sociolinguistic conventions resting on the subjectivity of writing and speaking. All this would sound like the death knell of humanistic studies were it not for the embrace of postmodernism by influential humanist intellectuals.

The postmodern found its way into the very heart of academic historical studies in the work of one man. For about twenty years, between 1980 and 2000, it was hard to find a history PhD dissertation without some reference to Michel Foucault. Foucault was a French left-wing public intellectual and sometime historical writer. His bête noir was the arbitrary tyranny of the modern state and its surveillance practices. He wrote incisively, if not always neutrally, about insanity, prisons, and authoritarianism. Foucault was the archetypal postmodernist, seeing discontinuities and absurdities where others had seen continuity and order. As he told an interviewer in 1984, the year of his death, "The work of an intellectual is not to mould the political will of others; it is, through the analyses that he does in his own field, to re-examine evidence and assumptions, to shake up habitual ways of working and thinking, to dissipate conventional familiarities, to re-evaluate rules and institutions."

Foucault's was a vision of history that freed susceptible students and scholars from modernist objectivism—what, in his *Truth in History* (1979), Oscar Handlin called "the capacity for advancing the approach to truth." Instead, Foucault's postmodern message was to use history as a weapon to destabilize existing institutions and customs. Insofar as it insisted "that knowledge is nothing but a manifestation of power" it was, in the judgment of Allan Megill, "a simplifying and ultimately vary dangerous claim." It politicized history. This was nothing new, of course, for the first great histories of Herodotus and Thucydides were in fact defenses of Greek imperialism and the policies of Athens during the Peloponnesian War. Until the middle of the seventeenth century Anglophone historians had no qualms about inventing conversations between men who never met, speeches that were never recorded, and the details of battles that were otherwise lost to memory. They moralized freely, took sides in political quarrels, and freely mangled historical evidence. Politicized history well served art. Slanted narratives like Raphael Holinshead's *Chronicles of England, Scotland, and Ireland* (heavily redacted by Queen Elizabeth's censors to promote Tudor legitimacy) became one basis of William Shakespeare's historical plays. Movie histories "based on a true story" still engage in this kind of fakery. In the 1640s, however, English Civil War historians vowed to check their sources and abandon invention. In the main, they adhered to that vow. Some postmodern history, influenced by the lure of trade press publication of historical novels and novelesque histories, is beginning to abandon that rule. Imagined conversations appear in italics. "They must have gone something like this." Zombies eagerly exploit such backsliding.

The following postmodern Zombies are not fully formed. They still look a lot like real people, events, and ideas. But give them time and they will infiltrate our history. The undead are persistent, and postmodern relativism gives them a leg up.

Conspiracy Theories

Conspiracy theories are as old as American history. They may result from too little information or too much information; have a basis in history, or exist only in a fevered imagination. They may be antistatist and thrive among the powerless, or thrive within elites and target outsiders. In 1692, prosecutors of the Salem accused assumed that a Satanic conspiracy threatened the Massachusetts Bay Colony. Colonial law made otherwise innocent conversations among angry slaves into felonious conspiracies. Many of the leaders of the American revolutionary movement were convinced that there was a conspiracy against liberty in George III's England. In the new nation, the Freemasons, the Church of Jesus Christ of Latter-day Saints (Mormons), Roman Catholics, Jews, and other religious groups were all suspected of conspiratorial activities at one time or another. A similar fear of conspiracy raged through the so-called fire-eaters of the antebellum South, who were convinced that the Republican Party and Abraham Lincoln were plotting to free all the slaves. The fear of this conspiracy was one among the many incitements for secession. In the Gilded Age, leaders of capital and leaders of organized labor accused one another of conspiring to violate the law. Anarchists and immigrants were targets of conspiratorial accusations in the first "Red Scare" during and after World War I, and a fear that Japanese Americans were plotting to aid their homeland to invade the US led to the "internment" of thousands of loyal Japanese Americans during World War II.

The conspiracy theory Zombie is an alternative history, one that did not happen. It gains its power from underlying anxieties about personal futures as well as the fate of public life. It most often takes a partisan form. Conspiracy theories have found a home in postmodern histories. The belief that Communists plotted to overthrow the democratic government of the United States after World War II was a potent part of the second "Red Scare," itself riven with conspiracy theories. Although there had been an active Communist Party of the United States before the war, with the inception of the Cold War anti-Communism was far more widespread than any remaining CPUSA activity, and, in any case, few American Communists sought a violent overthrow of any kind. Wisconsin senator Joseph

McCarthy sounded the tocsin in 1951: "This [Cold War] must be the product of a great conspiracy on a scale so immense as to dwarf any previous such venture in the history of man. A conspiracy of infamy so black that, when it is finally exposed, its principals shall be forever deserving of the maledictions of all honest men." As Richard Hofstadter characterized such fears in his *Paranoid Style in American Politics* (1952), they were themselves a conspiracy "directed against a nation, a culture, a way of life." This "distorted" and distorting way of viewing history was deeply ingrained in the American psyche. Hofstadter did not call the conspiracy theories Zombies, but that is what they are.

They have, however, made their way into our history books. A spate of books purporting to tell "the untold story" of McCarthy's fight against the real menace of Communism, and how a conspiracy of easily duped liberals and secret pinkos "blacklisted" him, are now best sellers among the fake news circle. Glen Beck, Ann Coulter, and other media figures have called the work essential reading. Similar works warn against the "big lies" that the dark government has told about a secret war on American character. Although the authors of this genre, like Diana West, M. Stanton Evans, and Coulter, are journalists, much history is written by journalists these days. One notes that these works cite one another as reliable sources, much as President Donald Trump would cite a Fox news story that cited a Breitbart opinion piece as though opinion were fact. What makes all of these into examples of conspiracy theory Zombies is the way they are argued—big lies, secrets, have kept the truth from being revealed.

The theory that President Lyndon Johnson was behind the John F. Kennedy assassination in 1963 (or that Fidel Castro was behind it, or that it was a well-organized effort with more than one shooter) has never been put to rest. Instead, it has entered into the history books. In fact, entire histories are devoted to the conspiracy to keep Americans from knowing the truth of what really happened. The Warrren Commission, led by Chief Justice Earl Warren, supposedly was part of the conspiracy to hide the truth. For example, in a series of histories, Michael Collins Piper offered evidence that the Israeli government and its agents were behind the assassination and the cover-up. The publisher, American Free Press, was the brainchild of Willis Carto, an avowed white supremacist, Holocaust denier, and founder of the anti-Semitic Liberty Lobby. The notion of conspiracy lay at the bottom of its publications—the idea that a vast and sinister Jewish conspiracy was behind war, disease, and poverty. One might simply dismiss the Kennedy conspiracy Zombie, until one discovers that histories incorporating one or another of its versions abound. With self-publishing now possible through Amazon, anyone can write a book, call it a history, and people will see it alongside legitimate scholarship. The more sensational its revelations, the more likely they are to attract attention.

Postmodern culture combined with the social media enable conspiracy theories to spread far faster than they can be contained or confuted. The speed with which current events are folded into histories empowers conspiracy theorists to feed their accounts to a gullible public. The conspiracy theory that the NASA moon landing was a fraud perpetrated to gain the space agency further funding has a large following. According to this alternative history, the landing was staged in a movie studio; evidence was altered or faked, and the space race with the Soviet Union was the motivation for the entire fraud. "Anti-Vaxers" accept the theory that a conspiracy of doctors, pharmaceutical companies, and the federal government is poisoning children or causing conditions such as autism with unnecessary and harmful vaccines.

The "birther conspiracy" is even more bizarre. Barack Obama was able to overcome many obstacles on his path to the White House and two terms as president of the United States. His foreign-sounding name, his racial identity, and his relative lack of experience in government (no longer an issue after the election of a successor who had no experience in government) all played a role in doubting the legitimacy of his candidacy. However, none of those items was nearly as powerful as the idea that, somehow, he was lying about his birthplace in order to meet the Constitution's requirement that a president be a "natural born citizen." The conspiracy theory Zombie became so widespread that its believers gained the name "birthers." Birthers contended that Obama's Kenyan father meant that Obama was born in Kenya and his certificate of live birth from Hawai'i was a forgery. It was supposedly an elaborate conspiracy so that an African American could cheat his way into the Oval Office. Left unsaid was why Obama's parents and supporters would have bothered concealing his birthplace given that, under US law, if one's mother was an American (as Obama's was), one is a natural born citizen. It was probably the concern with birthright citizenship under the Fourteenth Amendment and the so-called anchor babies of illegal immigrants that led to this focus on Obama's birthplace, but the birthers maintained their claim that Obama was not legitimate in spite of all of the contrary evidence.

After some befuddlement on his part about whether to dignify the matter, he produced his birth certificate. This was not enough proof for the birthers, who claimed it was a forgery. If he were not a citizen, he could not be president. As an irritant, the theory did little damage to his candidacy, but it did hint that racism was alive and well among certain groups of Americans, including supporters of Obama's opponents, and later the candidacy of Donald Trump. At first, polls showed that as many as a quarter of American potential voters disbelieved the proofs of Obama's Hawai'ian birth. He was forced to provide additional evidence, including the original forms, contemporary newspaper reports of the birth, and other documents, before the number of doubters dropped to a little over 10 percent of voters. The fact that disbelief continued to persist showed that the birther conspiracy theory was a powerful conspiracy Zombie. It had become part of American presidential history. It has already been added to history textbooks, dismissed as a hoax—thus far.

Not so easily dismissed are sets of conspiracies having to do with voter fraud. In American history, there have been a number of well-documented cases of the dead voting, multiple voting, and missing ballots sitting in warehoused voting machines. These may have begun as conspiracy theories but were later established by confessions or evidence at trial. More recently, a sitting president proposed that he had actually won the popular vote, even though the count did not support his claim. There was a conspiracy, he offered, citing the "deep state" of entrenched bureaucrats who had tampered with the results. Even more recently, conspiracy theories abound that Russian computer hackers had managed to alter the vote returns in key districts, or that members of one party or the other had similarly engaged in fraudulent practices.

The latest and surely not the last hiding place of conspiracy theory Zombies is the "whisper network." This is a largely web-based network of alleged victims of sexual harassment or abuse in the professions. There are also published, spreadsheet, and "crowd sourced" versions. Its purpose is to warn women of active, powerful abusers, but the network also affords women a measure of empowerment who have made formal complaints but have not received the outcome they sought. The clout of the whisper network lies in its ability to accumulate stories, much as the power of the Salem witchcraft crisis lay in its aggregation of accusations. There is no way that the accused can defend themselves against these accusations, as they are not made public until they have, in effect, been leaked. The whisper network version of conspiracy theory Zombie makes the accused into Zombies, present but unidentified until someone breaks the silence and speaks.

The conspiracy theory is a Zombie, and, like all Zombies, it is hard to kill. Postmodern history makes killing these Zombies very difficult. The anarchic, antirealist quality of postmodern history removes the reliability controls from accounts, making every version of history as good or bad as every other version. Return to the birther conspiracy. Long after Obama had provided the documentary evidence that proved his US birth, Republican politicians like Newt Gingrich, bloggers, and radio commentators on the right of the political spectrum continued to raise the issue. It had "legs" not because it undermined his legitimacy as chief executive, but because it said something about who belonged and who did not belong in the polity. All of the defenders of the birther conspiracy theory were white. Obama is mixed race. By raising the possibility that he was not native born, the birthers were engaging in race bashing. Insfar as white supremacy is a theme in history, the birther conspiracy could claim a pedigree. With every version of history as valid as popular opinion has determined it to be, no amount of evidence could entirely kill the birther. And that is how it became a Zombie.

The more outlandish the conspiracy theory Zombie, the more one should look behind its manifest content to the motives of its proponents. A second of these conspiracy Zombies suggests economic motives. The denial of global climate change is a conspiracy theory Zombie. There is little climatological doubt that the planet is warming, particularly the oceans, that the glaciers are melting, and that increasing heating has led to semipermanent and severe drought conditions in many areas of the world. The denial of the phenomenon itself and of the human component, particularly the use of fossil fuels, is a defense of the fossil fuels industry. Thus a conspiracy theory—arguing that scientists are deliberately lying about the climate—is actually an economic and political campaign for an industry by its lobbyists and those whom they support.

The ease with which conspiracy theories spread, their persistence despite factual proof to the contrary, and their impact on our public life suggest that there is something deep in our psyche that actually feeds conspiracy theories. They are fake explanations whose power over us comes from our need to find explanations. This makes them amenable to historical narrative—entirely legitimate emotional needs twisted by the conspiracy theory Zombie, which is, after all, what Zombies do. The way to prevent the conspiracy theory Zombie from taking over our history is to look closely at sources, to weigh the validity and the potential bias of those sources, and to ask whether the content of the conspiracy theory makes sense. In short, the way to dispose of this Zombie is exactly the same as the way to do good historical research.

Memes

The meme Zombie looks like a meme, because it is a meme. Memes are by their very nature not real. One definition is taken directly from the home of the meme Zombie—the internet: "an element of a culture or system of behavior that may be considered to be passed from one individual to another by nongenetic means, especially imitation. For example, a humorous image, video, piece of text, etc., that is copied (often with slight variations) and spread rapidly by Internet users." Got that—it is not real. The meme Zombie is pulled together from disparate sources, sometimes real images, sometimes cartoons. Why would anyone allow memes to enter historical scholarship if they are not real? In postmodern history, such questions need not be answered, because they are not asked.

Students of visual culture are beginning to realize that the meme is not just a joke with a kitten sticking out its tongue or Average Joe photoshopping himself into celebrity images online. As Limor Shifman explains it, memes can be the "building blocks" of much more complex stories than one-shot online images. As they can be "shaped by cultural norms and expectations" so they can, in the womb of time, shape those norms and expectations. Then they make their way into the blogosphere; and then into histories. The meme is a deliberate distortion. When the meme Zombie goes viral it can wreak havoc.

The most obvious meme Zombie is the photoshopped image. It is a composite of images that did not originally appear together. While it might be benign—for example to heighten a detail that is obscured or left out of the original—it can also fabricate an image. The first of these were the paranormal photographs of the nineteenth century, called "spirit photography," using double image development to make a ghost appear at the elbow of a real person. The superimposed image might be a departed loved one, often a dead child. These sold well even though the most famous of the nineteenth-century spirit photographers, William Mumler, was tried for fraud. (He was acquitted.) Computer-generated images in horror movies are the modern versions of these photographs.

History on the web is especially vulnerable to the photoshopped meme Zombie because online history is so visual and increasingly pervasive. So-called digital history is vulnerable to the meme Zombie because, unlike still visuals or re-creations, digital history is fabricated visuals from original materials, a genre of live action textbooks. A subtopic of digital humanities, the prospects for digital history are enormous, and various public and private funding agencies are investing in digital history projects at universities and libraries. Not everyone was on board. In 2003, Daniel Cohen and Roy Rosezweig's pioneering account of digital history promoted the project but admits its limitations. They found advantages and liabilities: "capacity, accessibility, flexibility, diversity, manipulability, interactivity, and hypertextuality (or nonlinearity)," on the one hand, and "dangers or hazards on the information superhighway: quality, durability, readability, passivity, and inaccessibility," on the other. Without accompanying text, images are almost too persuasive. Unsorted and unexplained by other means, they can convey incorrect interpretations of events and people. Yet the spread of computer-based history pedagogy in online distance education, PowerPoint lectures, and other essentially visual methods is not going away. In fact, it is becoming the norm. Thus the danger of meme Zombies infiltrating digital presentations is almost inevitable. As Rosenzweig and Anthony Grafton warned in 2011, traditional historical presentation made fakes and forgery difficult, but "digital media, tools and networks have altered the balance."

Rosenzweig and Grafton opined that such fakery or at least inauthenticity had proved to be a "phantom" problem, but meme Zombies now walk almost unafraid through our current events, and today's current events are tomorrow's history. The "doctored image" from the past using today's Photoshop tools and then posted on the web include the various versions of the inauguration crowds for Presidents Obama and Trump, in what became a hilarious barrage of tweets by Trump that his crowd was bigger than Obama's. This was silly, but the attempts by various political interest groups to photoshop their way to greater influence, or infamy, is not silly. If it becomes part of the historical record, it is the very opposite of silly. It is a victory for the Zombie.

There is another kind of meme that is a Zombie from its inception. This is the political cartoon or the advertising image that caricatures. While not history itself, this cartoon meme finds its way into histories. For example, in the wake of Reconstruction, cartoonists like Thomas Nast of *Harper's Weekly* produced seminal images of American political scenes. Perhaps best known for his GOP Elephant, he was also the creator of two versions of the freedman. The first, during Reconstruction, was ennobling, while the second, after the demise of Reconstruction, was demeaning. Neither was historically accurate, but both had the power to sway opinion.

Famous later "editorial" cartoonists like Tony Auth, Herb Block, and Pat Oliphant have created lasting memes of political figures and events. These are not history, however much they may please or anger us. They caricature the least attractive features of their subjects' faces or bodies— Lyndon Johnson's nose, Richard Nixon's five o'clock shadow, and Barack Obama's ears. They are Zombies.

Todays' meme Zombies have more persuasive power then they did in 2003 or 2011, and thus more potential for mischief, because so much more of modern culture is visual. Added to the visual impact of television and movies are the images one now sees on smartphones, tablets, and other machines connected to the internet. In so far as internet sources are not monitored, much less moderated, conspiracy theories in meme form can fly around and multiply with the speed of light. That means meme Zombies appearing everywhere, with little to check their misdeeds. The most recent of these is no laughing matter. An altered video of House Speaker Nancy Pelosi that appeared on FaceBook and elsewhere on May 24, 2019, seemed to show that she was slurring her words. President Trump and his legal advisor Rudy Giuliani both tweeted a rhetorical question of whether Pelosi, a critic of Trump, was ill. In fact, the video of her speaking had been slowed down to create a false impression. Although responsible social media sites agreed to either take it down or add a disclaimer, it had already gone viral. As the *Guardian* reported, "Concerns have been raised in recent years about the impact of 'deep fake' videos, where artificial intelligence technology is used to create disturbingly realistic videos."

Some responsible social media sites are now removing fake visuals, but only after they have been spotted. This gives them, and their makers, a chance to influence elections, among other key events, before the Zombies are erased. There is evidence that foreign powers have used memes with hidden persuaders (a meme introduced by advertisers in the mid-twentieth century) to sway undecided voters on social media like FaceBook and convince other potential voters to stay home.

Numbers

One of the required subjects in many college core curriculums is numeracy, or skill and understanding of arithmetic and mathematics. Once upon a time, the requirement was satisfied with introductory courses in algebra and calculus. Nowadays, statistics, computer science, and other, even more modern subjects will satisfy the requirement. Numbers are all around us, and familiarity with both descriptive statistics (averages, trends, and the like for a complete body of data) and inferential statistics (probability, sampling, and the like for representative or randomly selected bodies of data) helps everyone understand our world.

Historians have employed quantitative terms—more, less, fewer, many, increase, decrease, most, percentages, and averages—for as long as history has been written. Although quantification clearly had advantages in testing generalizations, as William O. Aydelotte, one of the pioneers in quantitative history, warned in 1966, the "fad" for it had already been "pushed too far." His concerns notwithstanding, with the arrival of computers and computer-assisted quantitative tools and software programs like SPSS (Statistical Package for Social Sciences) in the late 1970s, quantitative analysis of historically recorded data became much more sophisticated. For a time, quantitative historians hailed the new methods as the high road to historical truth and venues like the *Journal of Interdisciplinary History* and *Historical Methods* were all the rage, but over time most historians' numeracy has not particularly improved.

Among the "cliometricians" economic historians have led the way. Economic history is not the only form of quantitative analysis, but it may be the social science discipline most dependent on competence with numbers. Modern microeconomics (individual work and labor) and macroeconomics (the commerce, industry, and product of a nation or people) rests upon quantitative skills. But statistical skill is no substitute for sound history. If the data is poorly selected or poorly arranged, no degree of statistical sophistication can save an economic history.

To be sure, there are economists who do not believe that there is such a discipline as economic history. For them, numbers are only useful or trustworthy when they are embedded in theory. These economists regard their field as a branch of the sciences governed by ascertainable laws. That idea, of course, has a history going back to the first collectors of numbers, government agents like the late seventeenth-century English political economist William Petty. Petty's work for the English government involved rationalizing the collection of taxes and regulating the money supply, two themes of macroeconomics that are still subject to controversy. From the seventeenth century to our own, students of macroeconomics have tested their hypotheses by using numbers found in historical sources. For example, David Card and Alan Krueger demonstrated that theoretical claims about the minimum wage leading to a smaller workforce were empirically wrong. "Empirical studies of individual firms and markets," in effect, doing historical research on real people making real choices, contradicted theo-retical assumptions.

One can also derive theoretical models from historical evidence (in effect, going in the opposite direction from testing hypotheses with selective evidence). Classic works like Robert Fogel's *Railroads and American Economic Growth* (1964), which introduced counterfactual hypotheses about the relative value of rails and canals, and Douglass North's *The Economic Growth of the United States, 1790–1860* (1966), which argued that external trade and the exploitation of natural resources were the keys to the nation's rapid economic progress, were not just economics books—they were histories whose subject happened to be economics. Works like these spawned generations of narrower economic histories testing Fogel's and North's hypotheses.

Unfortunately, numbers derived from past records can have a false concreteness, as though they speak for themselves. When historians, economists, public policy wonks, and government officials fall prey to fake economic history, a Zombie is nearby. Critics of quantitative measures in history, including economic history, wail about them if they were mindless collections and presentations of numbers. Good economic history recognizes that historical evidence never speaks for itself. First it must be verified. The collection of numbers can be fabricated, bent by the bias of the recorder, incomplete, or not exactly on point. Numbers can be misused to prove or disprove a predisposition. In all of these ways, numerical conclusions can be the false face of history Zombies. Even first-rate economic historians can stumble into these wolf pits.

Robert Fogel and his coauthor Stanley Engerman fell into this trap with their prize-winning two-volume *Time on the Cross* (1974). Their numerical evidence about the profitability of slavery, the efficiency of slave labor, and the dollar value of food, clothing, housing, and other features of slave life compared to the life experiences of antebellum industrial workers relied too heavily on numbers, and not appropriately on social and cultural evidence. In particular, their conclusions, again from the numbers, about the breakup of slave families similarly did not value the impact of small numbers of sales of family members on large numbers of slave relatives. The response was more and better economic history, however. In *Reckoning with Slavery* (1976) a battalion of economic historians led by Peter Temin and Paul David weighed numbers differently to counter the Fogel-Engerman thesis.

The response to *Time on the Cross* should have warned cliometricians of the seductive dangers of numbers. So striking were their findings that Fogel and Engerman forgot their human context. For example, considering the matter of punishing or rewarding slaves, they wrote, "The analysis of the trade-off which faced planters in choosing between force and pecuniary payments [i.e., monetary rewards] is a complex but standard problem of economics . . . slaves actually shared in the gains from economies of scale—so far as pecuniary income was concerned." From this they concluded that force was not the principal basis of getting slaves to work. Seriously? With the use of force always looming in the background, various positive incentives cannot be considered on their own, or on balance, the more important motivation for slave labor. Fogel later recanted, after a fashion, in his *Without Consent or Contract*: "Which instrument of 'government' a given master chose at any moment in time depended on many considerations, some rational [i.e., economic] and some irrational. . . . The mix of controls varied greatly from plantation to plantation, turning in large measure on the personality of the master." The shift from generalization to particularization and from economic calculus to personality was a major concession to the critics of *Time on the Cross*, and about as far as Fogel was willing to go. But putting the numbers in context was a step in the right direction. The numbers Zombie was still there, but it was now looking in, rather than being in.

When politicians and blog pundits offer historical numbers, Zombies run riot. The attack on Social Security funding was one example, with opponents of Social Security, Medicare, and other entitlement programs taking the programs out of their historical context (the New Deal and the Great Society, respectively) and playing with fictive numbers. Representative Paul Ryan led the charge against these programs, telling Congress that they were spending the country into ruinous debt. The numbers he offered were plain: the fund for FICA (the tax that funds Social Security and Medicare) was in peril. As the workforce got older, more and more workers would draw Social Security payments. The theory of bankruptcy is that the fund will run out of cash when the number of retirees exceeds the number of people still paying into the system. That is a number Zombie, made so by those who oppose federal pension funding, those who oppose the federal government, and those who oppose the Social Security private-public solution. In fact, the fund will be able to pay out fully through 2034, partially through 2090, and can be revised by Congress to raise the retirement age for full benefits, increase the employer or the payee contribution, or shift funds to Social Security from other federal entitlements. The false chronology of coming bankruptcy is what adds verisimilitude to the argument. A history with numbers is supposedly more persuasive that simply demanding a rollback of the welfare state. That numbers Zombie has slunk back into the shadows. For now.

Why will it never die? The Social Security program is one of the federal government's oldest entitlements. It was signed into law by President Franklin D. Roosevelt in 1935, part of an omnibus bill to assist the aged, the disabled, and the victims of industrial accidents. From its inception, it faced opposition from those who called it a form of socialism, those who saw it as a burden on business in favor of labor, and those who opposed any additions to the federal bureaucracy. The same objections pertain today, offered by many of the same kinds of critics. The act certainly was a wealth shifting or wealth redistribution device, but the recipients' payments into the plan represented a far larger portion of their income than the employers' contributions. In any case, the survival of Social Security has not prevented a widening gap in wealth and numbers between a few very rich and a much larger class of poor. The Zombie waits for another chance.

Big Data

Most history Zombies are humanoid in shape and size, but one history Zombie shakes the ground like Godzilla. This is the Big Data Zombie, also known as the Meta Data Zombie. It takes up a lot of space and other Zombies fear it, even its smaller cousin the numbers Zombie, because it proposes to ingest everything around it.

Students of twentieth-century history are both blessed and cursed with an avalanche of paper—official reports spewed out by government offices; newspapers and magazines; correspondence and diaries—and now joined by the visuals discussed above. To the rescue comes the Big Data Zombie. Like the movie and comic book *Transformers*, it is a composite of machines that gather and sort information. One of the tasks of historians is to decide what information to use and what to discard. The Big Data Zombie does that for the historian, whether he or she likes it or not. Zombies are pushy that way.

The offerings of Big Data are most articulately and insistently promoted in historian Jo Guldi and David Armitage's tract (hard to call something as arrogant as theirs anything else) *The History Manifesto* (2014). It seems fair to quote extensively, as the work is open sourced:

Traditional research, limited by the sheer breadth of the non-digitised archive and the time necessary to sort through it, becomes easily shackled to histories of institutions and actors in power, for instance characterising universal trends in the American empire from the Ford and Rockefeller Foundations' investments in pesticides, as some historians have done. By identifying vying topics over time, Paper Machines allows the reader to identify and pursue particular moments of dissent, schism, and utopianism—zeroing in on conflicts between the pesticide industry and the Appropriate Technology movement or between the World Bank and the Liberation Theology movement over exploitative practices, for example. Digitally structured reading means giving more time to counterfactuals and suppressed voices, realigning the archive to the intentions of history from below.

I suppose the advice is meant to be useful to working scholars, but first they have to translate the advice into plain English. Paper Machines is a tool that Guldi helped develop, and a search for the term reveals this less than helpful description: "Paper Machines is a plugin for the *Zotero* bibliographic management software that makes cutting-edge topic-modeling analysis in Computer Science accessible to humanities researchers without requiring extensive computational resources or technical knowledge. It synthesizes several approaches to visualization within a highly accessible user interface." I worry about using the term "cutting edge" in conjunction with Zombies, knowing what they are wont to do with cutting edges. So I went off, with some trepidation, to find out about Zotero. Despite the futuristic character of the term, Zotero turns out to be a bibliographical guide, something like a more focused Google search machine. In the end of all our searching, we return to where we began (kudos to T. S. Eliot) with a search for usable date on the web.

Why then the need for the Big Data Zombie? The answer lies in *The History Manifesto* itself. Like its cousin, the *Communist Manifesto* (shorn of the redistributive and moralistic implications—well, not entirely shorn, because both authors do not hide their liberal predilictions), *The History Manifesto* tells historians what the future will be—the future of historical studies and the future of society both. The work pretends to be descriptive of the value of broad studies of big issues, but it is actually prescriptive. Join or die, it warns. Historians and histories that do not buy into the longue durée approach, who provide only cross-sectional, monographic, and sharply focused pictures of the past, will be discarded. Histories of this kind have already lost the public's interest, and risk burying the discipline itself: "History's relationship with the public future lies in developing a longue-durée contextual background against which archival information, events, and sources can be interpreted." You historians have only to lose your chains: "If long-term historical thinking is to fulfil the promise we have proposed for it here, then we will need a rubric for thinking big with adequate skill and historical finesse." But what constitutes a critical eye for looking at long-term stories?

What characteristics unite the models that we are told to choose? How would a classroom training young minds to think far back and far forward in time operate? "Looking to the past to shape the future offers an important call to historians, historical sociologists, historical geographers, and information scientists in particular. It also provides a roadmap for thinking prospectively to all of those institutions—government, finance, insurance, informal, self-organised, citizen-scientific, and other—that we call upon to guide us as we seek the road to better futures." Sounds like the footsteps of the Big Data Zombie are coming closer. "To put these challenges in perspective, and to combat the short-termism of our time, we urgently need the wide-angle, long-range views only historians can provide. Historians of the world, unite! There is a world to win—before it's too late."

Political Correctness and White Privilege

Political correctness is a term that the allegedly political correct never use. That is a characteristic of a Zombie. Calling members of the Society of Friends "Quakers" and radical reform Protestants "puritans" are ways of dismissing or demeaning those who hold dissenting opinions. The targets of those insulting phrases turned the tables on their accusers by adopting or at least accepting the terminology. Political correctness is a term used to pillory people and measures who avoid verbal or physical harm to disadvantaged or vulnerable minorities. For example, when liberal groups seek to protect minority groups with speech codes or safe spaces or other steps that may restrict freedom of speech or assembly, conservatives have descried political correctness. Thus a term that on its face seems friendly or supportive (what could be wrong with correctness?) became a term of opprobrium or invective. That kind of transformation of language warns us that a Zombie is near.

In the so-called culture wars of the 1980s and 1990s, the political correctness Zombie hovered alongside public school history teaching and course plans. National Endowment for the Humanities chair Lynne Cheney and others were appalled that high school students did not know the basic dates and facts about American leaders. They arranged funding for a committee, centered at UCLA, to prepare standardized course designs in American and world history. They selected UCLA historian Gary Nash, one of the first US textbook authors to feature social history and ethnic minorities in his work, to head the project. It was to be a controversial decision. Nash and his collaborators at UCLA brought in teachers and scholars from all over the country, and they worked for more than two years on standards and example exercises. The result in the early 1990s was a series of guides that included both good and not so good in American and world history, the famous, and the ordinary. Above all, the new recommendations were inclusive. Native peoples, immigrants, women, minorities, and working people appeared alongside the politicians, generals, intellectuals, and explorers. The standards also described historical facts as subject to periodic revision. Facts were arguments built on evidence, not bricks that could be mortared together into permanent structures.

The National History Standards were finished in 1994 and presented along with suggested exercises that year. Opponents of the National History Standards exploded in righteous wrath. They fumed that history had been hijacked by a conspiracy of radicals. To some supporters turned critics, like Cheney, the Standards and even more the exercises published along with the Standards had gone too far away from what was important. There were truths in history that were not simply impositions of the powerful on the oppressed. What might have been a serious discussion among history teachers about what children should know in history and about history became a political free-for-all by people who had a stake in the outcome of the culture wars. "Thought police of the right," according to Nash, now clashed with classroom teachers who had prepared sample exercises for the guides in what had become "a media event." Political correctness Zombies now roamed throughout the controversy, doing what they do best—causing confusion. In 1995, the US Senate voted to condemn the standards, 99 to 1, an unprecedented politicization of history teaching and surely an ironic inversion of political correctness! The members thought that the facts of history were fixed in present time as well as in past time. In vain, the national committee that wrote the standards pleaded that facts were subject to reinterpretation.

In 1997, after much of the controversy had subsided, Nash described the National History Standards he and his coworkers developed: "This collaboration and consensus-building between K-12 teachers and college historians was altogether unprecedented. Never in the long history of public education, reaching back more than three hundred years, had such an attempt been made to raise the level of history education. Never before had such a broad-based group of history educators from all parts of the country gathered to work collaboratively on such an enterprise." Asked many years later about the episode by the present author, he was still upset.

The political correctness Zombie was an effort to pillory attempts to bring ordinary people into the story we tell our school children. It failed, as teachers took the standards (if not the examples) as guides. But in the heightened atomosphere of identity scholarship after the election of Donald Trump, proponents of equity, inclusion, and diversity in the teaching of history did what critics of the National History Standards failed to do: they made a mockery of equity, inclusion, and diversity. What other explanation can there be for the new UCLA equity, diversity, and inclusion policy: "In recent years, UCLA has taken important steps to promote more equitable and inclusive faculty hiring. In the spirit of continuous improvement [UCLA was] announcing a new initiative: starting in the 2018–19 academic year, all regular rank faculty searches must require candidates to submit an 'EDI Statement' that describes the candidate's past, present, and future (planned) contributions to equity, diversity, and inclusion. This policy will extend to both standard searches and those employing search waivers. Also, please note that UCLA will implement a similar practice in the context of ladder rank faculty promotions beginning in the 2019–20 academic year." As a matter of fact, the author of the UCLA ukase is a medieval historian, Scott Waugh, whose two books on English kingship would not have passed the new UCLA test had he been a candidate for a history slot today. Although not quite the same as the HUAC opening question to suspected radicals, "Are you now or ever have you been a member of the Communist Party?," the UCLA test would presumptively rule out candidates whose work did not promote equity, diversity, and inclusion (whatever a hiring committee deemed those terms to mean). As Rita Koganzon has recently written in the *Chronicle of Higher Education*, reviewing historian Hanna Gray's deeply moving and highly sensible memoir:

As the internal workings of universities have come under the scrutiny of the increasingly all-encompassing ideologies of the left and right, even the most routine college happenings have become tinder for national conflagrations. Dissatisfied with your dining hall offerings? Frame it as part of movement politics and *The New York Times* will obligingly air your concerns to the nation. Don't like the people yelling on the quad? Film them and send it to your cause's national organization to disseminate. Publicizing such complaints is now easy because the constituencies that can be *activated* to fan the flames of campus controversies have expanded far beyond those who have any personal investment in higher education. Everyone has an opinion, and troll armies for both sides stand ever ready to dismantle privilege or trigger snowflakes. Not even the most established members of these institutions—the faculty—seem able to resist the temptation to behave like protesters, circumventing the institutional channels of redress created for them and appealing directly to this ambivalent "public."

Alongside the political correctness Zombie lurches the white privilege Zombie. This was the argument that whites, as whites, had to shoulder blame for the ills of the nation because whites always oppressed minorities. The claim that an entire class of people—whites—were responsible for the mistreatment of others because they belonged to a racial category was an almost eerie parallel, though hardly as damaging, to the Jim Crow assertion of black inferiority and a myriad of other racialist stereotypes. Indeed, the white privilege Zombie reintroduced the very idea of racial categories that a previous generation of social justice advocates had tried to eliminate from the public policy vocabulary. For the latter, the use of race to discriminate was the source of many ills. For the white privilege Zombie, whiteness itself is the source of the problem.

A moral and political stance, the white privilege Zombie invariably exaggerates the misconduct of everyone who happens to be born with European ancestry. As Peggy McIntosh, a founder of Seeking Educational Equality and Diversity (SEED) and a national spokesperson for the project, put it, "white privilege is an invisible package of unearned assets." Of course, because it is as invisible as it is inevitable, poor whites who come from disadvantaged backgrounds may not know they have it. Technically, such reasoning is essentialist. It assumes that an external categorization, and an arbitrary one at that (color), is the cause of what are, in fact, far more complex relationships. What is more, to say that the poor white farmers of the upper plains, or the miners of the Appalachians, or the white workers in the inner cities, are to blame for discrimination against (other) minorities is simply fake history. But the danger—and this is a truly dangerous Zombie—is that it reintroduces the very same sort of argument as underlay the Nuremburg laws, Jim Crow, and other racialist strategies, including white supremacy. Although, like all Zombies, it tries to pass as harmless, or even benevolent, its seeds are weeds.

Ironcially, the appearance of the white privilege Zombie in social media and college protests energized the slumbering white supremacy Zombie. In the elections of 2016 and 2018 it became clear that many voters (and presumably many who did not vote) considered America as a white nation and voted to keep it that way. The enemy, as in 1607, and in 1861, was the person of color, or, in 1848, the person whose first language was Spanish or Nahuatl or Mayan. They were invaders, criminals, sponges, or whatever the haters hated, and had to be stropped at the borders or found and deported from inside the nation.

The white supremacy Zombie assumes that whiteness is somehow a causal force in history. Deployed by promoters of European colonialism, shared by Union and Confederate leaders, assumed by the moguls of the Gilded Age, promoted by Progressives and many New Dealers, white supremacy meant that genetically or culturally or by divine mandate whites were the "ruling race" and should remain so.

Setting two Zombies—white privilege and white supremacy—to do battle is not, however, the best way to rid the land of Zombies. As a matter of historical fact, Jill Lepore has it right:

> Making political claims that are based on identity is what white supremacy is. To the degree that we can find that in the early decades of the country, it's the position taken by, say, John C. Calhoun or Stephen Douglas arguing against Abraham Lincoln. The whole Lincoln-Douglas debate in 1858 comes down to Douglas saying, *Our forefathers founded this country for white men and their posterity forever.* And Lincoln, following on the writings of black abolitionists like Frederick Douglass and David Walker and Maria Stewart, says, *No, that's just not true!* Lincoln read in the founding documents a universal claim of political equality and natural rights, the universality of the sovereignty of the people, not the particularity. Anyone who makes an identity-based claim for a political position has to reckon with the unfortunate fact that Stephen Douglas is their forebear, not Abraham Lincoln or Frederick Douglass.

What animates these Zombies? Bigotry. Blaming individuals in a group because of something that has nothing to do with activities of the individual; labeling, profiling, expressing prejudice because of color, or creed, or sexual identity—this is the force that propels these postmodern Zombies through our culture and into our history.

Dismay and Despair

The last postmodern Zombie in this catalogue may be the most insidious. The despair Zombie is invisible. You can feel its presence, but it lurks just out of sight, like the strange shape that darts just on the edge of our peripheral vision. It can go anywhere, almost unnoticed. It turns all history bitter in our mouths, drives away students and lay readers, and cynically derides all aspiration for a better future. In a world continually at war with terror and terrorists, with climate change deniers occupying places of power in the economy and government, and renewed evidence of pervasive racial, gender, and ethnic prejudice at every turn, it is easy to see how despair Zombies can multiply. Left to their own devices, they drain us of hope and lead some of us to wish for an all powerful leader to tell us what to do. With our moral compass failing, we welcome isolation from the world. We seek safety behind walls.

I am not disputing narratives of victimization and oppression. There is more than enough evidence of the pervasiveness of these in our history. I have in previous pages herein cited examples. They are dismaying. But when historians insist that we are the inherent beneficiaries of these oppressions, and that, despite our conscious and unconscious commitments to equality and opportunity, we continue to oppress in thought and deed, indeed cannot resist our basest urge to oppress, then we make new Zombies. When our idea of our history is infected with this Zombie's blood, narratives become unrelenting chronicles of hypocrisy, male dominance, white supremacy, and brutalization of the other. The despair Zombie destroys hope for a better present and future, because the despair Zombie implants the notion that our past sins are like original sin—they are essential elements of our flawed humanity. Who would or should purvey ideas of history that doomed us to eternal perdition?

Now, let me distinguish dismay from despair. Dismay is sad concern. Despair is hopelessness. One can find examples in all our newspapers and periodicals, in social media and documentaries, in the accusatory tone of postmodern political campaigns. The examples I have chosen below come from a much narrower band of these sources. All of the following I take from widely praised recent historical works, written with passion and based on thorough research. They are, in a word, considered among the very best of recent work. I teach them and respect the labor and care that went into them.

Colin Calloway is one of our finest chroniclers of Native America. His survey of early Indian-white relations dismayingly concludes, "white pioneers who arrived in the wake of smallpox [epidemic of 1776] and other epidemics engaged in heroic baby making, and most of their babies survived. The Indians' high mortality rates and low fertility rates . . . make the outcome seem inevitable." This is not despair, for the "seem" is the key word. We know that despite the removals and the massacres of Native peoples they persevered. They hid in plain sight; they intermarried; they are not gone. And it is this realization, which history affords us alongside the stories of outrage, that prevents dismay from becoming despair.

We have long accepted the American Revolution and the nation-building that followed as our birth story, but Robert G. Parkinson's remarkable diligence and passion has revealed a dismaying rot at the core of this celebratory metanarrative. Relying on an exhaustive survey of notices filling the middle pages of newspapers, he reveals that the American revolutionary unity was built, in part, on a shared fear of Indian raids and slave uprisings. As a result, "The refusal to extend to African Americans and Indians the benefit of emerging concepts of liberal subjectivity in the form of citizenship had ghastly consequences, for it legitimated and excused the destruction of vast numbers of human beings." The despoliation of Indian homes and the expansion of chattel slavery went hand in hand with Manifest Destiny, the march of American democracy across the continent. It is the irony of this—idealism alongside cynical exploitation—that gives Parkinson's work its power, but our dismay is not despair. For there were points of light in the darkness—attempts to protect Indians and to end slavery. These give the reader hope.

One of the most honored of our generation of historians, Alan Taylor, to whom this author owes more than one debt, has weighed in on the "legacies" of the American Revolution in his *American Revolutions* (2016): "Historians debate how revolutionary the revolution was in its consequences. . . . North America was riven with competing allegiances and multiple possibilities. Would the continent ultimately belong to an expansive republic or to British and Spanish empires allied to native peoples? The empires and natives were the better bet," he offered, "for the republican union was withering and internal conflict imperiled the state governments." It is surely dismaying to learn that the course of the republic was never smooth; indeed, the future of the new nation was never even secure. There was a British colony (Canada) on the northern border of the new nation and Spanish colonies to the south and west. Within the new nation, farmers raised rebellion against federal tax collectors and slaves raised rebellion against their masters. But in this, as in Calloway's and Parkinson's equally dismaying accounts, there were rays of hope: "Republicanism opened all forms of social inequality and domination to criticism in the name of individual rights." Rights talk gradually replaced admissions of privilege and deference to "betters." The world was changing, bit by hesitant bit, toward greater equality, if not all at once for all, but more and more for a greater number.

Who can but feel dismay at the sad, rhapsodic conclusion to Richard White's much admired *Railroaded: The Transcontinentals and the Making of Modern America* (2011): "What are the results of a world dominated by large, inept, but powerful failures whose influence could not be avoided?" For the moguls of the great railroads of the Gilded Age were failures, weren't they? "So many powerful people and influential people are so ignorant and do so many things so badly and yet the world still goes on." That it does distinguishes White's dismay from despair. For the deployment of a vast system of railroads reduced freight costs and promoted a national market, improving the quality of life for many. Take next White's peroration at the end of his majestic survey of the Gilded Age, *The Republic for Which It Stands* (2017): "The guarantee that freed people would enjoy rights equal to those of white citizens had proven largely empty. Despite the ex-slaves' successful resistance to the restoration of gang labor and impressive political mobilization, Reconstruction had not achieved its larger ambitions, having been undermined by stubborn racial prejudice and overwhelmed by terror and violence." That battle goes on today, but in fields of struggle far removed from those of 1877. Today and tomorrow people of color in federal and state government lead the forces of reform. There is yet hope for a better world.

These are examples of what students of late seventeenth-century Puritan sermons called declension narratives. Ministers told their congregations that their failing faith was evidence of G-d's displeasure. At the center of the Puritan version was a decline in piety. But the ministers held out the hope that a return to piety and G-d's law was possible, at least for a few. Some, after all, were saved. At the core of the modern historians' accounts is a similarly profound moral vision and the accompanying sense that expressions of equality and opportunity were cynical or had been betrayed. Jill Lepore's nearly 1,000-page history of the United States, *These Truths* (2018), is a beautifully crafted example of this kind of pleading. Her ending leaves the reader reeling: "The ship of state lurched and reeled. Liberals, blown down by the slightest breeze, had neglected to trim the ship's sails, leaving the canvas to flap and tear in a rising wind, the rigging flailing. Huddled belowdecks, they had failed to plot a course, having lost sight of the horizon and their grasp on any compass. On deck, conservatives had pulled up the ship's planking to make bonfires of rage: they had courted the popular will by demolishing the idea of truth itself." A dismaying vision of a vessel tossed about because its crew has abandoned their posts, is not a lost ship, however, for "it would fall to a new generation of Americans, reckoning what their forebears had wrought, to fathom the depths of the doom-black sea." They could, and they would, save the ship.

Dismay seems endemic among many of our best historians as among the public in general. But we must not succumb to despair. In our willingness to tell and to credit admonitory stories that yet hold out hope is the hope for the future of our entire people. True, for students and their teachers living in a world of academic and pedagogical anxiety, a world of universities and colleges increasingly led by businessmen and women who see higher education's prime goal as teaching job skills, it is hard to hope. With the humanities, including history, appearing to circle the drain, who can blame anyone for dismay? But despair is a Zombie that kills historical mindedness in even the best educated of our students.

I prefer poet and storyteller Stephen Vincent Benet's version of American history. In 1936, with the nation mired in the midst of a Great Depression, and the ominous shadows of Fascism and Nazism reaching across the sea toward our shores, he crafted "The Devil and Daniel Webster." In it, we find Webster pleading for the soul of Jabez Stone, a New Hampshire farmer as Webster's father once was. Stone has made a pact with the Devil to trade his soul for prosperity (sound familiar—it should), and called upon Webster to save him from going down to Hell. Historians may joke that Webster would never have argued against the sanctity of contract, but here, to a jury drawn from Hell itself by the Devil, Webster pleads Stone's—and our—cause: "He talked of the early days of America and the men who had made those days. It wasn't a spread-eagle speech, but he made you see it. He admitted all the wrong that had ever been done. But he showed how, out of the wrong and the right, the suffering and the starvations, something new had come. And everybody had played a part in it."

I would have liked to close this chapter on an upbeat note. But I too dismay for the future of academic history. According to data from the American Historical Association statement on the "History BA since the Great Recession: The 2018 Majors Report," history majors numbers have suffered the most precipitous decline, some 34 percent, of all undergrad majors since 2008. The authors of the survey hint that the drop is related to the 2008 crash and the shift in interest from humane studies like history to science, technology, engineering, and math (STEM). If, as some university administrators insist, the student is a consumer and the product is a degree that will bring employment, the decline does make sense. Student perceptions of job-related degrees surely play a part in the choice of major, despite the fact that history majors get jobs in all sectors of the economy. Hidden in the data is another more alarming possibility. If we are riven with guilt and doubt about the value of history and the virtues of our past, and communicate the guilt and doubt to our students in hundreds of ways, we lose the prospect of teaching them how to save the world. We tell them that they are the evil beneficiaries of the sins of previous generations; and that the ill effects of these sins are not only still with us, but will be with us for the foreseeable future. Students then are either victims or vicarious beneficiaries of persecution, and neither of those fates are attractive. Perhaps the steep decline in our history majors is our own fault, and corresponds as much to the rise of self-doubt and self-guilt in the history profession as to the economic dip of 2008? It is something to think about.

Epilogue

Where Zombies Go to Rest

Do Zombies need rest? If they do, where can Zombies rest in safety? Or are they fated to wander endlessly through our histories, occasionally bursting into view, hoping to replace the living? The answer is yes, tired Zombies can find refuge among neologisms, lopsided history texts, College Board Educational Testing Service's AP exams, and online social media and blog sites.

Neologisms

Technically speaking, a neologism is a newly coined word, term, or expression. If one is the first person to coin a new term and it catches on, one's fame is assured—or so the academic folk wisdom reports. Actually, the term "neologism" came into common usage because of the fame of those who coined the term, not the reverse. For example, the early nineteenth-century novelist and essayist Washington Irving invented one Diedrich Knickerbocker to tell the history of the Dutch settlement of what became New York, and Knickerbocker became synonymous with the city folk of a certain ancestry and social standing. (Knickers were a type of baggy pants and knickerbockers were the people who wore them.) The book was a satire of many things, including the old New York Dutch. The term not only caught on, it became a part of the city's culture.

Diedrich Knickerbocker was not a Zombie. He was a caricature that all Irving's intelligent readers recognized. A neologism becomes a history Zombie when it overstates, predetermines, or source-mines to gain an author credit for novelty where there is, in fact, none. The neologism Zombie appears almost cuddly compared to some of its more destructive relatives, but it is still fake and it makes history into fakery. Neologisms like the "tipping point" (aka when a major shift occurs in events), the "hinge factor" (aka chance and contingency), "American exceptionalism" (American political institutions and ideas are unique and made the US the first new nation), and "intersectionality" are all examples of quirky reasoning and questionable veracity. The tipping point is an example of hindsight. One looks back at the past and decides, based on considerations other than a rule or definition for tipping points, where the tip occurred. The old version of the "hinge factor" is "for want of a horse's shoe the battle was lost." What about all the other horses, not to mention their riders, weapons, leadership, the terrain, and so on? They are examples of the fallacy of the lone fact. The author simply picks one shoe and one horse. A more modern version is chaos theory, in which the wind currents created by a butterfly's wings change the world (the "butterfly effect"). Overgeneralization, in which the author picks and chooses those facts the author wants to assemble into a grand theory, is equally fallacious. American exceptionalism fits this characterization. In it, the author already knows what she or he wants to prove, and looks for friends in the past to prove it. Intersectionality is the neologism for the coming together of sexual, racial, and class oppression. There is no doubt that all three sometimes converge. Those who employ the term argue, however, that the three are always present, the fallacy of overdeterminism.

These are not Zombies per se, but they often accompany bunkum—statements that are simply jibberish. Made assertively, repeated by the author and by reviewers, received into the blogosphere, retweeted thousands of times, these neologisms gain the authority of deep truth. Because the neologism by its very nature is almost impossible to refute and because we celebrate novelty, the neologism that falsifies history easily transforms into a history Zombie the way that Saruman manufactured Uruk-hai in *The Two Towers*, the second book of *The Lord of the Rings*. Fame and power (or at least tenure and promotion) await the successful coiner. But complex events resist encapsulation in neologisms, and so should we.

Textbooks

The best textbook authors are college history teachers. But the marketing of textbooks (publishers have to make a living from them after all) invites

Zombies to find homes in the textbook. To ensure that the book is widely adopted, the authors' draft is sent to two dozen or so outside readers, who are (in the estimation of the publisher) potential adopters. A few teach at Research 1 universities, but the majority teach at branch campuses, junior colleges, and other schools that require a textbook. Some of these schools even impose a single book or a short list of books on the teaching staff. The outside readers are paid to read and comment on two or three of the draft chapters. What they want is a book that fits the level of their students and includes material in their courses' syllabus. The result is going to be a hodgepodge of topics.

From these outside readers' reports, rather than from the authors' own sense of the book, the publisher imposes its stamp on the project. Publishers frame textbooks to fit a variety of markets, depending on the strength or weakness of the intended audience. Some textbooks aim at the Research 1 university student. Others are intended for the less well prepared student in junior colleges. Some have a regional or a subject matter emphasis. There are social history and political history oriented books. All of this influences what can and what cannot go in the book. During one session with a developmental editor, the author of the present volume was told, "this book is not going to have a yurt." Meaning that the animal-skin-covered shelter that hunter gatherers carried with them would not be described or even mentioned in the volume. When it was done, the book would have the largest potential for adoption—hence for profit for the publisher—because it would have something for everyone (except housing for hunter gatherers). The result of these impositions from without and within the press on the textbook authors turned the book into a dumbed-down Zombie.

Despite the way in which the market constrained the authors, the first edition of a textbook often has a vision for itself, setting it off from all its competitors. The problem that ensues for even the most innovative of textbooks is that the publisher and the authors only earn when students buy new copies. When students begin to purchase used copies, the press and the authors no longer earn anything. (Only the bookstore and the warehouse profit from used or rented books.) So the textbook must be revised and a second edition issued, usually within three to four years of the previous edition. The result is a formless market-driven Zombie. That Zombie eats volumes that cannot or will not follow the dictates of the market. Some of the very best of textbooks were killed by this Zombie. For example Merritt Roe Smith, Daniel Kevles, Pauline Maier, and Alexander Keyssar, a group of MIT historians, produced *Inventing America* for W. W. Norton in 2002, a superb and original take on American history, but after a second edition, the book could not be had. It was devoured by the market Zombie.

In the meantime, the old rule that limits the size of textbooks remains in place. It requires that if anything is added, something of equal length must be omitted. Some issues cannot be adequately covered if their context cannot be expanded. This is particularly true of American history textbooks, for new material must be added to at the end of each new edition to keep it current. Thus the treatment of older events and issues must be elided or omitted. As newer scholarship on later issues grows, the textbook authors are caught between the rock of limited length and the hard place to bring the book up to date, and the book transmogrifies into the everything-is-as-important-as-everything-else Zombie.

The most recent iteration of textbook Zombieism is crowdsourcing. These books, online and free for the student to download, are written by squads of unpaid graduate students. Little control over plagiarism and less over content verification mark their pages. Their noble purpose, to reduce the cost of education for students already burdened by loan interest, fees, and tuition, is undercut by their debased value. In effect, courses that rely on these books are being taught by students themselves. They have, in effect, "flipped" the textbook. Rarely do these offerings have anything new or vital to say, and often they are simply one fact after another, in similar fashion to the old high school history "review books." The crowd-sourced textbook marks the triumph of the worth-nothing Zombie. In short, you get what you pay for in them.

Finally, in some state systems, the choice of a textbook is not the classroom teachers', but a state board of education's. Noteworthy in this respect are high school history textbooks. The members of these elected boards dominate the review and adoption of textbooks, and the books they approve cannot have any disparaging remarks about the history of the state. Thus one leading high school textbook was unacceptable because it mentioned that there were prostitutes in some of the nineteenth-century Texas cowboy towns. The result is textbooks that are "everything-is-awesome" Zombies, walking through the past whistling happy tunes.

I am not the first reader and user of textbooks to spot Zombies. James Loewen's provocative *Lies My Teacher Told Me: Everything Your American History Textbook Got Wrong* (rev. eds. 1997, 2007, 2018) is a no-holds barred assault on high school history textbooks. Loewen's editions have sold thousands of copies according to the author. Loewen has prudently declined to be the "arbiter" of what is right (unlike the author of the present book) and refuses to expand his book to "cover every distortion in error in history as traditionally taught." A closer look, however, reveals that this killer of Zombies is one of their own. From too close and too long contact with Zombies, he has become infected.

His basic premise is a Zombie. He asserts that "history is the least-liked subject in American high schools." If my experience is any guide (teaching American history since 1967), Americans love history. Students tell me that history is their favorite subject, perhaps just polishing the apple, but I believe them. His sample for this enormous generalization was the comments of readers of the first edition of his book. Now why would these respondents join him in condemning "false history"? Maybe because they already agreed with his screed?

After an introduction to the second edition celebrating his best-seller status, he gets down to the nitty-gritty. He argues that textbooks are written to please as many potential adopters of the textbook as possible. This is true of the standard textbook composition and adoption process. The author of the present volume knows this from (painful) personal experience with more than one textbook publisher. Loewen contends that the process leads to bland, fact-driven accounts, often with the effect of "making students stupid." This is an overstatement for effect, as he surely knows (I hope).

Loewen has never written a major textbook, but finally reveals where he is coming from: "As a sociologist . . ." He does not teach history, and his only formal foray into the field was *Mississippi: Conflicts and Change* (1974), a coedited volume. In his *Lies* he misstated the title as *Conflict and Change*, and suggests that it was an original volume rather than an anthology. He reported that it so enraged the white members of the state school board that they banned it from their classrooms. (He has no source for this, but let's believe him.) He related that the two black members of the state school board wanted it adopted. (Again no source, but we get the idea.) His point was not that history had to be nuanced or that historical writing had to be historical minded (seeing the world as the people in your story see it). It had to trash everyone else's work. *Lies* is a Zombie, portraying itself as fact.

Howard Zinn blurbed the first edition of Loewen's *Lies My Teacher Taught Me*: "Every teacher, every student of history, every citizen should read this book." Zinn, a political scientist whose radical revisions of the American history textbook so affrighted conservatives that they demanded no teacher use his work in class, was the Zombie killer extraordinaire. Zinn wrote that history is a weapon against tyranny and injustice. It can be. But what if the Zombie slayer is seduced by that ideal, and decides to use his or her history to slay unpleasant facts in the cause of higher purpose? Or to erase history to remove evildoers from our record? Or to emphasize or twist facts to fit a theory of social justice, economic oppression, or some other higher truth (in his or her mind)? All of which Zinn did with gusto.

Zinn's *A People's History of the United States* (first published in 1980) found nothing much to like in American history. From the first, everyone wanted to despoil everyone else. (A sort of Hobbesian world, I assume.) "Show me the gold" Columbus supposedly asked the first natives he met. Zinn decided that the cure for overzealous celebration of American history was the opposite medicine. One example is pretty much typical. Zinn's chapter on "Drawing the Color Line," began "there is not a country in world history in which racism has been more important, for so long a time, as the United States." This is a chapter on the introduction of slavery into the first English colonies. So why begin it with a generalization about a country that would not exist for the next 165 years and is not in fact discussed in the chapter? Shock value—the weapon of the Zombie. Note that the sentence blames but does not explain. For the color line was invented not by anyone in the United States, but long before 1776 by Portuguese and Spanish slave traders. It was brought to North America by Europeans, seeking to justify their trade in human flesh. It was just not racism, but greed, that drove these distinctions, for the slave trade and slave labor was highly profitable to those skilled in its management. Racism was useful as a justification. That some (not all) white Americans continued to believe that color was a justification for oppression was not a product of nation building or a product of the events creating the nation. It was instead a lasting and continuing feature of European capitalism's relentless self-centeredness. Nor in modern times did the United States have a monopoly on racial discrimination. Anyone familiar with the history of Japan and Germany knows that attitudes in those countries toward supposed racial inferiors infused their empire building and their genocidal acts. In his eagerness to lay blame and cause shame, Zinn did not bother with real people. He preferred the everyone-is-rotten Zombie. Thus another slayer fell victim to the very malady he set out to remedy.

The Advanced Placement Test

When one turns to the Advanced Placement Test in American History, one finds Zombies galore. In line with shifts in college teaching of history toward a more diverse, bottom-up view of the lives of ordinary people, and the mixed multitudes of Americans, the AP advisory committee laid out the overall design of the test in 2013.

> The AP U.S. History course focuses on the development of histori-
> cal thinking skills (chronological reasoning, comparing and contex-
> tualizing, crafting historical arguments using historical evidence,
> and interpreting and synthesizing historical narrative) and an un-
> derstanding of content learning objectives organized around seven
> themes, such as identity, peopling, and America in the world. In line
> with college and university U.S. history survey courses' increased
> focus on early and recent American history and decreased emphasis
> on other areas, the AP U.S. History course expands on the history
> of the Americas from 1491 to 1607 and from 1980 to the present. It
> also allows teachers flexibility across nine different periods of U.S.
> history to teach topics of their choice in depth.

In 2014, the Republican National Committee, whose expertise in American history is certainly not the first characteristic of that body that comes to mind, weighed in on earlier versions of the exam. The old exams appeared to them to offer a "radically revisionist view of American his-tory that emphasizes negative aspects of our nation's history while omit-ting or minimizing positive aspects." The criticisms were the same as those Lynne Cheney and other critics raised in 1995, when the National History Standards were released: not enough great men; not enough military suc-cess; not enough praise for veterans; too much class, gender, and race. A supporting letter from the conservative think tank American Principles in Action spelled out similar concerns: "Instead of striving to build a 'City upon a Hill,' as generations of students have been taught, the colonists are portrayed as bigots who developed 'a rigid racial hierarchy' that was in turn derived from 'a strong belief in British racial and cultural superiority.' . . . The new Framework continues its theme of oppression and conflict by re-interpreting Manifest Destiny from a belief that America had a mission to spread democracy and new technologies across the continent to something that 'was built on a belief in white racial superiority and a sense of Ameri-can cultural superiority.'"

The Educational Testing Service (ETS) responded that it would not compromise the integrity of the exam in the face of partisan ideological pressure. Then it did just that, claiming to make the exam "more balanced."

What's New in the 2015 Edition of the AP U.S. History Course and Exam Description?

Every section in the new framework has been reviewed and improved. The following areas received the greatest public comment, and reflect the most significant changes:

American national identity and unity

American ideals of liberty, citizenship, and self-governance, and how those ideals play out in U.S. history

American founding political leaders, including George Washington, Thomas Jefferson, John Adams, James Madison, Alexander Hamilton, and Benjamin Franklin

Founding Documents—including the Declaration of Independence, the Constitution, and the Federalist Papers—as reflected in a new recommended focus section

Productive role of free enterprise, entrepreneurship, and innovation in shaping U.S. history

U.S. role in the victories of WWI and WWII, particularly the contributions and sacrifices of American servicemen and women in those wars

U.S. leadership in ending the Cold War.

The newer version looked as if the American Enterprise Institute and the Republican National Committee had collaborated with Newt Gingrich to prepare the talking points. Now if one is wondering how this nearly complete revision of the AP test occurred, don't expect the College Board to tell it like it is. Revised, yes. Improved, well, not so fast. Yes, they explained the changes, but they never mentioned the well-orchestrated conservative upsurge of criticism, or the threat by a number of conservative-dominated state school boards, like Texas, to stop offering AP American History courses (which would have gutted the finances of the ETS). Instead, behold the Zombie:

Q: Why did the College Board redesign AP U.S. History?
AP U.S. History teachers were the major motivating factor in the course redesign process that the College Board began in 2006. Many AP teachers expressed frustration that the previous course did not provide sufficient time to immerse students in the major ideas,

events, people, and documents of U.S. history, and that they were instead required to race through topics. The redesign was aimed at addressing this concern, resulting in a course framework that teachers and students began using in fall 2014.

Q: Why was the AP U.S. History exam updated in 2015?
The 2014 edition of the AP U.S. History Course and Exam Description (CED) sparked significant public conversations among students, educators, historians, policymakers, and others about the teaching of U.S. history. The College Board gathered feedback over the past year—including a public review period—and on July 30, 2015, released a new edition of the CED that includes improvements to the language and structure of the course.

The changes from 2014 to 2015 were not an "update." The material added was actually older than the material it replaced. The change was a reversion, not a revision, in form and spirit. Despite the ETS report that feedback came from a wide variety of sources, some sources (school boards) were more influential than other sources (the teachers). In fact, the majority of AP teachers did not call for any revision. The three AP teachers that the ETS website quoted came from Georgia, Oklahoma, and Texas, all states in which a conservative school board demanded changes in the 2014 version of the test. How can a highly professional institution like the ETS and the College Board, representing not school boards or any political group, cave in so thoroughly? How can the AP teachers and the historians who made up the test accede to such clearly misleading explanations? Funding, or the threat of the withdrawal of same, is the answer. In this case, the ETS turned into a hive of Zombies.

Online Zombies

Everyone familiar with Zombies knows that they shamble, a slow-walk, rolling pace that allows all but the most terrified potential victims to flee. What happens when some Zombies learn to move at the speed of light—literally? Students, teachers, and anyone else interested in history topics now routinely turn on the laptop and begin a web-based search for online sources. The online history Zombie is the most dangerous of all the breed, for it lurks in everyone's computer and can spread false information with every click of the keyboard.

Not every webbit (a bit of information on the web) is a wascally webbit, to borrow Elmer Fudd's characterization of Bugs Bunny. But how are we to tell which webbits to chase and which to ignore? We cannot shoot at them all. The browsers or search engines may be Google, Yahoo, or some other managed provider, and the major sources like YouTube are themselves collections of sources. Wikipedia and various other wikis are created by crowdsourcing—individuals or groups posting on the website. Wikipedia entries have some pedigree because much of the references to early history come from various out-of-copyright encyclopedias (the *Encyclopedia Britannica* is a favorite). Other sites may not be so trustworthy. Beware. The Were-webbit may be easy to spot (he's ten feet tall and lives in the world of Wallace and Gromit); the online Zombie webbit is much harder to find.

The Stanford History Education Group has a reliable website tutorial for students and teachers on how to tell online fake history from reliable information. The three golden rules are "Who's behind the information," "What is the evidence for it (cited or quoted in the online source)," and "What do other sources (online and archival or published) say?" Just as a journalist looking to confirm a story does not rely on one informant, so no one should rely on one online site.

When the sites we find are not only biased in some way, but simply wrong or intentionally lying, the Stanford rules are fairly easy to apply. Those sites are Zombies. They pretend or promote themselves as reliable gateways to sound facts. Instead, they are twisted or invented versions of events, biographies, and other historical materials. After a year and half of field testing with students and teachers, the Stanford History Education tion Group developed a checklist to verify the trustworthiness of sites that presented themselves in online searches. Key discriminators are, Does the site have advertising? Can one distinguish between ads and news items or information? Are pieces of evidence, for example photos or quotations, relevant, in context, and probative (having direct relation to cause or effect)? Is the website a form of social media? If so, is the post reproducible—that is, can one find evidence for it in non-social-media sites? Above all, does the online post make sense?

Entirely fake websites are another matter. Studies at MIT and elsewhere have shown that totally fake posts on social media still convince nearly 20 percent of those who read them. Just ask the Russian hackers who flood social media with fake information on fake sites during the 2016 presidential campaign. Even when the post is at variance with the readers' political or social ideas, seeing becomes believing. This is particularly true of websites like Twitter and Facebook, where gaining followers or friends may outweigh the reposter's common sense. Thus outrageously untrue information may be more likely to be reposted simply to gain popularity.

Some of the sources cited in online websites may be nonexistent. Some of the organizations supposedly generating the information may exist, but only online. This is particularly true of news sites that are little more than blogs. Some of these blogs are legit, but many are not trustworthy. One way to test for Zombies is to find out who is on the board or other managing directorate of the blog. In a digital world, one must be especially vigilant for Zombies, because they are so easily mistaken for the real thing.

The most frightening of all the history Zombies is the one who wants us to forget. Not just forget about Zombies, but forget about our history. No reparations. No apologies. Nothing to be ashamed of. Nothing but praise and celebration. This willful amnesia about the unpleasantness in past events is deliberate. It is an invitation to ignore the past because the past offers some very dire lessons. This Zombie does not trust any of the other Zombies to do the job. Any knowledge of the past must be scrubbed from public arenas, classrooms, and political memory. This Zombie simply does not want us to know any history, because knowing itself is dangerous.

Zombie history will not triumph in the end. In the penultimate scene of *The Two Towers*, the middle film of Peter Jackson's *Lord of the Rings* trilogy, Aragon says to a young soldier on the eve of battle, "there is always hope." The teaching of history, the reading of history, and the doing of history all have a sticky quality. They have been with us since the dawn of recorded history—in fact, we only know about that dawn because people thought its story was important to remember. We are history and have always been history, and in that fact there is always hope that history teaching and learning will, one day, resume a central place in our self-education.

Bibliographical Essay

The following brief bibliographical essay lists references for the chapters. Page numbers following sources refer to quotations in the text. Some of the sources are grouped in miniature essays, an alternative style to endnotes that I have used elsewhere. A note to historians who may find themselves mentioned in this book: just as my comments in the text may be controversial, so the entries here are entirely my judgment calls. Not everyone (again, perhaps not anyone) will agree with all of them. Historians disagree all the time, and that is not untoward. If it may seem that I have sometimes crossed the line of professional civility, mea culpa. Constructive disagreement makes all of us better scholars.

Preface

Eric Foner, *Who Owns History? Rethinking the Past in a Changing World* (New York: Hill and Wang, 2003), 4; media flubs: Naomi Wolfe on "death recorded" in nineteenth-century criminal sentences (not!) and Cokie Roberts on abortion services advertisements absent from nineteenth-century newspapers (duh—look for code words like "unlock menses"), see Karin Wulf, "Made by History—Perspective: What Naomi Wolf and Cokie Roberts Teach Us about the Need for Historians," *Washington Post*, June 11, 2019; Hannah Arendt, *Between Past and Present: Eight Exercises in Political Thought* (rev. ed., New York: Penguin, 2006), 228, 246. For cases of misconduct among academic historians in academe, see Peter Charles Hoffer, *Past Imperfect* (2nd ed., New York: PublicAffairs, 2008), and Ralph E. Luker, "Clio's Malpractice, or, What's a Fallen Girl to Do?," History News Network, https://historynewsnetwork.org/article/1696.

Introduction

William Henry Seward, speech at Rochester Republican Party gathering, October 25, 1858, http://www.nyhistory.com/central/conflict.htm; T. R. R. Cobb speech to the Georgia Secession Convention, November 12, 1860, georgiainfo.galileo.usg.edu/thisday/cwhistory/11/12/t.r.r.-cobb-speech-supporting-secession; Andrew Dixon White's presidential address appears on the American Historical Association website, at www.historians.org/about-aha-and-membership/aha-history-and-archives/presidential-addresses/andrew-dickson-white-(1884). Jefferson Davis, *Short History of the Confederate States of America* (New York, 1890), 1.

The account of the textbooks here begins with Frances Fitzgerald, *America Revised: History Schoolbooks in the Twentieth Century* (New York: Random House, 1979). Quotes in text from David Saville Muzzey, *An American History* (Boston: Ginn, 1911), 15, 18, 19; Woodrow Wilson, *A History of the American People* (New York: Harper & Brothers, 1918), 1:22, 25, 28; 5:18, 19; James Axtell, "Europeans, Indians, and the Age of Discovery in American History Textbooks," *American Historical Review* 92 (1987): 622, 624; and Patricia Limerick, "The Case of the Premature Departure: The Trans-Mississippi West in American History Textbooks," *Journal of American History* 72 (1992): 1382. See also James M. Loewen, *Lies My Teacher Told Me* (New York: Simon and Schuster, 2007).

Deborah Lipstadt's tale can be found in her own *Denying the Holocaust: The Growing Assault on Truth and Memory* (New York: Free Press, 1993) and *History on Trial: My Day in Court with David Irving* (New York: Harper Collins, 2005).

A woeful tale of social media assault: Kat Rosenfelt, "The Toxic Drama on YA Twitter," cited in Jesse Singal, "How a Twitter Mob Derailed an Immigrant Female Author's Budding Career," www.tabletmag.com/jewish-news-and-politics/279806/how-a-twitter-mob-destroyed-a-young-immigrant-female-authors-budding-career.

Chapter One

Opening quotations from Jonathan C. H. King, *First Peoples, First Contacts: Native Peoples of North America* (Cambridge: Harvard University Press, 1999), 10, and Colin Calloway, *First Peoples: A Documentary Survey of Native American History* (New York: Macmillan, 2008), 3.

The first accounts of native history were kept orally by the First Peoples themselves. They were long after written down by Spanish missionaries in Mexico and the Southwest, European travelers like Thomas Harriot and John White at Roanoke in the sixteenth century, Jesuit and Recollet missionaries in Canada in the seventeenth century, and Moravian missionaries in Pennsylvania and Ohio in the eighteenth and early nineteenth centuries. In the later nineteenth century, New Yorkers Henry Schoolcraft and Henry Morgan undertook studies of Indian customs. The focus of the first accounts was native religion and family life. They were sympathetic. Not so, Francis Parkman, *The Jesuits in North America* (1868), reprinted in Samuel Eliot Morison, ed., *The Parkman Reader* (Boston: Little, Brown 1955), 52, nor Theodore Roosevelt, *Winning of the West* (New York: Putnam, 1881), 1:1, 5, 8. For the kinder, gentler modern version, see David McCullough, *The Pioneers: The Heroic Story of the Settlers Who Brought the American Ideal West* (New York: Simon and Schuster, 2019), 8, 13, 230.

The recovery of Indian history, a people no longer considered mindless savages, victims, or history's losers, but adaptable and able, came, I think most notably, in the work of Gary Nash, *Red, White, and Black* (Boston: Prentice Hall, 1974), the first textbook of early America that gave equal space to the Indians. James Merrill, in *The Indians' New World* (Chapel Hill: University of North Carolina Press, 1989) and *Into the American Woods* (New York: Norton, 1999), reentered the space between the two worlds of European and native with sensitivity and literary flair. James Axtell's *The Invasion Within* (New York: Oxford University Press, 1985), the first of a series on native peoples, was a detailed Indian ethnohistory using French, English, and Indian evidence on how the Indians tried to persuade (or pressure) Europeans to accept an Indian point of view.

Perhaps the most vivid of the defenders of the Indian point of view was Francis Jennings, starting with his *The Invasion of America* (Chapel Hill: University of North Carolina Press, 1975). Jennings was one of the first ethnographers working at the Newberry Library. His works introduced the idea of Indian agency—that Indians had found creative ways to respond to the encounter. On John Wesley Powell and Tu Pu, see Wayne Journell, "An Incomplete History: Representation of American Indians in State Social Studies Standards," *Journal of American Indian Education* 48 (2009): 18–19.

On the origin of the Red Man, see Wesley Frank Craven, *White, Red, and Black: The First Virginians* (Charlottesville: University of Virginia Press, 1971), 38; Nancy Shoemaker, "How Indians Got to Be Red," *American Historical Review* 102 (1997), quotes on 627–28; on the English view of Indian bodies, see Karen Ordahl Kupperman, *Indians and English: Facing*

Off in Early America (Ithaca, NY: Cornell University Press, 2000), 63; on eighteenth-century colors and animosities, see Peter Silver, *Our Savage Neighbors: How Indian War Transformed Early America* (New York: Norton, 2007), xx; and Daniel Richter, *Facing East from Indian Country* (Cambridge: Harvard University Press, 2001), 181–85.

The pejorative connotation of Red Man remains the savage. See C. Richard King, *Redskins: Insult and Brand* (Lincoln: University of Nebraska Press, 2016). For the cancellation of the Redskins trademark, see *Amanda Blackhorse, Marcus Briggs-Cloud, Philip Gover, Jillian Pappan, and Courtney Tsotigh v. Pro-Football, Inc.* _____ Cancellation No. 92046185 (2014), http:// ttabvue.uspto.gov/ttabvue/v?pno=92046185&pty=CAN&eno=199. For an account of the 2019 AHA panel on Elizabeth Warren's contested indigenous identity, see Elizabeth Poorman, "White Lies: Indigenous Scholars Respond to Elizabeth Warren's Claims to Native Ancestry," *Perspectives on History* 57 (2019): 9–11. On decolonization, see "What Is Decolonization?," https://abbemuseum.wordpress.com/about-us/decolonization/.

Columbus has the misfortune of spawning two Zombies, who spend much of their time trying to slay one another. The first is the Columbus of Samuel Eliot Morison's Pulitzer Prize–winning two-volume biography, *Admiral of the Ocean Sea* (Boston: Little, Brown, 1942). Morison was a sailor as well as a Harvard college professor and he retraced Columbus's voyages. His Columbus is not without fault, but he is hardly the Columbus of environmental historian Alfred W. Crosby's "ecological imperialism." Crosby's Columbus brings with him rats, cockroaches, measles, mumps, chicken pox, smallpox, pigs, and just about every other plague that decimated Indian crops and reduced Indian population by millions. "Thus, within a few score years of Columbus's first American landfall, the Antillean aborigines had been almost completely annihilated." Crosby, *The Columbian Exchange: Biological and Cultural Consequences of 1492* (New York: Praeger, 2003), 75. The Knights of Columbus weigh in on the man and his religious views in Alton Pelowski, "Why Columbus Sailed," Knights of Columbus Columbia online, an interview with anthropologist Carol Delaney, at http://www.kofc.org/en/columbia/detail/2012_06_columbus_interview.html. A few hardy souls have tried to dispose of the twin Columbus Zombies. As Carla Rahn Phillips and William D. Phillips wrote in the introduction to *The Worlds of Christopher Columbus*, "it was the magnitude of the processes he unleashed," that is, the consequences of his voyages, that are the essence of his significance. Phillips and Phillips, *The Worlds of Christopher Columbus* (New York: Cambridge University Press, 1992), 4.

For the technology Zombie, see, for example, David Landes, *The Wealth and Poverty of Nations* (New York: Norton, 1998), 62–63, and William E. Burns, *Science and Technology in Colonial America* (Westport, CT: Greenwood, 2005), xv. An alternative idea is that of adaptation. Native Americans adapted the products of European metallurgy, for example, to modify older weapon types, with the result that Indian weapons were more durable. See, e.g., Colin F. Taylor, *Native American Weapons* (Norman: University of Oklahoma Press, 2005), 9. When a technology was useful, for example, hunting on horseback and raiding on the plains, Indians not only adopted it, they mastered it. See, e.g., Peter Mitchell, *Horse Nations: The Worldwide Impact on the Horse on Indigenous Societies, Post-1492* (Oxford: Oxford University Press, 2015), 110.

On Puritans, the best survey in my opinion is Michael P. Winship, *Hot Protestants: A History of Puritanism in England and America* (New Haven: Yale University Press, 2019), quotations in text from 80, 168–69. On religious liberty: David Beale, *The Mayflower Puritans* (Greenville, SC: Ambassador-Emerald, 2000), 137; John M. Barry, *Roger Williams and the American Soul: Church, State, and the Birth of Liberty* (New York: Penguin, 2012), quotes from Parrington and Morgan on 390–91; on theocracy, see Thomas Jefferson Wertenbaker, *The First Americans* (New York: Macmillan, 1927), 97–99; Sidney E. Mead, *The Lively Experiment: The Shaping of Christianity in America* (New York: Harper and Row, 1963), 24; Darren Staloff, *The Making of an American Thinking Class: Intellectuals and Intelligentsia in Puritan Massachusetts* (New York: Oxford University Press, 1997), 196. Note, perhaps, that Wertenbaker was a Virginia historian who had little good to say about New England (and regarded theocracy as tyranny), and that Mead wanted to show the rise of religious toleration in America, and needed theocracy as the wicked starting point for the journey toward liberty.

Rick Santorum's speech quoted in Scott Jaschik, "Santorum's Attack on Higher Ed," February 27, 2012, Inside Higher Ed, www.insidehighered.com/news/2012/02/27/santorums-views-higher-education-and-satan; on the many explanations for the Salem witchcraft crisis, see, e.g., Peter Charles Hoffer, *The Devil's Disciples: Makers of the Salem Witchcraft Crisis* (Baltimore: Johns Hopkins University Press, 1996), and Mary Beth Norton, *In the Devil's Snare: The Salem Witchcraft Crisis* (New York: Knopf, 2003). There are over one hundred other books in scholarly, trade, young adult, and fiction lists on the subject, and more appear each year. This does not include copies of Arthur Miller's dramatization, *The Crucible*, and books about it.

For examples of prosecutions of devil worshippers, see, e.g., Lawrence Wright, *Remembering Satan: A Tragic Case of Recovered Memory* (New York: Random House, 1994), 74–75 (cases of devil worship).

Chapter Two

Michael Kammen, *A Season of Youth: The American Revolution and the Historical Imagination* (Ithaca, NY: Cornell University Press, 1978), 121, warns of our desire to reshape the past to fit present needs.

For skulking Zombies: see Francis Parkman, *The Conspiracy of Pontiac* (New York: Collier, [1851] 1961), 382, 131, and Daniel Boorstin, *The Americans: The Colonial Experience* (New York: Random House, 1958), 359, 355.

On America as the asylum: "A Defense of the African Slave Trade, 1740," *London Magazine* 9 (1740): 493–94; Christopher Tomlins, *Freedom Bound: Law, Labor, and Civic Identity in Colonizing English America, 1558–1865* (New York: Cambridge University Press, 2010), 218 ("low end of the social order" emigrated), and Gary B. Nash, *The Urban Crucible: Social Change, Political Consciousness, and the Origins of the American Revolution* (Cambridge: Harvard University Press, 1979), 8–10 (working conditions). Quotations from Marilyn C. Baseler, *"Asylum for Mankind": America, 1607–1800* (Ithaca, NY: Cornell University Press, 1998), 54; Alan Taylor, *American Colonies: The Settling of North America* (New York: Penguin, 2001), 303; Eric Nelson, *The Royalist Revolution* (Cambridge: Harvard University Press, 2014), 111, and Tom Paine, *Common Sense* (1776), edited by Isaac Kramnick (New York: Penguin), 43. On the arguments that Thomas Jefferson, John Dickinson, and John Adams made for the American origins of liberty, see Peter Charles Hoffer and Williamjames Hull Hoffer, *The Clamor of Lawyers: The American Revoluton and Crisis in the Legal Profession* (Ithaca, NY: Cornell University Press, 2018), 96–113. For Roger Ekirch, see "Asylum Once Defined America, Now, It Seems Imperiled," *Guardian* online, September 3, 2017, www.theguardian.com/commentisfree/2017/sep/03/asylum-america-founding-fathers.

The frontier Zombie lurks in the pages of Frederick Jackson Turner, "The Hunter Type" (1890), essay reprinted in Wilbur R. Jacobs, ed., *Frederick Jackson Turner's Unpublished Essays: America's Great Frontiers and Sections* (Lincoln: University of Nebraska Press, 1965), 153. For further elaboration, see Turner, "The Significance of the Frontier in American History" (1893), in Turner, *The Frontier in American History* (New York: Holt, 1921),

4. About Turner: Ray Allen Billington, *Frederick Jackson Turner: Historian, Scholar, Teacher* (New York: Oxford University Press, 1973), 109–10 (on immigrants), 436–37 (anti-Semitism). For the idea of borderlands, see Jeremy Adelman and Stephen Aron, "From Borderlands to Borders: Empires, Nation-States, and the Peoples in Between in North American History," *American Historical Review* 104 (1999): 815–41.

George III's personal papers are now available online, at Royal Collection Trust website, www.rct.uk/collection/georgian-papers-programme/papers-of-george-iii. The "wicked history" of King George III is Philip Brooks, *King George III: America's Enemy* (New York: Scholastic Books, 2009), quote on 12. On Grenville, see Philip Lawson, "George Grenville and America: The Years of Opposition, 1765-1770," *William and Mary Quarterly*, 3rd ser., 37 (1980): 567. For more on ministers of state and their kings, see David McCullough, *John Adams* (New York, Simon and Schuster, 2001), 337; George Bancroft, *History of the United States* (Boston: Little, Brown, 1858), 4:386; and Thomas Slaughter, *Independence: The Tangled Roots of the American Revolution* (New York: Hill and Wang, 2014), 126. Note that political scientist Eric Nelson, in *The Royalist Revolution: Monarchy and the American Founding* (Cambridge: Harvard University Press, 2014), 5, offers an alternative theory, which he calls "patriot royalism." In it, supposedly, until the eve of Independence key revolutionary leaders actually clung to loyalty to the crown as the antidote to a wicked Parliament.

On slavery in the American Revolution: Simon Schama, *Rough Crossings: The Slaves, the British, and the American Revolution* (New York: Harper-Collins, 2006), 16; Robert G. Parkinson, *The Common Cause: Creating Race and Nation in the American Revolution* (Chapel Hill: University of North Carolina Press, 2014), 628 (on naturalization); Alan Taylor, *The Internal Enemy: Slavery and War in Virginia, 1772-1832* (New York: Norton, 2013), 18–30; Alan Taylor, *American Revolutions* (New York: Penguin, 2017), 151; Alan Gilbert, *Black Patriots and Loyalists* (Chicago: University of Chicago Press, 2012), 248; Robert Middlekauff, *The Glorious Cause: The American Revolution, 1763–1789* (New York: Oxford University Press, 1982), 357; and Gordon S. Wood, *The Radicalism of the American Revolution* (New York: Knopf, 1991), 186.

The Age of Democratic Revolution Zombie appears in R. R. Palmer, *History of the Modern World* (Princeton: Princeton University Press, 1950), 289, and *The Age of Democratic Revolution: The Challenge* (Princeton: Princeton University Press, 1959), 19. For voting in early states, see Richard Beeman, *The Varieties of Political Experience in Eighteenth-Century America* (Philadelphia: University of Pennsylvania Press, 2004), 276–92; for suppression of free speech during and immediately after the Revolution, see Leonard Levy, *The Emergence of a Free Press* (New York: Knopf, 1985), 173–220. On the shift to the ideal of democracy among American thinkers, see Gordon S. Wood, *The Radicalism of the American Revolution* (New York: Knopf, 1991), 229–304. For the consensus school, see Peter Novick, *That Noble Dream: The "Objectivity Question" and the American Historical Profession* (New York: Cambridge University Press, 1988), 333–35; Sidney Hook, "The Future of Socialism," *Partisan Review* 14 (1947): 36; Louis Hartz, *The Liberal Tradition in America* (New York: Harcourt, Brace, 1955), 74; and Daniel Boorstin, *The Americans: The Colonial Experience* (New York: Random House, 1958), 362. On Boorstin and Hartz, see John Patrick Diggins, "Knowledge and Sorrow: Louis Hartz's Quarrel with American History," *Political Theory* 16 (1988): 370, and Michael Kraus and Davis D. Joyce, *The Writing of American History* (rev. ed., Norman: University of Oklahoma Press, 1990), 321–29.

Populist histories of a radical American Revolution include Gary B. Nash, *The Unknown American Revolution: The Unruly Birth of Democracy and the Struggle to Create America* (New York: Penguin, 2005), 183; T. H. Breen, *American Insurgents, American Patriots: The Revolution of the People* (New York: Hill and Wang, 2010), 19, 25, and after; T. H. Breen, *The Will of the People: The Revolutionary Birth of America* (Cambridge: Harvard University Press, 2019); Alfred F. Young, Gary B. Nash, and Ray Raphael, "Introduction," in *Revolutionary Founders: Rebels, Radicals, and Reformers in the Making of the Nation*, edited by Alfred F. Young, Gary B. Nash, and Ray Raphael (New York: Knopf, 2012), 11–12; and Peter McPhee, "Teaching about the Age of Revolutions," in *Understanding and Teaching the Age of Revolutions*, edited by Ben Marsh and Mike Rapport (Madison: University of Wisconsin Press, 2017), 30.

On slavery at the Constitutional Convention: David Waldstreicher; *Slavery's Constitution; From Revolution to Ratification* (New York: Hill and Wang, 2009), quotations at 91 and 153; Paul Finkelman, *Slavery and the Founders: Race and Liberty in the Age of Jefferson* (3rd ed., New York: Routledge, 2014), 3–45; and Sean Wilentz, *No Property in Man: Slavery and Anti-Slavery at the Nation's Founding* (Cambridge: Harvard University Press, 2018), 59. On slavery and progress, David Brion Davis, *Slavery and Human Progress* (New York: Oxford University Press, 1984), suggests that slavery was not widely condemned until the early nineteenth century.

Chapter Three

For the American national Zombie, see Daniel Boorstin, *The Americans: The National Experience* (New York: Random House, 1967), 1. For the second quotation, see Jonathan Gienapp, *The Second Creation: Fixing the American Constitution in the Founding Era* (Cambridge: Harvard University Press, 2018), 73; for the third quotation, Gordon S. Wood, *The Radicalism of the American Revolution* (New York: Knopf, 1991), 310, 308.

On "free markets": William J. Novak, "Public Economy and the Well-Ordered Market: Law and Economic Regulation in 19th-Century America," *Law and Social Inquiry* 18 (1993): 2; Francis Wayland, *The Elements of Moral Science* (school edition, Boston: Gould and Lincoln, 1860), 115; Charles G. Sellers, *The Market Revolution: Jacksonian America, 1815–1848* (New York: Oxford University Press, 1992), 53–54; and Daniel Walker Howe, *What God Hath Wrought: The Transformation of America, 1815–1848* (New York: Oxford University Press, 2007), 560.

For the rise of sentiment, consult Edward Shorter, *The Making of the Modern Family* (New York: Basic, 1975), and Benjamin Rush, *Thoughts upon Female Education* (Boston: Folsom, 1787), 6, 20–21. On women's history: Arthur Meier Schlesinger, *New Viewpoints in American History* (New York: Macmillan, 1928), 126–27; Gerda Lerner, "Placing Women in History: Definitions and Challenges," *Feminist Studies* 3 (1975): 5–14; Joan Wallach Scott, *Gender and the Politics of History* (New York: Columbia University Press, 1988), 15; and Scott, *The Fantasy of Feminist History* (Durham, NC: Duke University Press, 2011), 5. Nancy Cott attributes the strong version of her separate spheres thesis to the women's consciousness raising efforts at the time she wrote the first edition of the book, in 1972. Cott, *The Bonds of Womanhood: "Women's Sphere" in New England, 1780–1830* (2nd ed., New Haven: Yale University Press, 1997), xi–xiii. On Schlafly and the ERA: Donald T. Critchlow, *Phyllis Schafly and Grassroots Conservatism: A Woman's Crusade* (Princeton: Princeton University Press, 2018), 235–38. The Eagle Forum website features the brochure from which the quotation is drawn, at https://eagleforum.org/about/brochure.html.

For sambo Zombies happily shuffling along, see George Fitzhugh, *Cannibals All, or Slaves Without Masters* (Richmond, VA: A. Morris, 1857), 30, eagerly followed by Mrs. Henry Schoolcraft, *Black Gauntlet* (Philadelphia: Lippincott, 1860), 30. The Civil War and Reconstruction could not kill the sambo Zombie, and it slouched through Samuel Eliot Morison, *Oxford History of the United States* (New York: Oxford University Press, 1928),

2:8; Ulrich Bonnell Phillips, *American Negro Slavery* (New York: Appleton, 1918), 278; and Eugene Genovese, *A Consuming Fire: The Fall of the Confederacy in the Mind of the White Christian South* (Athens: University of Georgia Press, 2009), 4.

It took three generations of historians to begin to slay the sambo Zombie, beginning with Kenneth Stampp, *The Peculiar Institution* (New York: Knopf, 1956), and George Rawick, *From Sunup to Sundown: The Making of the Black Community* (New York: Praeger, 1973), thence to Ira Berlin *Many Thousands Gone: The First Two Centuries of Slavery in North America* (Cambridge: Harvard University Press, 1998), and Philip Morgan, *Slave Counterpoint: Black Culture in the Eighteenth-Century Chesapeake and Low Country* (Chapel Hill: University of North Carolina Press, 1998), and more recently to work by Edward Baptist, Erica Armstrong Dunbar, Ariela Gross, Tera W. Hunter, Walter Johnson, and Deborah Gray White. All of these works shared a willingness to use firsthand slave testimony and an empathy for the slaves' experience.

Rebel Zombie slayers: Patrick H. Breen, *Land Deluged in Blood* (New York: Oxford University Press, 2016), 167 (Nat Turner Rebellion); Daniel Rasmussen, *American Uprising* (New York: Harper, 2011) (German Coast Rebellion); Douglas Egerton, *He Shall Go Out Free* (Madison, WI: Madison House, 1999) 224 (Vesey Rebellion); and James Sidbury, *Ploughshares into Swords* (New York: Cambridge University Press, 1997), 257 (Gabriel's Rebellion). The leaders, followers, and victims of the slave rebellions all had stories to tell us, and, if we can, we should listen.

On the industrial North and the agrarian South: Charles and Mary Beard, influenced by World War I, thought that the Civil War was a struggle between the industrial North and the agricultural South. *History of the United States* (New York: Macmillan, 1921), 129. A modern and far more nuanced version of this economic thesis is Marc Egnal, *Clash of Extremes: The Economic Origins of the Civil War* (New York: Hill and Wang, 2009), 256, arguing that the economic priorities of the two parties made the clash inevitable, particularly the economic interests of the newly formed Republican Party. The "mostly industrial North" still appears in textbooks. See Carol Sheriff, "Virginia's Embattled Textbooks," *Civil War History* 58 (2012): 40.

On abolitionists: Joel Olson, "The Freshness of Fanaticism: The Abolitionist Defense of Zealotry," *Perspectives on Politics* 5 (2007): 685, 686; Leonard L. Richards, *The Slave Power: The Free North and Southern Domination, 1780–1860* (Baton Rouge: Louisiana State University Press, 2000), 140;

Manisha Sinha, *The Slave's Cause: A History of Abolition* (New Haven: Yale University Press, 2016), 219; David Donald, *Charles Sumner and the Coming of the Civil War* (New York: Knopf, 1960), 265 (symptoms), 271 (suspicion of fraud); Stanley Elkins, *Slavery: A Problem in American Institutional and Intellectual Life* (Chicago: University of Chicago Press, 1959), 212; James H. Hutson, "The Origins of the Paranoid Style in American Politics," in *Saints and Revolutionaries: Essays on Early American History*, edited by David D. Hall (New York: Norton, 1984), 371–72. In 1969, Merton L. Dillon chronicled the rise and fall and rise of the abolitionists' reputation in "The Abolitionists, A Decade of Historiography, 1959–1969," *Journal of Southern History* 35 (1969): 500–522. Manisha Sinha, *The Slave's Cause: A History of Abolition* (New Haven: Yale University Press, 2016), describes the historical writing on abolition, giving proper due to the efforts of blacks.

Gordon S. Wood, *The Radicalism of the American Revolution* (New York: Knopf, 1991), 359, is the source of the final quotation in the chapter.

Chapter Four

The corruption of the 1850s is well documented in Mark W. Summers, *The Plundering Generation: Corruption and the Crisis of the Union, 1849–1861* (New York: Oxford University Press, 1988), but Summers did not buy the conclusions in James G. Randall, "The Blundering Generation," *Mississippi Valley Historical Review* 27 (1940): 3–28. Randall blamed the Civil War on the moral blindness of the party leaders. Perhaps Randall was thinking about the US entry into World War I and the blunders of President Woodrow Wilson's prewar diplomacy that made the declaration of war almost inevitable. In this, Randall was not alone. A new generation of historians, schooled in the moral credo of the Four Freedoms of 1940, concluded the exact opposite, however. As Arthur M. Schlesinger Jr. wrote in 1945, the war's cause was "differences growing out of the system of Negro bondage." Schlesinger, "Casting the National Horoscope," *Proceedings of the American Antiquarian Society* 55 (1945): 71; in accord, see James M. McPherson's magisterial *Battle Cry of Freedom: The Civil War Era* (New York: Oxford University Press, 1988), 7: "The greatest danger to American survival at midcentury . . . was sectional conflict between North and South over the future of slavery." Randall's own followers thus faced a dilemma—cling to prewar views or, painfully, reverse themselves. See, e.g., Avery O. Craven, "The 1840s and the Democratic Process," *Journal of Southern History* 16 (1950): 162: "This is not saying, as some have charged, that great moral issues were not involved." Craven was a subscriber, before the war, to Randall's blundering generation theory. After the war, he revised himself, but one can see him struggling to do so in this unlovely double negative.

Ralph Ellison, *Invisible Man: A Novel* (New York: Modern Library, [1952] 1994), 78. The motives of the soldiers themselves are revealed in Bell Wiley, *The Life of Johnny Reb* (Baton Rouge: Louisiana State University Press, 1943) and *The Life of Billy Yank* (Baton Rouge: Louisiana State University Press, 1952), quote from 15; Shelby Foote, *The Civil War*, 3 vols. (New York: Random House, 1983–86); and Bruce Catton, *Army of the Potomac*, 3 vols. (New York: Doubleday, 1953–58), and *The Civil War* (New York: Doubleday, 1960). All of them offer touching stories of the common experiences and motives of soldiers and officers on both sides.

Slavery was not, at first, one of these motives. As Bruce Catton reported of the Union men, "They had little sympathy with the slave as a person" (*The Civil War* [1960], 174). But with time, and with the battlefield contributions of black troops, the "sable arm," race became a more salient issue on both sides. See James McPherson, *For Cause and Comrades: Why Men Fought in the Civil War* (New York: Oxford University Press, 1997), 106–10, 117–30.

On the cost to the slaveholders of the Emancipation, see, e.g., Edward L. Ayers, *In the Presence of Mine Enemies: The Civil War in the Heart of America, 1859–1863* (New York: Norton, 2003), 18.

States' rights: Thomas Jefferson, Kentucky Resolution, draft before October 4, 1798, *Papers of Thomas Jefferson* (Princeton: Princeton University Press, 2003), 30:536; James Madison, Virginia Resolution, December 21, 1798, *Papers of James Madison* (Charlottesville: University of Virginia Press, 1991), 17:187; Alexander Stephens, *A Constitutional View of the Late War between the States* (Philadelphia: National Publishing, 1868) 1:10; "South Carolina Declaration of the Immediate Causes . . ." December 24, 1860, Avalon Project, http://avalon.law.yale.edu/19th_century/csa_scarsec.asp.

On the doctrine of states' rights itself, see Sotirios A. Barber, *The Fallacies of States' Rights* (Cambridge: Harvard University Press, 2013), and, contra, Adam Freedman, *A Less Perfect Union: The Case for States' Rights* (New York: Harper Collins, 2015). A survey of antebellum states' rights thinking is Forrest McDonald, *States' Rights and the Union: Imperium in Imperio, 1787–1860* (Lawrence: University Press of Kansas, 2000). For an example of Reconstruction Era historians' views of states' rights, see, e.g., David B. Scott, *Smaller Schoolbook History of the United States to 1876* (New York: Harper, 1881), 163. The text on the Southern Manifesto above is adapted from Peter Charles Hoffer, *The Search for Justice: Lawyers in the Civil Rights Revolution, 1950–1975* (Chicago: University of Chicago Press, 2019), 102–18.

Lincoln frees the slaves: Richard Striner, *Father Abraham: Lincoln's Relentless Struggle to End Slavery* (New York: Oxford University Press, 2006), 3; Eric Foner, *The Fiery Trial: Abraham Lincoln and American Slavery* (New York: Norton, 2010), 166 (need for border state loyalty); David E. Long, *The Jewel of Liberty: Abraham Lincoln's Re-election and the End of Slavery* (Mechanicsburg, PA: Stackpole, 1994), 262–63 (Lincoln sees 1864 reelection as mandate for emancipation); and James Oakes, *Freedom National: The Destruction of Slavery in the United States, 1861–1865* (New York: Norton, 2013), 95–99 (Butler), 157–59 (Fremont). My own account appears in *Uncivil Warriors: The Lawyers' Civil War* (New York: Oxford University Press, 2018), 125–48.

For more on carpetbaggers and scalawags, see Richard N. Current, *Those Terrible Carpetbaggers* (New York: Oxford University Press, 1988), and James Alex Baggett, *The Scalawags: Southern Dissenters in the Civil War and Reconstruction* (Baton Rouge: Louisiana State University Press, 2004). Quotes on the lost cause are from Edward Pollard, *The Lost Cause* (New York: E.B. Treat, 1866), 727, 729; and Fred Arthur Bailey, "The Textbooks of the 'Lost Cause,'" *Georgia Historical Quarterly* 75 (1991): 508, quotations from the History Committee reports at 512.

The Reconstruction Zombie maker in academic robes quoted above is William A. Dunning, *Reconstruction, Political and Economic, 1865–1877* (New York: Harper, 1907), xv. See also Claude Bowers, *The Tragic Era: Reconstruction after Lincoln* (New York: Literary Guild, 1929), vi, and E. Merton Coulter, *The South during Reconstruction* (Baton Rouge: Louisiana State University Press, 1947), 1.

Although the Dunning school was rejected by a number of historians as early as the 1930s, works signaling the turn of the tide were John Hope Franklin, *Reconstruction after the Civil War* (Chicago: University of Chicago Press, 1961), quotation on 133, and Kenneth M. Stampp's *The Era of Reconstruction, 1865–1877* (New York: Knopf, 1966), quotes on 4, 5. Ironically covering the same period for the New American Nation series as Dunning had in the American Nation series a half century earlier, Stampp summarized revisionist historical scholarship, reexamined the role of the Radical Republicans, and argued that they made positive changes to southern society even as corruption, tax increases, and racism ensured the demise of their efforts. Mark Summers brought all this together in his *The Ordeal of the Reunion: A New History of Reconstruction* (Chapel Hill: University of North Carolina Press, 2014), quotation on 316.

Franklin and Stampp tried to slay the Zombie carpetbagger and scalawag by returning to the words of the freedmen and women. These can be found in Ira Berlin, Barbara J. Fields, Steven F. Miller, Joseph P. Reidy, and Leslie S. Rowland, eds., *Freedom: A Documentary History of Emancipation, 1861–1867* (New York: Cambridge University Press, 1982–).

Eric Foner's *Reconstruction: America's Unfinished Revolution, 1863–1877* (New York: Norton, 1988) is the seminal work of the modern school, seeing the good, the bad, and the ugly on all sides, but giving full credit to the vision of equality that some in North and South shared. As he concluded his work, "few interpretations of history has had such far-reaching consequence as this [Zombie] image of Reconstruction. For it "did much to freeze the mind of the white South in unalterable opposition to outside pressures for social change and to any thought of breaching Democratic ascendancy, eliminating segregation, or restoring suffrage to disenfranchised blacks" (598).

Foner did not stand alone in this generation. Leon F. Litwack's *Been in the Storm So Long: The Aftermath of Slavery* (New York: Knopf, 1979) documented the challenges and adjustments to freedom the newly freed faced. George C. Rable, *But There Was No Peace: The Role of Violence in the Politics of Reconstruction* (Athens: University of Georgia Press, 1984), looked at the other side of the story, at how many southerners continued the war into peacetime, by resisting the new Reconstruction governments, terrorizing the freedmen, and making no effort at all to accept the outcome of the rebellion. Heather Cox Richardson's *The Death of Reconstruction: Race, Labor, and Politics in the Post–Civil War North, 1865–1901* (Cambridge: Harvard University Press, 2001) demonstrated how class and race conflict played complementary roles in ending Reconstruction, including their part in the decision of many northerners to leave the fate of the freedmen to their former masters.

Chapter Five

The quotations in the introduction to the chapter are from Richard White, *The Republic for Which It Stands: The United States during Reconstruction and the Gilded Age, 1865–1896* (New York: Oxford University Press, 2017), 477, 315.

Current standard textbook accounts of the Gilded Age are White, *The Republic for Which It Stands*; Vincent P. De Santis, *The Shaping of Modern*

America, 1877–1920 (3rd ed., Wheeling, IL: Harlan Davidson, 2000); Mark Wahlgren Summers, *The Gilded Age, or, The Hazard of New Functions* (Upper Saddle River, NJ: Prentice-Hall, 1997); Charles William Calhoun, ed., *The Gilded Age: Perspectives on the Origins of Modern America* (Lanham, MD: Rowman and Littelfield, 2007); and Elisabeth Israels Perry and Karen Manners Smith, *The Gilded Age and Progressive Era* (New York: Oxford University Press, 2006). The business side of big business is the subject of the classic by Alfred D. Chandler, *The Visible Hand: The Managerial Revolution in American Business* (Cambridge: Harvard University Press, 1977).

On Veblen and racialism (race distinctions without prejudice), Rick Tillman, *Thorstein Veblen and His Critics, 1893–1963* (Princeton: Princeton University Press, 2014), 161; for a defense of Jim Crow, see Woodrow Wilson, *History of the American People* (New York: Harper, 1901), 5:17. For reasons why Jim Crow gained support among whites, see Charles Postel, *The Populist Vision* (New York: Oxford University Press, 2007), 176; Michael McGerr, *A Fierce Discontent: The Rise and Fall of the Progessive Movement in America, 1870–1920* (New York: Oxford University Press, 2005), 183; Ira Katznelson, *Fear Itself: The New Deal and the Origins of Our Time* (New York: Norton, 2013), 159; *Alabama: A Guide to the Deep South* (New York: R. R. Smith, 1941), 5, 3, 4, 52–53; and James Grossman, "Whose Memory? Whose Monuments?," *Perspectives on History* (February 1, 2016): 3.

Machines tear through Upton Sinclair, *The Jungle* (New York: Doubleday, 1906), 40, and Frank Norris, *The Octopus: The Epic of the Wheat* (New York: Doubleday, 1901), 50. On technology: Jonathan Rees, *Refrigeration Nation: A History of Ice, Appliances, and Enterprise in America* (Baltimore: Johns Hopkins University press, 2013), 190–91; Merritt Roe Smith, "Introduction" in *Does Technology Drive History: The Dilemma of Technological Determinism*, edited by Merritt Roe Smith and Leo Marx (Cambridge, MA: MIT Press, 1994), 5; and David Kennedy, *Freedom from Fear: The American People in Depression and War* (New York: Oxford University Press, 1999), 619.

The "robber baron" image (though not the term) predated the Civil War, became common in the work of the "muckrakers" Ray Stannard Baker's stories of corruption of the cities and Ida Tarbell's history of Standard Oil, and was canonized in Matthew Josephson's *The Robber Barons: The Great American Capitalists, 1861–1901* (New York: Harcourt, Brace, 1934), 293. See also Howard Zinn, *A People's History of the United States* (New York: Routledge, 2015), 255, and Richard White, *Railroaded: The Transcontinentals and the Making of Modern America* (New York: Norton, 2011), 230, 232.

On Jay Gould, see Maury Klein, *The Life and Legend of Jay Gould* (Baltimore: Johns Hopkins University Press, 1997). On Rockefeller, see Allen Nevins, *John D. Rockefeller: The Heroic Age of American Enterprise*, 2 vols. (New York: Charles Scribner's Sons, 1940); Gerald L. Fetner, *Immersed in Great Affairs: Allan Nevins and the Heroic Age of American History* (Albany: State University of New York Press, 2012), 107, 120; and Ron Chernow, *Titan: The Life of John D. Rockefeller* (New York: Random House, 1998), xx, 676.

Chapter Six

The idea of a fin de siècle or mauve decade or other turn of the century caption was contemporary. For the naysayers, see Oswald Spengler, "Preface to the Second Edition (1921)," *The Decline of the West: Form and Actuality* (complete ed., New York: Knopf, 1926), xiii, and Henry Adams, "The Tendency of History," in Elizabeth Stevenson, ed., *A Henry Adams Reader* (New York: Doubleday, 1959), 346–347.

The classic work on immigration in turn of the century America is Oscar Handlin, *The Uprooted* (Boston: Little, Brown, 1951), quotations in the text from 3, 5, 285. See the critique of the work by Rudolph Vecoli, "Contadini in Chicago: A Critique of *The Uprooted*," *Journal of American History* 51 (1964): 404–17. A more modern (and better annotated) account of immigration is Roger Daniels, *Coming to America: A History of Immigration and Ethnicity in American Life* (3rd ed., New York: Harpers, 2019). The *New York Tribune* quotation (1882) and the congressional testimony of Martin Dies (1898) are taken from John Higham, *Strangers in the Land: Patterns of American Nativism, 1860–1925* (rev. ed., New Brunswick: Rutgers University Press, 2002), 36, 171. Note that the two quotations were separated in time but not in ideology.

On the scab, see "Scab," in Robert E. Weir, ed., *Workers in America: A Historical Encyclopedia* (Santa Barbara, CA: ABC-CLIO, 2013), 1:688; Melvyn Dubofsky, *Labor in America: A History* (Hoboken, NJ: Wiley-Blackwell, 2017), 141; Katherine Scott Sturdevant, "Colorado Labor Wars," in Melvyn Dubofsky, ed., *The Oxford Encyclopedia of American Business, Labor and Economic History* (New York: Oxford University Press, 2011), 129; and Nelson Lichtenstein, *State of the Union: A Century of American Labor* (Princeton: Princeton University Press, 2003), 137.

Henry M. Littlefield, "The Wizard of Oz: Parable on Populism," *American Quarterly* 16 (1964): 47–58, suggested the hidden identity of the characters, something that Frank Baum never said. For the metallic Zombies, see James Ledbetter, *One Nation under Gold: How One Precious Metal Has Dominated the American Imagination for Four Centuries* (New York: Liveright, 2017), 63; Ernest L. Bogart, *Economic History of the United States* (New York: Longmans, 1908), 349; Hugh Rackoff, "Banking and Finance, 1789–1914," in Stanley L. Engerman and Robert E. Gallman, eds., *Cambridge Economic History of the United States* (New York: Cambridge University Press, 2000), 2:662–63; and Sebastian Edwards, *American Default: The Untold Story of FDR, the Supreme Court, and the Battle over Gold* (Princeton: Princeton University Press, 2018), 46.

Marxism: Karl Marx, *Contribution to the Critique of Political Economy* (Moscow: Progress Publishers, [1859] 1977), iii; Marx, *Manifesto of the Communist Party* (Moscow: Progress Publishers, [1848] 1969), 14; Gerald A. Cohen, *Karl Marx's Theory of History: A Defense* (Princeton: Princeton University Press, 1978), 278; E. P. Thompson, *The Making of the English Working Class* (New York: Vintage, [1963] 1966), 807. [Daniel DeLeon], Socialist Labor Party of the United States of America, National Platform, June 8, 1900, www.marxists.org/history/usa/parties/slp/1900/plat1900. pdf; Constitution of the Communist Party of America, September 7, 1919, www.marxists.org/history/usa/parties/cpusa/1919/09/0907-cpa-constitution.pdf. On Marxism in the 1930s: Harvey Klehr, *The Heyday of American Communism: The Depression Decades* (New York, Basic, 1984), 372. MARHO and such: Jonathan Wiener, "Radical Historians and the Crisis in American History, 1959–1980," *Journal of American History* 75 (1989): 399–434; T. J. Jackson Lears, "Radical History in Retrospect," *Reviews in American History* 14 (1986): 17, 18; and E. P. Thompson, "Agenda for Radical History," *Critical Inquiry* 21 (1995): 302. On standpoint theory: T. Bowell, "Feminist Standpoint Theory," Internet Encyclopedia of Philosophy, www.iep.utm. edu/fem-stan.

Chapter Seven

On modernism, see Tim Armstrong, *Modernism: A Cultural History* (Cambridge: Polity, 2005).

For the ghetto: Bonnie Yochelson and Daniel Czitrom, *Rediscovering Jacob Riis* (New York: New Press, 2007), 250; Jacob Riis, *The Battle with the Slum* (New York: Macmillan, 1902), 3; Frederick Lewis Allen, *Only Yesterday: An Informal History of the 1920s* (New York: Harper and Row, 1931), 41; Alexander von Hoffman, "The Lost History of Urban Renewal," *Jour-*

nal of Urbanism 1 (2008): 282; James L. Roark, Michael P. Johnson, Patricia Cline Cohen, Sarah Stage, and Susan M. Hartmann, *The American Promise* (5th ed., New York: Bedford, 2012), 93; and Mary Beth Norton, Jane Kamensky, Carol Sheriff, David W. Blight, and Howard Chudacoff, *A People and a Nation* (10th ed. Stamford, CT: Cengage, 2014), 852. On the image of the ghetto, see Mitchell Duneier, *Ghetto: The Invention of a Place, the History of an Idea* (New York: Farrar, Straus and Giroux, 2016), ix; Douglas W. Rae, *City: Urbanism and Its End* (New Haven: Yale University Press, 2008), 282; and Lance Freeman, *There Goes the 'Hood: Gentrification from the Ground Up* (Philadelphia: Temple University Press, 2006), 127.

Muggers walk in the shadows in Roger Lane, *Roots of Violence in Black Philadelphia, 1860–1900* (Cambridge: Harvard University Press, 1986), 140, 169; Mary F. Brewer, *Staging Whiteness* (Middleton, CT: Wesleyan University Press, 2005), 174; Evan Stark and Ann Flitcraft, "Social Knowledge, Social Policy and the Abuse of Women," in *The Dark Side of Families*, edited by David Finkelhor, Richard J. Gelles, Gerald T. Hotaling, and Murray A. Strauss (London: Sage, 1983), 335; and James Burfeind and Dawn Jeglum Bartusch, *Juvenile Delinquency: An Integrated Approach* (New York: Routledge, 2014), 120–33.

Fear stalks the land in Fredrick Lewis Allen, *Since Yesterday: America in the 1930s* (New York: Harper and Row, 1940); Carl Lotus Becker, "What Is a Liberal" (1932), reprinted in Philip L. Snyder, ed., *Detachment and the Writing of History: Essays and Letters of Carl L. Becker* (Ithaca, NY: Cornell University Press, 1958), 199, 200, 212; Charles and Mary Beard, *America in Midpassage* (New York: Macmillan, 1939), 2:539, 540, 911, 917; and Charles Beard, *President Roosevelt and the Coming of the War: Appearances and Realities* (New Haven: Yale University Press, 1948), 3, 8, 11.

Reds and Red baiters abound in Ellen Schrecker, *Many Are the Crimes: McCarthyism in America* (Boston: Little, Brown, 1998), 256–64 (Army hearings), and David Oshinsky, *A Conspiracy So Immense: The World of Joe McCarthy* (New York: Free Press, 1983), 109–17, 205.

For eggheads: James T. Patterson, *Grand Expectations: The United States, 1945–1974* (New York: Oxford University Press, 1996), 254; Aaron Lecklida, *Inventing the Egghead: The Battle over Brainpower in American Culture* (Philadelphia: University of Pennsylvania Press, 2013), 193; and Richard Hofstadter, *Anti-Intellectualism in American Life* (New York: Knopf, 1963), 23–25.

Chapter Eight

On postmodernism: Stephen R. C. Hicks, *Explaining Postmodernism* (rev. ed., Roscoe, IL: Ockhams's Razor, 2011), 2–3; Christopher Butler, *Postmodernism: A Very Short Introduction* (New York: Oxford University Press, 2003), 4–5; Michel Foucault, interview, 1984, quoted in Allan D. Kritzman, "Introduction: Foucault and the Politics of Experience," in *Michel Foucault: Politics, Philosophy, Culture: Interviews and Other Writings, 1877–1984* (London: Routledge, 1988), xvi; Oscar Handlin, *Truth in History* (Cambridge: Harvard University Press, 1979), 405; and Allan Megill, *Historical Knowledge, Historical Error: A Contemporary Guide to Practice* (Chicago: University of Chicago Press, 2007), 13.

On the rise of the fact and fact-checking in history, see Barbara J. Shapiro, *A Culture of Fact, England, 1550–1720* (Ithaca, NY: Cornell University Press, 2000), 34–62. Ironically, another Barbara Shapiro writes historical fiction as B. A. Shapiro.

Conspiracy theories: Richard Hofstadter, *The Paranoid Style in American Politics* (New York: Knopf, 1952), 4, 6; and Robert Alan Goldberg, "Conspiracy Theories in America: An Historical Overview," in Peter Knight, ed., *Conspiracy Theories in American History: An Encyclopedia* (Santa Barbara, CA: ABC-CLIO), 1:1–12. On the conspiracy against McCarthy, see M. Stanton Evans, *Blacklisted by History: The Untold Story of Senator Joseph McCarthy* (New York: Crown, 2009), and Diana West, *American Betrayal: The Secret Assault on Our Nation's Character* (New York: St. Martin's, 2009) 63–65 (citing Evans). On the Kennedy assassination: Michael Collins Piper, *Final Judgment: The Missing Link in the JFK Assassination Conspiracy* (N.p.: American Free Press, 2017).

Memes and history: Limor Shifman, *Memes in Digital Culture* (Cambridge, MA: MIT Press, 2013), 33–34, and Daniel I. Cohen and Roy Rosenzweig, *Digital History: A Guide to Gathering, Preserving, and Presenting the Past on the Web* (Philadelphia: University of Pennsylvania Press, 2005), quotation from 3. Rosenzweig added to the corpus of books on digital history with Anthony Grafton in *Clio Wired: The Future of the Past in the Digital Age* (New York: Columbia University Press, 2011), quotations from 13 and 144. "Facebook Refuses to Delete Fake Pelosi Video Spread by Trump Supporters," *Guardian*, May 24, 2019, www.theguardian.com/technology/2019/may/24/facebook-leaves-fake-nancy-pelosi-video-on-site?fbclid=IwAR0EpHJ02NsN0k8jJ3Iy0b_NhOPdCiomgDTfq03ySeqkxZeYKEsOQPn29iY.

Numbers: William O. Aydelotte, "Quantification in History," *American Historical Review* 71 (1966): 804; Jerome Clubb and Allan Bogue, "History, Quantification, and the Social Sciences," *American Behavioral Scientist* 21 (1977): 172; and David Card and Alan Krueger, *Myth and Measurement: The New Economics of the Minimum Wage* (Princeton: Princeton University Press, 1995), 9. Quantitative historical methods are surveyed in Pat Hudson and Mina Ishizu, *History by Numbers: An Introduction to Quantiative Approaches* (London: Bloomsbury, 2017).

Some of the more famous examples of economic history are Robert W. Fogel, *Railroads and American Economic Growth* (Baltimore: Johns Hopkins University Press, 1964), and Douglass C. North, *The Economic Growth of the United States, 1790–1860* (New York: Norton, 1966). For time on the cross, see Robert William Fogel and Stanley L. Engerman, *Time on the Cross: The Economics of American Negro Slavery* (Boston: Little, Brown, 1974) 1:239; Robert M. Fogel, *Without Consent or Contract: Conditions of Slave Life and the Transition to Freedom, Technical Papers* (New York: Norton, 1992), 2:195; and Paul A. David, Herbert G. Gutman, Richard Sutch, Peter Temin, and Gavin Wright, *Reckoning with Slavery: A Critical Study in the Quantitative History of American Negro Slavery* (New York: Oxford University Press, 1976). On Social Security: Eric Laursen, *The People's Pension: The Struggle to Defend Social Security since Reagan* (Oakland, CA: AK Publishing, 2012), and Nancy J. Altman and Eric R. Kingson, *Social Security Works!* (New York: New Press, 2015).

Big Data is the centerpiece of Jo Guldi and David Armitage, *The History Manifesto* (Cambridge: Cambridge University Press, 2014), Cambridge Core, https://www.cambridge.org/core/books/history-manifesto/AC1A1EC711AE91A4F9004E7582D79AFD. This is an open access book, or really a web text, so there are no page numbers. The easiest way to find the quotations is to do a keyword search of chapter 4 and the conclusion. For a view of the criticisms (I am not alone in finding problems), see Pseudoerasmus, "The Long Puree," https://pseudoerasmus.com/2014/11/10/la-longue-puree/; Deborah Cohen, "Critique of the History Manifesto," http://www.deborahacohen.com/profile/?q=content/critique-history-manifesto; and Richard Blakemore, "Some Thoughts on the History Manifesto" https://historywomble.wordpress.com/2014/10/14/some-thoughts-on-the-history-manifesto/.

On political correctness and white privilege, see Lynne Cheney, *Telling the Truth* (New York: Touchstone, 1995), 197; Gary Nash, Charlotte Crabtree, and Ross Dunn, *History on Trial: Culture Wars and the Teaching of the Past* (rev. ed., New York: Random House, 2000), 104, 207; Scott L. Waugh, "New EDI Statement for Regular Rank Faculty Searches," May 24, 2018, /equity.ucla.edu/news-and-events/new-edi-statement-requirement-for-regular-rank-faculty-searches/; Rita Koganzon, "Who Will Defend the University: Hanna Holborn Gray and the Lost Art of Academic Governance," *Chronicle of Higher Education*, November 12, 2018; Jill Lepore in Evan Goldstein, "Interview with Jill Lepore," *Chronicle of Higher Education*, November 13, 2018, www.chronicle.com/article/The-Academy-Is-Largely/245080; and Peggy McIntosh, "White Privilege and Male Privilege," 1988, https://nationalseedproject.org/white-privilege-and-male-privilege.

Dismay and despair: Colin Calloway, *One Vast Winter Count: The Native American West before Lewis and Clark* (Lincoln: University of Nebraska Press, 2003), 428; Robert G. Parkinson, *The Common Cause: Creating Race and Nation in the American Revolution* (Chapel Hill: University of North Carolina Press, 2014), 665; Alan Taylor, *American Revolutions* (New York: Penguin, 2017), 351, 458; Richard White, *Railroaded: The Transcontinentals and the Making of Modern America* (New York: Norton, 2011), 509; and White, *The Republic for Which It Stands: The United States during Reconstruction and the Gilded Age, 1865–1896* (New York: Oxford University Press, 2017), 855–56.

The AHA report can be found at Benjamin M. Schmidt, "The History BA since the Great Recession," *Perspectives on History* 56 (December 2018): 19–23. It is deeply worrisome. But see James Grossman, executive director of the AHA, "Talk to Historians: What's behind the Current Lamentations over History," *Perspectives on History*, March 7, 2019.

Epilogue

On the (il)logic of neologisms: David Hackett Fischer, *Historians' Fallacies: Toward a Logic of Historical Thought* (New York: Harper and Row, 1970), is a classic. For examples of the neologism Zombie in book titles (and throughout the text), see Malcolm Gladwell, *The Tipping Point: How Little Things Can Make a Big Difference* (Boston: Little, Brown, 2000); Erik Durschmied, *How Chance and Stupidity Have Changed History: The Hinge Factor* (New York: Arcade, 2000); and Seymour Martin Lipset, *The First New Nation: The United States in Historical and Comparative Perspective* (New York: Norton, 1963). A neologism wannabe appears in Kimberlé Crenshaw, "Mapping the Margins: Intersectionality, Identity Politics, and Violence against Women,"

Stanford Law Review 42 (1990): 1241–1300, and Crenshaw, "Demarginalizing the Intersection of Race and Sex: A Black Feminist Critique of Antidiscrimination Doctrine, Feminist Theory, and Antiracist Politics," *University of Chicago Law School Legal Forum* 19 (1989): 139–68.

On textbooks: much of what I have written relies on my own experience with the genre, working with Pearson Higher Education, D. C. Heath college textbook division, Houghton Mifflin textbook division, and Oxford University Press higher education division on various projects. See also James W. Loewen, *Lies My Teacher Told Me: Everything Your American History Textbook Got Wrong* (rev. ed., New York: Simon and Schuster, 2007, 2018), quotations at 356, iii, 9. Loewen added a new preface to a new edition in 2007 in which he reminded us of how important his work and he is. In the many editions of Howard Zinn's *A People's History of the United States* (reprint, New York: Harper, 2005), 8, 23, little was changed, as new scholarship was not as important as old, long-rehearsed criticisms.

There is no survey for college-level texts comparable to Loewen's for school texts, but new and revised books were for a time reviewed in the *Journal of American History*. The rule of thumb on bias is the older the textbook, the more likely it is to be conservative. Newer textbooks tend to be more open in their treatment of oppressed minorities. Compare Thomas A. Bailey's *American Pageant*, first published in 1956, with John Mack Faragher, et al., *Out of Many*, first published in 1994, or the first of the social-emphasis histories, Gary Nash, et al., *The American People: Creating a Nation* (1986). Are these histories of the same people? The answer is yes.

Today, with free online alternatives ("open textbooks") and the skyrocketing prices of print texts, the traditional textbook may be on the way out. Publishers like Prentice Hall have left the college textbook field. Others like Houghton Mifflin have been sold and resold so many times that they have lost their editorial identity. For more on how the standard multiauthored textbook was composed, see Gary J. Kornblith and Carol Lasser, "'The Truth, the Whole Truth, and Nothing But the Truth': Writing, Producing and Using College Level American History Textbooks," *Journal of American History* (March 2005): 1380–83.

AP tests in history can be found, surprise, surprise, on the web. The Educational Testing Service explains and extols the changes, with each edition of the text apparently better than its predecessors. (https://advancesinap.collegeboard.org/english-history-and-social-science/us-history/2015-ced).

Online history is all over the web. Who can one trust? Certainly not student-created "quizlets" (unless the students have posted questions and answers for online exams). The rules for assessing bias in primary sources apply to history websites. Is the website professionally created/moderated or an amateur production? Does it feature the work of recognized professional authorities, or are the posts anonymous or by nonspecialists? Does the site and its authors have a recognizable bias or ideological purpose? How dramatic/prejudicial is the prose? To whom does the website seem addressed? Do its materials seem slanted by its perception of its audience? What impact does the website have on you? The Stanford University Web Credibility Project has a series of guides for the perplexed at https://credibility.stanford.edu/resources.html. It's well worth visiting.

Index